To Live Here, You Have to Fight

THE WORKING CLASS IN AMERICAN HISTORY

A list of books in the series appears at the end of this book.

To Live Here, You Have to Fight

How Women Led Appalachian Movements for Social Justice

JESSICA WILKERSON

UNIVERSITY OF ILLINOIS PRESS
Urbana, Chicago, and Springfield

Publication supported by a grant from the Howard D. and Marjorie I. Brooks Fund for Progressive Thought.

1 2 3 4 5 C P 5 4 3 2 1
∞ This book is printed on acid-free paper.

Library of Congress Cataloging-in-Publication Data
Names: Wilkerson, Jessica, 1981– author.
Title: To live here, you have to fight: how women led Appalachian movements for social justice / Jessica Wilkerson.
Description: [Urbana, IL: University of Illinois Press, 2019] | Series: The working class in American history | Includes bibliographical references and index.
Identifiers: LCCN 2018032364| ISBN 9780252042188 (cloth : alk. paper) | ISBN 9780252083907 (pbk. : alk. paper)
Subjects: LCSH: Women—Political activity—Appalachian Region, Southern. | Social action—Appalachian Region, Southern. | Appalachian Region, Southern—Social conditions--20th century.
Classification: LCC HQ1236.5.A6 .W55 2019 | DDC 320.082/0975—dc23 LC record available at https://lccn.loc.gov/2018032364

Ebook ISBN 978-0-252-05092-3

Pray for the dead, and fight like hell for the living.
Mary Harris "Mother" Jones

To stay here, you're going to have to fight like hell.
Bessie Smith Gayheart

Contents

Acknowledgments

This book is the culmination of many people's stories. I am grateful to those who shared their own stories, preserved stories, wrote other people's stories, and supported my story.

My grandmother Fay Loy Spitzer gave me my first lessons on Appalachian and labor history. She also gave me my first books, took me to the library and museums, and sent me newspaper clippings when I was away at college. The day that I delivered my master's thesis to her she wept. I understood then how truly fortunate I was that I got to do what I loved, and that so many women before me had grieved those lost opportunities even as they celebrated for their daughters and granddaughters.

This book would not be possible without the generosity of people who shared their life histories in interviews. From the moment I met Sue Ella Kobak in 2010, she supported this project. I am grateful to her for sharing her vast knowledge of place, her deep love of Appalachian history, and her commitment to justice and fairness. The day she took me on a tour of Poor Bottom is one of my most memorable research trips and invigorated me as I headed into final writing stages. Many others invited me to their homes and offices, told stories, and shared sources. Special thanks to Eula Hall, the staff at the Eula Hall Health Center, Helen Matthews Lewis, Loyal Jones, Sally Ward Maggard, Helen Rentch, John Rosenberg, Maxine Kenny, Steve Brooks, Jeanette Knowles, Mildred Shackleford, Thelma Witt, June Rostan, and the many others who sat for interviews or spoke with me informally.

I am deeply indebted to the professors who taught me when I was an undergraduate at Carson Newman College. Jeff Daniel Marion introduced me to the poetry of the Appalachian South. Beth Van Landingham, Susan

Underwood, Andrew Hazucha, and John Wells cheered my budding interest in women's and gender history and encouraged me to attend graduate school, pointing me in the direction of Sarah Lawrence College. There, Priscilla Murolo demonstrated how to be a scholar. She also introduced me to labor and working-class history and reassured me that there was a place for me in academia if I wanted it. Many thanks to Mary Dillard for introducing me to the method of oral history, and to Komozi Woodard, Lyde Sizer, Tara James, Abby Lester, and the women's history class of 2006 for their support. Sarah Lawrence also gave me my forever-friend Sonia Arora. Thanks, Sonia, for your unyielding friendship.

I am grateful for the people and vibrant intellectual communities that I encountered in Chapel Hill. Jacquelyn Hall, in her bones, understood the value of my research. Her excitement for historical research is contagious, and her commitment to her students admirable. She fosters community like nobody I know. My scholarship, indeed my life, is enriched because of her. Thanks also to Jim Leloudis, Zaragosa Vargas, Nancy MacLean, and, especially, Laura F. Edwards, for their encouragement and advice. For friendship and collegiality, thanks to my sister-scholar Joey Fink, as well as Jennifer Donnally, Sarah McNamara, Nora Doyle, Rachel Hynson, Brad Proctor, Joshua Lynn, and David Williard. My writing group extraordinaire—Anna Krome-Lukens, Liz Lundeen, and Shannon Eaves—has made this a better book. Their support and friendship mean the world to me. My only regret is that we don't get to live in the same town and work at the same place for the rest of our lives. The Working Group in Feminism and History was a vital space. So was UNC's Southern Oral History Program (SOHP) and the Center for the Study of the American South. The SOHP in particular had a profound impact on how I think of myself as a scholar in the world, and its influence is etched into this manuscript. Thanks to David Cline, Beth Millwood, Seth Kotch, Della Pollock, Rachel Seidman, Malinda Maynor Lowery, Bill Ferris, Jaycie Vos, and my fellow research assistants there.

This book is possible due to the work of archivists, oral historians, and documentarians. Special thanks to archivists and staff at Appalshop, the Southern Appalachian Archives at Berea College, the Appalachian Center at the Southeast Kentucky Community and Technical College, Wilson Library at UNC, the Louie B. Nunn Center for Oral History at the University of Kentucky, the State Historical Society of Wisconsin, the Archives of Appalachia at East Tennessee State University, the Lyndon Baines Johnson Library, and the Schlesinger Library at Harvard. I am grateful to the interviewers who recorded and archived oral history interviews with men and women who lived, worked, and fought for a better world in eastern Kentucky.

I had help imagining the historical period of which I wrote thanks to the filmmakers Elizabeth Barrett, Barbara Kopple, Anne Lewis, Mimi Pickering, and Lucy Massie Phenix; documentarians Guy and Candie Carawan; and photographers Phil Primack and Earl Dotter.

I am grateful to Jacquelyn Hall for meticulously reading the manuscript at various stages. For reading all or parts of the manuscript, thanks to Ted Ownby, Sue Ella Kobak, Shennette Garrett-Scott, Sue Grayzel, Ken Fones-Wolf, Daniel Horowitz, Barbara Ellen Smith, Sally Ward Maggard, Melissa Estes Blair, Megan Black, Katherine Turk, Elizabeth Payne, Sarah McNamara, Shannon Eaves, Anna Krome-Lukens, Liz Lundeen, Melody Ivins, and members of the Delta Women Writers' Symposium. I owe a special debt to Katherine Mellon Charron for helping me find my way to a title. Portions of chapter six appeared previously in "The Company Owns the Mine But They Don't Own Us: Feminist Critiques of Capitalism in the Coalfields of Kentucky in the 1970s," in *Gender & History* 28, no. 1 (April 2016), and I would like to thank the editors of *Gender & History* and anonymous readers for their helpful feedback.

Thanks to James Engelhardt and the staff at the University of Illinois Press, especially Alison K. Syring, for shepherding me through the publishing process. Thanks also to Susan Youngblood Ashmore and Julie Greene for their careful reading of the manuscript and incisive feedback in the late stages of writing.

The faculty and staff of the Arch Dalrymple III Department of History and the Center for the Study of Southern Culture at the University of Mississippi have been tremendously supportive, and I thank you all. I am especially grateful to Kelly Brown Houston, Sherra Jones, Donna Crenshaw, and Sarah Dixon Pegues for helping me navigate university bureaucracies. I am grateful for friends and colleagues who have supported me in large and small ways since I moved to Oxford: Amy McDowell, Alberto Del Arco, Catarina Passidomo, Jodi Skipper, Shennette Garrett-Scott, Sue Grayzel, Katie McKee, Barb Combs, Darren Grem, Jaime Harker, Jarod Roll, Rhiannon Stephens, Brian Foster, Charles Reagan Wilson, Zack Kagan-Guthrie, Hanna Lee, Ellie Campbell, Margaret Gaffney, and Mary Hartwell Howorth.

For comments and conversations at conferences, I am indebted to Laurie Green, Annelise Orleck, Lane Windham, Naomi Williams, Keona Irvin, Ileen DeVault, Jon Free, Megan Schockley, Bob Korstad, Lisa Levenstein, Marisa Chappell, Jay Driskell, Ken Fones-Wolf, Chana Kai Lee, Clay Howard, Jennifer Mittelstadt, Priscilla Murolo, Kathy Newfont, Amy Zanoni, and Mary Klann. I am fortunate to have vibrant intellectual networks through the Labor and Working-Class History Association, the Southern Association for

Women Historians, the Berkshire Conference of Women Historians, the Oral History Association, and the Southern Labor Studies Association. Thanks to the following folks who invited me to give talks: Tara James at Sarah Lawrence College; Rob Ferguson and his colleagues at Western Carolina University; and Dave Anderson at Louisiana Tech University.

I was fortunate to receive a fellowship from the American Academy of Arts & Sciences, which granted me time and a quiet space in which to write. Thanks to the visiting scholars for their feedback on the manuscript, and to Lawrence Buell and Paul Erickson for fostering a collegial environment. Thanks to Joe Ward, Noell Wilson, Ted Ownby, and Jeffrey Watt for advocating on my behalf and to the University of Mississippi College of Liberal Arts for providing the funding to make the fellowship possible. Thanks also to the other institutions that supported my research and writing with generous funding. These include the American Association of University Women, the Arch Dalrymple III Department of History, and the Center for the Study of Southern Culture. The Appalachian Sound Archives Fellowship at Berea College and the Moody Research Grant from the LBJ Library made travel to those archives possible.

I give my deepest thanks to my family. I owe a debt of gratitude to Brian Sherry, whose capacity for caregiving inspires me and informed this book in countless ways. Margie and Pat Sherry embraced me completely from day one, and I look forward to sharing this book with them and the entire Sherry team—Nicole, Tyson, Scott, Shannon, Owen, and Erin. My grandmother Laverne Wilkerson asks at the beginning of each visit when the book will be done and reminds me that she would like a copy, for which I'm grateful. My siblings Tess and Jud put all things in perspective, and I am thankful for them, Jeremy, Heather, Addison, Ella, and Deacon. My greatest debt of gratitude is to my parents, Martha and Dennis Wilkerson, who have been nothing but unwavering in their support. They have always made me believe that I would be good at anything that I try. This book is dedicated to them.

Acronyms

AFDC	Aid to Families with Dependent Children
AGSLP	Appalachian Group to Save the Land and People
ASOC	Appalachian Student Organizing Committee
AV	Appalachian Volunteers
AWRO	Appalachian Women's Rights Organization
BLA	Black Lung Association
CAA	Community Action Agency
CAP	Community Action Program
CEP	Coal Employment Project
CSM	Council of the Southern Mountains
EKWRO	Eastern Kentucky Welfare Rights Organization
HEW	Department of Health, Education, and Welfare
HUAC	House Un-American Activities Committee
KUAC	Kentucky Un-American Activities Committee
KWRO	Kentucky Welfare Rights Organization
MCHR	Medical Committee for Human Rights
ML&W	*Mountain Life & Work*
NMU	National Miners' Union
NOW	National Organization for Women
NWRO	National Welfare Rights Organization
OEO	Office of Economic Opportunity
SCLC	Southern Christian Leadership Conference
SNCC	Student Non-Violent Coordinating Committee
SSOC	Southern Student Organizing Committee
UMWA	United Mine Workers of America
VISTA	Volunteers in Service to America

To Live Here, You Have to Fight

Introduction

In 1962, Frances "Granny" Hager rushed to the Appalachian Hospital in Harlan, Kentucky. There she met her husband Ab Hager, who was having "a real bad spell," she later recalled. Ab had worked forty-eight years in the coalmines. His body had been "mashed" and his lungs had filled with coal dust, causing coalminers' pneumoconiosis, or black lung disease. The doctor told Granny that Ab's lungs looked "like concrete." A midwife by training, Granny had nursed her ailing spouse over the years, as his breathing became labored, his organs hardened, and his body weakened. But her ability to care for her loved one had become more difficult in recent months. The Hagers had lost their health insurance when the United Mine Workers of America (UMWA), Ab's union, restructured its retirement policies, leaving many retired coalminers and their families without health care. The hospital turned the Hagers away, citing their inability to pay a fifty-dollar deposit. Granny Hager took Ab home and "sat right there by him for three weeks and watched him slowly die."[1]

Months after Ab's death, Granny Hager—who first joined union picket lines in the 1930s—partnered with retired miner Ashford Thomas to organize what they called "roving pickets." Widows and retired miners traveled from mine to mine urging workers to strike and force the coal companies to improve working conditions. A few years later, Hager met antipoverty workers who helped miners and widows, like her, to force the federal government and the coal industry to recognize the existence of black lung disease. Together, they successfully lobbied for the Mine Health and Safety Act of 1969. In subsequent years, Hager and others participated in protests, marches, and

Figure 1. Frances "Granny" Hager. Courtesy of Berea College Special Collections and Archives; Berea, Kentucky.

public hearings to improve compensation for sick miners and their families, and Hager went door-to-door to inform people of their rights as workers.

Ten years after Ab's death, Granny Hager was known around the region for her activism. In June 1972, she spoke at a union rally for Miners for Democracy, a grassroots movement of rank-and-file coalminers to reform the UMWA. The rally took place at the site of a 1931 labor skirmish in Harlan County dubbed the Battle of Evarts. Hager had been there, yards from where one man was shot and killed for his pro-union stance. Now she sought to inspire the uprising of miners in Harlan County and across eastern Kentucky as they spearheaded a new union campaign.[2]

During her 1972 speech, Hager declared, "People say to me, 'Well, Granny, why are you out working and doing this when you've got no kids, nobody but yourself?' I said, 'Yeah, but there're old people who needs their miners' retirement pension, there're old people who need their Social Security, there're fathers who has died and left their little children, they need their black lung [benefits]. And if I can help one person that really needs it to get something to live on, buddy I think it's worth all these here forty years that I've been on the job.'"[3] Central to her "job" of forty years was a commitment to helping working-class men and women understand and take advantage of their citizenship rights.

Granny Hager's life and activism exemplifies the fusion of an *ethic of care* with an ethos of citizenship. Hager was part of a tradition of Appalachian women's activism that linked the daily acts of sustaining life to democratic participation. Charting the life histories and activism of Hager and others like her, this book argues that caring labor is fundamental to understanding the limitations and successes of social and political movements that sought to expand democracy and citizenship rights.

• • •

This book tells the story of women in the Appalachian South who joined and led progressive movements in the 1960s and 1970s.[4] Most of the historical actors in this story are white women who lived and worked in poor and working-class communities, and who became part of an unfolding drama. It featured conservative and liberal politicians with whom they sparred over antipoverty funding; black and white civil rights activists they joined in poor people's campaigns; striking miners with whom they marched on picket lines; and welfare rights and feminist activists with whom they united to fight for fairness and equality. Their story thus enables us to understand the region, the nation, and the time period from new perspectives.

A yearning to understand Appalachian women activists' political motivations, desires, and relationships inspired this study. Many of the women whose stories follow have been memorialized in story, film, music, and images. Indeed, it was through these mediums that I first learned about them. Yet I was mystified when I read histories of the region that, with few exceptions, rarely considered these women in any depth or as primary historical actors. I wanted to know: Who were women activists before the political campaigns, labor strikes, and protests? How did those dramatic moments change their lives? How did they make history? What visions did they have for themselves, their children, and their communities? If they made only fleeting appearances in Appalachian history, they have been virtually invisible in twentieth-century American history. Yet their stories help us rethink major debates in American history and about poverty, social movements, capitalism, feminism, and more. One of the primary goals of *To Live Here, You Have to Fight* is to position Appalachian women as political actors who were part of social movements, joined in ideological debates, offered fresh visions of democratic participation, and faced sometimes-crippling political struggles.[5]

The women at the center of this history participated in what scholars have called the "grassroots war on poverty"—the mobilization of poor communities across the nation. Building on the foundations of the federal War on Poverty, they developed community-run organizations, helped to implement new antipoverty legislation, and mounted democratic campaigns in the second half of the twentieth century.[6] When President Lyndon B. Johnson announced a War on Poverty, Appalachia became its main stage. As antipoverty programs emerged in mountain communities, local women joined and shaped them to respond to the daily and entrenched problems that they observed. And as Johnson's Great Society legislation expanded the welfare state, women helped implement its policies in their communities. Most scholars date the top-down, federal War on Poverty from 1964 to 1968, but the grassroots war on poverty reverberated for over a decade. Its legacies continue into the present.

White women in the Appalachian South sustained antipoverty programs, which came under increasing attack in the late 1960s. This book shows how, in subsequent years, they continued the work of implementing and improving federal legislation in their communities, and they also mounted an array of democratic campaigns addressing the complex ways that class and gender disparity played out in the region. Galvanized by the War on Poverty and inspired by the civil rights movement, women fostered diverse coalitions and crisscrossed 1960s and 1970s social movements. They became leaders and foot soldiers in a regional poor people's movement, the welfare rights movement, a community health movement, environmental justice protests, unionization campaigns, and a grassroots women's movement.

Caregiving defines the central and consistent theme in these women's lives and activism, something that becomes clear only when we foreground women's participation in 1960s social movements and examine policy campaigns in the Mountain South through the lens of gender. Antipoverty activism in eastern Kentucky, the primary site of this study, initially addressed daily challenges of living in the coalfields, where the coal industry had dominated politics since the late nineteenth century and had amassed huge quantities of wealth on the backs of working people. Historically, male employment was inconsistent, and the single-industry economy offered few labor opportunities for women. To make matters worse, coalmining wreaked havoc on miners' bodies. Many suffered from crippling disabilities, including broken bones and crushed backs. Coalminers' pneumoconiosis led to premature aging and death. This crisis in workers' health only compounded the health and psychological impacts of environmental destruction as the coal industry altered the landscape, polluted waterways, and dumped waste down mountainsides. Caregiving became the unifying thread for women who tended to disabled fathers, husbands, and sons; struggled to nourish children in toxic environments; managed household budgets; handled state-sponsored social provisioning; and assisted other men and women in their trials and tribulations.

Activists drew on their social positions as caregivers as they articulated the goals of a multitude of grassroots campaigns. They exposed the harsh realities of life under coalfield capitalism—characterized by the concentration of power and wealth in the hands of mine owners, investors, and corporate coal's executives. To make sense of Appalachian women's gendered and class-conscious activism that challenged this system, I turned to the interdisciplinary scholarship on caregiving and reproductive labor. Sociologist Evelyn Nakano Glenn describes social reproduction as the "array of activities and relationships involved in maintaining people both on a daily basis and intergenerationally."[7] These activities include raising and socializing children, caring for the elderly and disabled, caring for oneself, preparing food, cleaning living quarters, buying consumer goods, and maintaining ties of family and kin. The majority of this labor—both paid and unpaid—has historically fallen to women.[8]

Feminist philosophers have outlined how caring work—who does it and how society values it—brings up questions of social responsibility and political will. As Eva Feder Kittay posits, caregiving and the human dependency that it reveals is central to how we understand equality and citizenship, typically in the sense that we erase it from consideration altogether. Kittay offers a "dependency critique of equality." She calls into question the idea that it is possible for humans to function as free and equal citizens because humans depend on the care of another human at least several points in life.[9] In the history recounted here, women performed life-sustaining labor and provided end-of-life care. They did so without adequate resources, setting in relief the limitations of arguments for rights and equality that ignored the necessity of caregiving.

As women became activists, they exposed the ways in which unpaid caregiving labor was—and is—among capitalism's "background conditions of possibility" at the same time that it is devalued and destabilized.[10]

Caregiving labor did what industrial capitalism could not—it sustained life. Yet, paradoxically, capitalist accumulation strained and threatened social reproduction; it created conditions in which caregiving labor became difficult if not impossible to perform. When we center women's caregiving as a political activity and as a motivation for democratic campaigns, we raise the question: what would it mean to imagine the average American not as a citizen worker, as has been the case in modern U.S. political history, but as a citizen caregiver?[11]

To do so should not negate the fact that many of the women whose lives are examined here were also paid workers. Many took great pleasure in fighting hard against sexist barriers to gain access to employment, or "public work." They also stood on the frontlines of labor struggles and fought for the collective bargaining rights of all working people. This has been the case even as Appalachian women have often been reduced to simple gender identities, as in the common phrases "coalminer's wife" and "coalminer's daughter." For example, journalists portrayed women who joined miners on picket lines in the 1970s as "miners' wives," even as many of them also worked for wages and others used affirmative action to secure jobs in the mines for themselves. Others claimed identities as mothers, daughters, and wives, but they also yearned for the independence entailed in earning wages. Consider Eula Hall, for whom paid employment was one necessary step in divorcing her violent husband. Some, like Edith Easterling, did not particularly enjoy housekeeping. She sought employment that satiated her interest in politics and that improved the quality of life in her community.

To refer to the central figures in this study as "citizen caregivers" is to acknowledge the fact that women in the Appalachian South—indeed, working-class and poor women in the United States—bore responsibility for caregiving in their families and in their communities. They did so not because women are inherently more caring or nurturing than men, but because they lived in a society that assigned them that social position through institutions, culture, and laws. As they became activists, they infused social and political movements with those experiences of taking care of parents, husbands, children, and neighbors in the hostile environment created by coalfield capitalism.

• • •

Understanding white women's activism in Appalachia is impossible without attending to the history of race in America. The women about whom I write lived in harsh places filled with difficult challenges. Nonetheless, gendered white privilege often served as a cornerstone to their lives. They lived in communities where laws, ordinances, customs, and racial violence had driven out many, but not all, African Americans. Working-class white communities benefited from that process, even when they also faced economic and environmental injustices.[12]

Racial privilege was not gender-neutral, however. In coalmining communities, white women experienced racial privilege that was mediated through gender in three primary ways.[13] First, they gained a tenuous economic security through wages, housing, and land through their male kin, who were the first hired for relatively well-paying jobs or who inherited or were able to buy property freely. Access to economic stability came as an exchange: women committed to relationships of economic dependence, in which they would trade reproductive labor for largely male-controlled property and wealth.

Second, while working-class white women faced barriers to employment in male-dominated industry, they had a wider range of work opportunities than black women. For instance, some found employment in factories, restaurants, schools, and hospitals. Others moved to cities to work, as some did during World War II, when they were employed in factories that refused to hire black women.[14]

Last, married white women had greater access to the welfare state than people of color and single white women. The state tied the most generous social provisions—those designated as entitlements—to specific kinds of employment, to which white, able-bodied men had exclusive access. It deemed entitlements such as the Social Security program for retired workers the right of white male citizens and their families. Policy makers excluded many single mothers, African Americans, and other nonwhite people from entitlement programs and channeled them into needs-based programs or left them out entirely. In Appalachia, the racial contours of these programs persisted into the 1960s. Federal and regional policy makers imagined the region as white, and they designed and implemented 1960s-era antipoverty policies in such a way that targeted poor white communities.[15]

These and other benefits of racist structures did not equal privilege in the sense that poor and working-class whites in the Mountain South had discernible access to power, rank, or wealth. And it is in part for that reason—the knotty intersection of class and race—that leftist activists in the 1960s looked to the region to build progressive, interracial social movements. By the spring and summer of 1964, white civil rights activists who had worked alongside black activists in the Deep South turned their attention to white working-class communities. They drew explicit links between the civil rights movement and the War on Poverty.[16] Many young white activists joined the antipoverty programs in the Appalachian South, where they hoped to build on a legacy of union activism and contribute to an "Appalachian Movement" that would contribute to a multiracial movement for economic fairness.[17]

Many local whites identified the importance of class stratification in their lives and the series of barriers to upward mobility. Some went on to identify common class goals and join interracial alliances in poor people's campaigns and the welfare rights movement. The activism of working-class whites fell along a spectrum: some saw the practicality of interracial movements, others were sincerely devoted to cross-racial solidarity, and some, the minority of the activists represented here, practiced antiracism. The latter group actively sought to challenge systems of American racism. I have made a point of highlighting these moments of interracial coalitions to counteract the narrative of Appalachia as "white" and to gesture toward the spirit of cooperation and the range of activism that emerged as communities came together to improve policies combating poverty.[18]

Yet Appalachia was not a place of white racial innocence. Like the rest of the United States, the Mountain South has a long history of ethnic and racial oppression. White settlers forced removal of Native Americans, and many owned and traded enslaved African Americans. In the late nineteenth and early twentieth centuries, whites led campaigns of violence and terror against freedmen. White-controlled state and local governments passed laws and ordinances that prevented the settlement of African Americans and impeded their occupational mobility, patterns that existed well into the twentieth century. These and other factors led to black outmigration, giving the appearance of a white Appalachia by the mid–twentieth century. As sociologist Barbara Ellen Smith argues, the myth of white racial innocence strengthened in the 1960s and 1970s because Appalachia saw relatively little in the way of civil rights protests, and white activists in the region tended to focus on the actions of corporate and government outsiders rather than internal systems of white supremacy. She writes that in much of the literature, "The contemporary predominance of whites in Appalachia becomes a benign demographic fact, rather than a product of active practices characterized in part by persistent white supremacy."[19]

The activists I write about varied in their consciousness of and their responses to racial ideas about the Mountain South. Many participated in processes that reinforced the idea of Appalachia as a white enclave absent of racism, for instance, when they identified with the struggles of black civil rights activists, but avoided discussion of racial discrimination or the legacy of racial violence in their own communities. Other activists, black and white, countered images of Appalachia as a mythic white space. They did so by casting regional campaigns as part of broader, national struggles that saw racism, poverty, and oppression as interwoven. By tracing activist campaigns, but also by contextualizing activism within the racial and political history of the United States, I show how movements in Appalachia produced, responded to, and sometimes countered racial myths.

• • •

In the 1930s, Kentucky folksinger Sarah Ogan Gunning composed the song "I Hate the Capitalist System." She described a life of hardship brought on by corporate greed and class divisions. "They call this the land of plenty / To them I guess it's true," she sang. "But that's to the company bosses / Not workers like me an' you."[20] Drawing on the stories of women like Gunning, Chapter One foregrounds women and gender, along with race and class, in the development of the Appalachian coal economy. In the early twentieth century, farming declined and industry expanded. Mountain communities felt the effects of single-industry economies, from timbering to coalmining. Private industry built towns, amassed huge quantities of land, controlled resources, and circumscribed access to political power, creating deep social divisions as wealth concentrated in the hands of a few and flowed out of the region.

In the first half of the twentieth century, extractive industries overwhelmed the region; communities experienced tolls in the form of workplace death and disability; workers organized into unions and faced corporate backlash; and by the 1950s, mechanization again transformed industry and unemployment rates soon rose. Women's caregiving transformed alongside industry, as male workers faced injury and death, and poverty crept around the edges of the boom-and-bust economy. Women activists emerged in these early years. They testified about corporate domination, protested environmental destruction, and organized for worker rights, often connecting their protest to the caregiving labor they performed. They provided the cultural and intellectual foundations for future waves of activism. Chapter One places the passage of War on Poverty legislation in 1964 within these decades of social unrest in the Mountain South. It then examines the racial and gender contours of federal policies in the region and how, despite limitations, the notion of "community action" at the heart of the War on Poverty held promise for many poor and working-class people and their allies.

Among the women who took advantage of War on Poverty legislation, Edith Easterling reminisced in later years that becoming politically active and speaking out against injustice made one "feel like a free person."[21] Born in 1925 to a mountain family, Easterling was among the first in her community to participate in federal antipoverty programs. She made an ideal leader with her local connections, abiding interest in community improvement, and charisma. She had long been active in local politics in Pike County, Kentucky, one of the heaviest coal-producing counties in the country. She considered herself among the "self-educated" people who joined local antipoverty efforts, in her case the Appalachian Volunteers funded by the Office of Economic Opportunity, created by the signature legislation of the War on Poverty.[22] Chapter Two traces Edith Easterling's path to the Appalachian Volunteers and her efforts, alongside allies, to organize her community, provide for the needs of poor people, and expose the reasons why entrenched poverty existed in the first place. She also joined efforts to challenge corporate control of the land and to make a case for welfare as an entitlement of American citizenship, campaigns that countered the long-held assumption that blamed Appalachians for poverty. Those campaigns quickly thrust her into a wider world of southern social justice activists. The history of community action in Pike County reveals how federal resources opened up new opportunities to attack antidemocratic politics and power imbalances in the coalfields.[23]

The story of Edith, her family, and their relationships with activists from across the country calls into question the insider/outsider framework that has been widely accepted in the study of the Appalachian War on Poverty.[24] Appalachian studies scholars have long concentrated on a legacy of missionary work in Appalachia, dating to the early twentieth century, in which outsider reformers and missionaries characterized mountain dwellers as "yesterday's people" who were poor in part because they refused to adjust to modern society.[25] Scholars have lumped these missionaries together with the antipoverty workers of the 1960s and 1970s. By doing so they have suggested that mountaineers never trusted the War on Poverty or the outsiders and that cultural insensitivity on the part of outsiders undermined the antipoverty programs. That framework has obscured the ways that Appalachian women leaders helped to build a multidimensional movement that relied on strong alliances, traversed boundaries, and forged both regional and national connections that were crucial to sustaining their activism.[26]

Centering insider/outsider relationships and the internal conflicts that they wrought, some historians concluded that, by the end of the 1960s, organizations had failed due to political infighting. Yet this is not the whole story. As Chapter Three shows, antipoverty programs came under sustained attack by local and state officials. They organized quickly to stop the expanding grassroots war on poverty.[27] In Kentucky, a state-funded red-baiting campaign called the Kentucky Un-American Activities Committee targeted white antipoverty workers in eastern Kentucky, including Edith Easterling. The committee used racist appeals to undermine community organizing in Pike

County and across Kentucky. A close examination of those hearings reveals how the Appalachian movement's intersection with civil rights organizers, along with its pointed indictment of coalfield politics, posed a serious threat to Kentucky elites.

The backlash weakened the Appalachian Volunteers, but it did not hamper the resolve of people in the mountains who looked for new avenues to organize for the expansion of democracy. Building on the ideas of the civil rights movement, in particular the Southern Christian Leadership Conference's Poor People's Campaign, white and black Appalachians joined together to make more militant calls for economic justice in the United States. They carried those ideas into the oldest social reform organization in the region, the Council of the Southern Mountains. As they transformed the Council, they also developed a progressive Appalachian identity, one that connected them to the multiracial movements of poor people, rejected stereotypes of backward and lazy hillbillies, and proved a foundation for more militant activism that emerged in the late 1960s and early 1970s.

Local activists and their allies who picked up the mantle of poor people's rights soon joined together in regional welfare rights organizations, the subject of Chapter Four. Among the local activists was Eula Hall, a white, middle-aged mother of four stuck in an abusive relationship. Eula Hall first saw the chance to change her life when she met Volunteers in Service to America (VISTA) workers in the Mud Creek community of Floyd County and learned of the War on Poverty. She had grown up poor and "knew what it's like. If it's cold, I've been there. If it's hunger, I've been there. If it was bare without clothes or shoes to wear to school, I knew." But she also had an abiding interest in social justice and often dreamed of ways to make life better for herself and her neighbors. The college students who moved to Appalachia to work in VISTA programs had resources that she knew could help her and her community, so she got involved. Together they "would organize groups, testify and march, picket, or whatever it took to try and get something done to make a difference in our living standards."[28] Access to welfare became one of the central issues in her community, where she and others led the Eastern Kentucky Welfare Rights Organization. Calls for "welfare rights" connected white Appalachian activists to the national welfare rights movement, spearheaded by black women, and led to a regional variation of welfare rights organizing. Chapter Four uncovers a wing of the welfare rights movement that neither scholars of Appalachia nor welfare have recognized.[29]

The welfare rights movement brought together single mothers, disabled miners, and elderly people, who, along with fighting for school lunch programs, food stamps, and fair treatment by social workers, identified access to health care as a primary factor in poverty. Chapter Five charts how Eula Hall and her allies helped to build a community health movement, calling for health care as a human right. Influenced by the Medical Committee for Human Rights, an organization that formed in response to health disparities in African American communities in the Deep South, health activists opened community-controlled medical clinics and connected them to a host of other community issues, including women's health concerns and local struggles for environmental justice. They argued that health patterns, employment, gender, and the environment were interrelated, and all played a part in a community's health outcomes.

Appalachian women activists helped to implement antipoverty programs in their communities and used them to ignite campaigns for welfare rights, health care, and environmental justice. Even when not central to a particular campaign, the relationship between capital and labor was always the backdrop to progressive activism in eastern Kentucky, in particular the labor struggles of coalminers. In 1973 miners in Harlan County went on strike for the right to unionize. They saw their campaign as an opening volley in the battle to unionize mines across the Mountain South. Women soon joined the picket lines. They also formed the Brookside Women's Club to support striking miners and their families. Chapter Six explores how they drew on the language that had circulated for a decade, calling not only for the right to join a union but also making a case for how unionized workplaces would benefit working-class families, with the concerns of women—in particular the challenges of social reproduction in the coalfields—a key theme of their protests. As they gave voice to their specific concerns as women, they also gave rise to a feminist consciousness in the coalfields.

In the mid-1970s women's rights exploded onto the scene. Although previous women's activism in the mountains was feminist in nature, in the sense that it promoted women's equality, an explicitly, self-identified feminist movement emerged during and after the Brookside Strike. White antipoverty and working-class activists incorporated the lessons of the War on Poverty and the labor struggle into their quest for women's rights.[30] Chapter Seven shows how their struggles against corporate abuse led to a regionally specific form of feminism, as some white mountain women connected their gendered positions—as mothers, workers, wives, and caregivers—to their class experiences of living and working in the coalfields.[31] Others fought for access to mining jobs, traditionally restricted to men, and changed the workplace once there.

Yet, as Chapter Seven shows, white, working-class women's understanding of feminism sometimes clashed with the ideas of middle-class feminists who shaped policy decisions. For instance, when the Appalachian Women's Rights

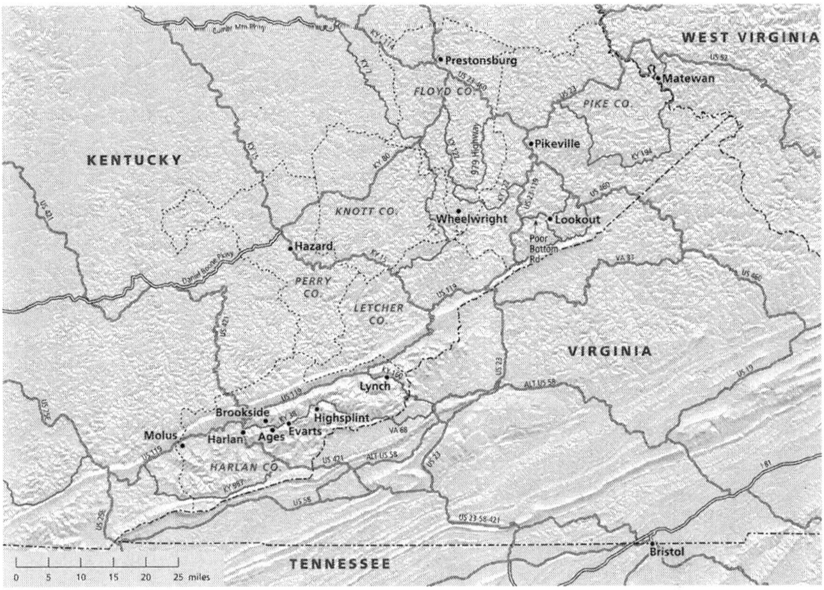

Figure 2. Map of eastern Kentucky. Courtesy of INCaseLLC.

Organization debated elite white women who were part of the governor-appointed Commission on Women in Kentucky, they encountered limited conceptions of women's rights that failed to integrate the concerns of rural, working-class, and poor women.[32] Women in the Mountain South did not simply give up on the women's movement, however. They continued to push for changes in their workplaces and communities that would benefit a greater number of women and the working-class communities where they lived.[33]

The activists whose stories follow were based in eastern Kentucky, where they were concentrated in predominantly white, working-class communities. Many of them lived in coal-producing counties Harlan, Floyd, and Pike, as well as Knott and Letcher. Residents in these places witnessed a large influx of activists and resources in the 1960s and 1970s, and a handful of women became especially prominent activists.

Telling their stories required creativity and a willingness to cast a wide net, as the perspectives of working-class and poor women rarely appear with any consistency in institutional records. I conducted oral history interviews with activists and their allies, and I also drew upon interviews conducted in the last three decades by documentarians and former antipoverty activists, invested in preserving memories of the 1960s. Captivating film footage and photographs preserved at regional cultural and media arts centers helped me imagine the period: the facial expressions of protesters, the timbre of women's voices, the landscape. All of these sources in combination with national and regional manuscript collections and print publications allowed me to trace women's activism across time and place and to stitch a multilayered, dynamic history of gender and social movements in the Mountain South.

Although I focus on specific women in particular places, whenever possible I illuminate broader themes across the Mountain South and show how activists in eastern Kentucky participated in regional and national organizing efforts. That is not to say that Appalachia is a monolithic place. While there were common themes across communities, like corporate control of land, plenty of places throughout the region were not dominated by the coal industry. Nonetheless, many struggled with entrenched poverty, like in western North Carolina, where debates swirled around federal land use, and agricultural communities in eastern Kentucky and Tennessee.[34] People of color in Appalachia were too often passed over by policy makers, who cast the entire region as a white enclave and sent the majority of resources into white communities. Moreover, variations in local politics and union membership influenced the strands of activism that emerged in specific places. Thus, this study is specific to particular communities in eastern Kentucky, but it also recognizes when, how, and why activists forged networks across the region and the nation.

• • •

By ignoring white mountain women, poor and working-class, historians have reinforced the idea that they stand apart or outside of history and politics. This book seeks to correct that misconception. In doing so, it also makes several contributions to our understanding of twentieth-century American history.

First, it reveals how vital the history of caregiving labor is to the histories of labor and capitalism.[35] The coalfields of the Mountain South may not be the norm, but the extreme labor conditions there throw into relief the necessity of social reproduction in capitalist production and how the expropriation of caregiving labors (as well as land and natural resources) has been fundamental to capitalist systems. When women politicized their caregiving labor and challenged the extraction of their work, they made their labor visible and generated critiques of capitalist logics.[36] Moreover, the history of women in the coalfields shows how caregiving labor is not static but has changed over time, in relation to the economy, federal legislation, and access to social provisions. Poor and working-class women felt changes acutely and fought for policy changes that grappled with the needs of working-class communities in their entirety. When mountain women joined the picket lines of male workers, organized welfare rights meetings with disabled miners, and brought their life experiences to bear in social justice campaigns, they blurred the lines between productive and reproductive labor in ways that are instructive to how we think about and write history.

Second, it reinforces how the expansion of the welfare state under the Great Society legislation, despite limitations, opened up possibilities for poor and working-class women to redress the worst abuses of capitalism, to chart new paths for themselves, and to address community crises. This is a story in part about how women activists interacted with various levels of government; how their expectations of citizenship were shaped by their caregiving labors; and how they navigated, changed, and were changed by federal power. They entered new jobs, built community institutions, and acquired legal resources to challenge injustices that they witnessed—from how decisions about land-use were made to how their children were treated in school. Historians of the New Deal have shown how the welfare state made vast improvement in many Americans' lives, for instance, by strengthening labor protections and creating Social Security. Yet, in studies of the Appalachian War on Poverty, the positive impact of the welfare state has been more muted. It is more difficult to deny that impact with women and gender at the center of the story. It is equally important to examine how women made policies more effective with their insights and strategies. Although they achieved numerous victories, they also encountered major setbacks, due to political backlash and transformations in the economy. But those setbacks should not eclipse the sense of political possibility that animated the lives of activists at the time.

Last, by tracing women's activism across time and place, this book shows how Appalachian activists stood at the nexus of mid-twentieth-century social movements, compelling us to reconsider the meaning and scope of the American women's movement. As antipoverty and feminist activist Eula Hall put it, "In Appalachia, there is nothing worse than being poor and a woman."[37] Yet "second-wave" feminism in the United States has primarily been cast as a middle-class, urban movement that made few real inroads in the South and was virtually nonexistent in the Appalachian South.[38] A close analysis of Appalachian women's organizing, however, reveals feminists struggling to define "women's issues" in a way that was capacious and encompassing, what one Appalachian feminist called *grassroots feminism*. This book joins a growing body of scholarship that examines how poor and working-class women and women of color offered alternative and radical visions of feminism that braided together class, race, and gender disparities.[39]

For working-class caregivers in Appalachia, labor struggles, welfare rights movements, and campaigns against environmental destruction were women's issues just as much as those typically identified as such, like reproductive health care and domestic violence.

In the story that follows, the War on Poverty galvanized women; they built strong alliances across communities; their hard-nosed activism changed the Mountain South; and that activism led many of them to a gender consciousness that influenced a wave of organizing in the South. Women in the Mountain South imagined a society in which interdependence is the defining feature driving political and economic decisions. Their vision allowed for various, overlapping, and productive coalitions. The chapters that follow place working-class caregivers in Appalachia at the center of history, allowing us to see the world through their eyes.

1 The Political and Gender Economy of the Mountain South, 1900–1964

Florence Reece watched from the cabin as her husband Sam cowered in the hillside cornfields. Her mind reeled. For weeks he had been harassed by "gun thugs," hired by coal operators and supported by the sheriff to thwart his organizing activities with the United Mine Workers of America in Harlan County, Kentucky. The men had ransacked the Reece's home on one occasion and arrested Sam under bogus charges. Now they surrounded the house and threatened to abduct him. While Florence was "a-watchin' for the thugs to come after him," she must have worried about the seven children who slept under her roof. Raising them was no easy feat in the Depression-struck coalfields of the early 1930s. She witnessed the dire poverty of her neighbors and knew that little separated her from them. In Molus, the coal town where the Reeces lived, food had become scarce. One day a neighbor came to their house in search of sustenance. She was "scaly all over," tale-tell signs of pellagra, a disease she got "at the table because she didn't have no food."[1]

Life had gotten worse since the Depression, but it had never been easy. Like many coalminers' wives, Florence fretted daily about her husband's safety. Miners would "go under that mountain every day, never knowing whether they'd come out alive."[2] Her own father had died in a slate fall in a Tennessee coalmine when she was fourteen years old. Fork Ridge, where Florence and her parents had lived, was controlled by a small group of antiunion, elite white men. From the time she was a child, Florence understood that the lives of mining families stood in stark contrast to those of company families, who considered themselves civic leaders, yet did little to challenge the horrendous conditions of so many coalmining communities.[3] Florence and Sam married and stayed in Fork Ridge, where Sam had worked as a miner since he was a boy. As a young man, he joined the wave of Appalachian union campaigns, leading workers out on strike in 1922. The company broke the union and fired Sam, and the Reeces moved to Molus where Sam found a job in the mines and continued organizing.[4] In Harlan County he faced coal operators who owned all but three of the incorporated towns and a sheriff, J. H. Blair, who pledged allegiance to coal operators.[5]

In the early morning hours, as her husband hid in the fields and she stood watch over her children, her mind turned from fear and anger to music. Lacking paper, she ripped the calendar from the wall and wrote "Which Side Are You On?" Set to the tune of the hymn "Lay the Lily Low," Florence's song later became the labor anthem, calling on workers to join the "good battle" and declaring that there is "no neutral" in Harlan County. Workers could choose the side of the union or the company's crony: "You'll either be a union man / Or a thug for J. H. Blair." The song also interwove the stories of women and children into the labor struggle, declaring that the company men's children "live in luxury, our children almost wild" and that the company will "take away our bread." The last verse and chorus referenced her father's death in the mines early in life: "My daddy was a miner / He's now in the air and sun / He'll be with you fellow workers / Till every battle's won / Which side are you on, Which side are you on?"[6]

Florence Reece's "Which Side Are You On?" is most often heralded as a song by and about workers. Labor organizers carried the song to industrial workers across the country. Pete Seeger and the Almanac Singers helped to make it famous in folk circles, and in the 1960s, civil rights organizers learned the anthem. As it passed through organizations and movements, its lyrics were revised to suit each situation. Yet part of the power of the song is in the portrait it offers of a wife and mother—the caregiver of the working-class community. Reece's song was about the labor struggle, yes, but that struggle encompassed more than a battle between workers and capitalists. It was a story about the working-class community in general and about the position of working-class women in particular, as the narrator calls on workers to unionize for the benefit of all.[7]

Reece's gendered and class perspective as a caregiver comes into sharper focus when we place her song in the context of her life and activism. While she is remembered most often for her labor anthem, she was also a lifelong activist. In the 1970s, she returned to Harlan County to support union workers who were on strike. As she led the workers in song at rallies, her husband suffered from black lung disease, which she connected to the long labor struggle. She also wrote new songs that supported the 1960s antipoverty movements and challenged the dominance of capitalism, again emphasizing a caring role: "If the sun would stand still / Till the people are fed, all wars

Figure 3. Florence Reece performs at a UMWA Coal Miner Memorial Day Observance, Evarts, Kentucky, 1974. Courtesy of www.earldotter.com ©.

cease to be / Houses, hospitals, schools a-built / We must have a new recipe." In an interview Florence Reece summed up her support of the workers' and antipoverty movements: "All in the world we people wanted was enough to feed and clothe and house our children. We didn't want what the coal operators had at all, just a decent living."[8]

Florence Reece was a part of a tradition of working-class white women whose activism was born out of daily life, configured in the particular class and gender dynamics at play in the Mountain South. To understand her and the dozens of women activists who were her contemporaries and those who came after, we must begin with the history of capitalist development and its impact on social relations in the coalfields of Appalachia. As coalmining dominated the economy of the region, women's work altered, and their caregiving roles strained under new pressures.

The Coal Industry Arrives

In eastern Kentucky in the late nineteenth century, white rural families lived in hollows, narrow valleys hemmed in by steep ridges and tall mountains. These mountain-sheltered valleys offered modest land to farm, hunting and foraging grounds, and streams. Wealthier residents of the region settled in wide valleys where they built towns, owned large farms and slaves, and developed commercial enterprises financed through land speculation and, later, through timber and mineral resources. Before the large-scale industrialization in the early 1900s, some industry flourished (relying in part on enslaved labor), including iron making, salt making, and the burgeoning resort industry. White rural families practiced subsistence agriculture but were also linked to market economies. They sold and purchased goods from merchants and borrowed money. Many went into debt. The men who did not own or rent land worked as farmhands or as laborers. Poor white women often joined men in the fields or labored in boarding houses and as laundresses. With the arrival of the railroad and new industries after the Civil War, the political economy underwent a sea change.[9]

The promise of coal drove the industrial engine in Appalachia. Eastern Kentucky, West Virginia, northeast Tennessee, and Southwest Virginia sit atop one of six geological coalfields that exist in North America. The term *coalfields* refers to the expansive deposits of carbonized plant debris that rest deep within the earth's surface and were formed over thousands of years. An important form of energy, coal has been used as a fuel to heat homes, power locomotives, generate electricity, and produce iron and steel. When railroads penetrated the region after the Civil War, semi-bituminous coal, previously inaccessible to large-scale American markets and industry, was ready for the taking.[10]

The change was swift and the scale unimaginable. The population increased dramatically as workers flooded new industries. For example, in Pike County the number of coal companies jumped from eight in 1916 to forty-five in 1920, spurred along by the United States' entrance into World War I.[11] Between 1900 and 1930, the population increased by 178 percent, and the influx did not cease until the 1950s. White, black, and central and eastern European immigrant workers migrated to the mountains or moved from mountain farms to coal towns, lured by the promise of steady work and wages. Once sparsely populated counties saw the rise of densely populated coal towns. An onslaught of workers brought new working-class cultures to the region. At the same time, politics came to reflect the interests of the industrial elite.[12]

The new politics ushered in by industrialization diverged from the patronage system of the nineteenth century, when kinship and personal contacts characterized business and political relationships. Middle-class families had long held clout, rooted in their control of banks and land, and they distributed resources as they saw fit. At the same time, political participation was high across mountain communities, so middle-class leaders did not hold absolute power. White male residents of the county traveled to town for court sessions, to hear campaign speeches, and to vote, and they often brought their whole families with them. New industrialists—many of whom were absentee property holders—relied on the political power of middle-class residents to maintain a political system and economic environment that favored industry. As less wealthy residents of the mountains moved from farms, relinquished property, and entered the world of wage work, they gave up prior affiliations. For those who were migratory, a lack of permanent residence weakened their franchise. And new voting laws, meant to disenfranchise African Americans, also eclipsed poor whites' access to the ballot box. Meanwhile, middle-class residents maintained their status and grew more powerful as their ties to corporations strengthened.[13]

The most evident indication of a new political system appeared in the form of coal operators' associations, founded by and presided over by coal operators and town elites. These associations fostered the concentration of political power in the hands of coal barons. They oversaw the police force, controlled company unions, regulated prices, and influenced elections and political parties at the local and state levels.[14] They did not rule uncontested, however, as striking workers, unions, and, later, antipoverty workers challenged their political dominance in the Appalachian South.

Caregiving in the New Economy

Gender patterns evolved alongside the labor system, as families moved from farms or straddled agriculture and industry. For many women, labor intensified as they managed farms and capitalized on new economies in the coal camps. Above all, the industrialization of the coalfields ushered in a new era of intensified caregiving, in which women navigated new sicknesses, disabilities, and threats of violence that stemmed from coalmining.

In the nineteenth century, women's labor (and often children's labor) was crucial in operating farms and making a livelihood. Along with caring for children, fetching water, doing laundry, cleaning, and cooking, women participated in informal labor markets and, to a lesser extent, formal wage labor. They proved to be among the most productive women in the nation in the 1840s, bringing in more income from goods than farmwomen nationally.[15] Women ventured into the forest to pick fruit, nuts, and wild herbs. Closer to home they kept gardens, chickens, bees, and milk cows, all of which offered sustenance and goods for trade. They sold milk, butter, cheese, eggs, and honey at markets. They manufactured cloth and sewed clothing and quilts. And they made other household goods like soaps, brooms, and baskets that they traded or sold. Others worked in factory-organized putting-out systems, for which they carded and spun wool and cotton, wove fabrics, or sewed and finished products. They also did fieldwork when widowed, when a husband was sick, or simply because more hands were needed. The poorest women worked as domestic servants in the homes of wealthier families, took in laundry, worked as field hands, or labored in commercial enterprises. In sum, the majority of white Appalachian households were, as one man remembered his childhood, "survival units" in which every member of the household was expected to contribute.[16]

White mountain women did not slow down their pace when men entered the coalmines and other industrial work. In fact, the transition ushered in a deepening of the gender division of labor, as men increasingly worked in industry while women and children maintained homes and farms. Malta Miller grew up on a farm on John's Creek near Van Lear, Kentucky, in the 1910s with her siblings and tenant farmer parents. Prior to entering the mines, Miller's father devoted all of his time to working the farm with the help of his children, including his daughters, who thinned corn and drove cattle. Her mother mostly tended the garden, from which "she sold a lot." Miller's family continued to live on the farm after her father started mining, and her mother and the children picked up the slack. After he was injured in the mines, Miller's father had to quit his waged job. The injury also prevented him from returning full-time to farming, although he was able to garden and work odd jobs. Miller's childhood memories suggest that her mother and the children were crucial to keeping the farm and freeing up her father's time so that he could garner wages in the mines and then provide for the family once he was disabled.[17]

With the increased population in the coal camps, many white women found an expanded market for their wares and food products. Mae Frazier's mother took advantage of a new customer base in the coal camps. She sold produce and eggs in the nearby mining town, and Frazier credited her mother's business savvy for her own upward mobility: That "was how she managed to raise us and get us all an education."[18] Malta Miller also participated in the coal camp economy once she was grown. After graduating, she became a teacher, but she quit her job after marrying a miner. She continued to bring in an income by sewing and selling dresses and skirts for girls and women, work shirts for men, and children's clothing.[19] Onda Lee Holbrook, born in 1917, worked in a shoe factory in Portsmith, Ohio, before moving to the coal camp Auxier with her husband. She had no access to similar wage work in Auxier, but she used her skills to become a seamstress in the informal economy.[20]

Along with the sale of foods and other goods, women provided laundry and boarding services for the influx of men who worked in mining, timber, and oil fields. One widowed mother operated a boarding house and laundry service for the "office men" of the mines. Her nine children helped with the daily tasks of running the boarding house. They prepared meals for ten to fifteen men, washed dishes, laundered clothes in the nearby creek, and ironed the men's shirts.[21] Marjorie Castle and her husband moved between mining towns and the family farm in the 1920s. They eventually moved to the coal town Van Lear so that her husband could work in the mines full time. They saved enough money to purchase a farm, which they rented out for two years while they continued to live in Van Lear. When mining slowed, they moved to the farm and Castle began operating a boarding house from her home, balancing housework and care for her five children. She organized her boarding house operation with a friend; her friend rented to the men who worked the day shifts, and Castle rented rooms to men who worked night shifts.[22]

For some white, rural families, the founding of coal towns brought new options for work, education, and leisure. Some companies built modern towns with large company stores, where mine employees and their families had access to an array of products, including food, textiles, tools, and household goods. One woman remembered the stores as carrying a variety of goods that covered "about a hundred percent of people's needs."[23] Even if the available products had expanded in her memory, her story highlights the contrast between the small stores of the past, where farmers bought only staple items, and the modern company stores. For the first time, rural white parents who desired formal education for their children could send children to school and, more rarely, college. Rural children often had access to school only through the eighth grade, but the larger industry towns operated high schools. Some companies also built community meeting spaces, churches, and post offices. For example, in Harlan County, U.S. Steel established the coal town of Lynch in 1917. The town included an impressive post office built from cut stone, segregated secondary schools (marking it as a modern southern town), a hospital, and a multistory company store. The houses sat in neat rows along urban streets with sidewalks. In sum, it was a modern, early-twentieth-century southern town, tucked in Appalachia.[24]

Coal towns were not the idyllic places that they might seem on the surface, however, as grave structural issues shaped women's and men's lives. The companies who owned these towns saw fit to circumscribe democracy: there was usually no local government to speak of, and many coal barons ruled with an iron fist. They controlled the workforce with company-hired police forces, and they often required that workers rent company homes (thus paying rent to their employer) and shop in the company stores using "scrip," the company-produced currency that mine owners paid to workers. Many coalmine operators manipulated the rent and price of consumer goods to ensure their own profits. And their system of control allowed them to keep an eye on workers and prevent unionization.

Coal companies also enforced racial segregation and systematized white supremacist policies. The black population increased in towns and coal camps between 1870 and 1940 as employment opportunities arose and coal operators recruited black workers. In larger towns, coal operators built racially segregated housing, churches, schools, and recreational spaces. Black people in Appalachia faced struggles similar to those of black people throughout the South, where Jim Crow structured economic, political, and social relations. While the coalmines offered an alternative to the sharecropping of the Deep South, mine bosses routinely employed black miners in the most dangerous jobs at the lowest pay, and rarely in foremen positions. As the population of African Americans increased, some whites reacted violently. White communities posted signs warning African Americans to leave before the sun set; whites expelled black residents in Cary and Corbin, Kentucky, following race riots; the Ku Klux Klan was active in the region; and a rash of lynchings between the late nineteenth century and the 1930s sent warnings to African Americans who dared challenge the racial status quo.[25] Despite harsh and unfair conditions, black Appalachians living in coal towns created separate, thriving communities, as in Lynch, Kentucky, where black coalmining families took great pride in their work and community.[26]

In contrast to the black miners and their families who moved into coal towns, rural black Appalachians lived in places that most Americans identified as totally "white." Yet, as scholars Dwight Billings and Kathleen Blee argue, "the racial homogeneity of Kentucky mountain society . . . was created over time." They show how the rural black population decreased in the decades after emancipation in eastern Kentucky, due to an inhospitable economy and "organized racial terrorism."[27] The low African American population throughout rural Appalachia was not inevitable but part of a longer process of discriminatory policies and racial terror.[28]

The small population of black Appalachians who lived in more rural locales found themselves on the extreme margins of society, without access to schools and other public institutions. For instance, residents of String Town, which was on the outskirts of Pikeville, had to travel the river by boat to get to town because they had no access to roads. They also lived under the threat that whites might commit violence against them with impunity. After arsonists burned down the community's only school, students had to travel ten miles away. Without adequate transportation, going to school became an all-day affair.[29] Racial boundaries and racism fundamentally shaped Appalachian places and dramatically influenced how people navigated spaces.

Labor conditions could lead to a common experience across race. Neither black nor white workers could escape the volatility of the coal industry, defined by periods of intense labor followed by stretches of unemployment. Communities also mourned together when disaster struck, and it often did. Coalmining is notoriously dangerous work, which explains in part the great pride miners and miners' families took in it, as well as the iconic image of the coalminer. To cross the mine threshold and drop into the "dark black bowels" of the earth, as Florence Reece described it, was an exercise in faith.[30] Coalminers and their families learned to live with the possibility of catastrophe almost as soon as the mines opened in the early part of the century.

Coalfield Disasters

In 1902, the Coal Creek Company mine exploded in Fraterville, Tennessee, marking one of the first catastrophic mining disasters of the twentieth century. Two hundred and sixteen miners died. Not all of the deaths were immediate. Twenty-six miners barricaded themselves in a chamber, hoping for rescue, but they eventually succumbed to "bad air." All but three of the adult men in the town died in the accident, leaving behind 1200 widows and children. Women and children gathered around the entrance to the mine in the hours after the explosion, where they saw heaps of slate and sheets of flames that prevented a rescue mission. The company reported a day after the accident that families had "nothing to eat and it is a matter of only a few days until there will be great suffering in the valley."[31]

The Fraterville explosion was among dozens of mine disasters that rocked coalmining communities. In 1907, at least 362 Italian immigrant miners died following an explosion at the Fairmont Coal Mine in Monongah, West Virginia, leaving behind approximately 250 widows and one thousand children. Seven years later, another West Virginia mine consumed 181 miners in an explosion, and in 1917, 62 miners died in a mine in Clay County, Kentucky.[32]

Along with large-scale disasters, smaller accidents—with death tolls between five and twenty—claimed dozens of miners' lives every year. In Kentucky alone there were over thirty-five incidents in which five or more workers died in an explosion, fire, or flood from 1900 to 1981. Even as technology and safety regulations made mines safer as the century progressed, disasters were quick reminders that mines were volatile. In 1968, seventy-eight miners died in the Farmington Mine Disaster in West Virginia. In 1969, congress passed the Federal Coal Mine Health and Safety Act, creating an agency to inspect mines for safety, yet enforcement was slow. Thirty-eight men died in a mine explosion in Hyden, Kentucky, in 1970. The Buffalo Creek Flood, the result of a broken coal slurry impoundment dam, claimed the lives of 114 miners in West Virginia. It also killed 125 residents along the Buffalo Creek and destroyed over 500 homes. In 1976, the Scotia Mine disaster in Kentucky caused 26 miner deaths, precipitating passage of the 1977 Mine Health and Safety Act that required more stringent federal oversight of the mining industry.[33]

Along with catastrophes that claimed lives in the blink of an eye, miners and their families faced the consequences of serious injury and disability. Opal Goble knew all too well how the mines could "gobble up" men. Her father was among the first wave of miners in Kentucky. In a slate fall, his chest was crushed and both legs broken. He survived, but one leg was permanently shorter than the other. Goble's miner husband survived two separate accidents, and in each he suffered a broken pelvis. "And he never was well since. But he went back to the mines then, till he retired" in 1968.[34] Along with crippling injury, miners risked developing coal workers' pneumoconiosis, or black lung disease. As their lungs deteriorated from exposure to coal dust, they slowly suffocated. Between 1968 and 2014, black lung disease contributed to the deaths of at least 75,000 miners; over 350,000 miners had succumbed in the decades prior, before coal companies and the federal government recognized the disease.[35]

Emotional and caregiving labor fell to women. Mothers, wives, and daughters cared for sick, injured, and disabled men, and they mourned the loss of loved ones. Nursing ailing men was one of the primary, unspoken responsibilities of women. For instance, labor activist Sudie Crusenberry cared for her father when he got sick with black lung disease. At one point he was "a-smothering down" and "he couldn't get no breath." So Crusenberry decided to take him to a hospital, despite flooding. "I had to wade through [the flood to get him] to the hospital," where the doctor told Crusenberry her father was dying. She took him home and nursed him until he died three days later.[36] When her husband was severely injured in a mine, doctors told him he would never walk again. Crusenberry brought him home from the hospital and worked with him daily, providing physical therapy until he was eventually able to walk with a cane.

The Rise of the Labor Movement

Miners and their families faced a dangerous industry that could squelch out a miner's life in an instant and send a family spiraling into economic distress. Many looked to the labor movement to help them improve their conditions. The 1920s and 1930s saw several intense labor battles in the Appalachian coalfields, as the United Mine Workers of America and, briefly, the National Miners' Union attempted to organize the workers of the Appalachian coal industry.

In the 1920s, Appalachian coalminers earned less than their unionized counterparts in the Midwest and Northeast. For instance, Harlan County coal loaders earned a fraction of the wages of Illinois and Indiana miners, at 42 and 35 percent, respectively. Throughout Appalachia, coal associations offset high freight costs with low wages.[37] Many workers believed that the coal bosses valued profit more than they did men's lives. An oft-told story by miners and their family members captured the ruthlessness of the industry. In the story, a boss tells the miner to make sure the work mules get out of the mines alive. When the miner says "What about me?" the boss replies, as singer and miner Nimrod Workman told it, "We can always hire another man, but you've got to buy that mule."[38]

During World War I, organizers from the UMWA were able to gain a foothold in Appalachia, with labor leader Mary Harris "Mother" Jones leading the charge. An Irish immigrant, who had lost her family to a yellow fever epidemic and her dressmaking business to the Great Chicago Fire, Jones committed herself to the movement for labor rights, earning the title "the miners' angel." In the first decade of the twentieth century she helped to inspire an interracial unionization campaign in the West Virginia coalfields, where coal operators refused to recognize unions and became increasingly aggressive in their efforts to prevent union organizing. In 1921, striking miners and their families were thrown out of their homes and harassed by private detectives. And the company hired replacement workers in order to break the strike. The labor struggle culminated in ten thousand armed workers facing off against police squads at the Battle of Blair Mountain near Matewan, West Virginia, now known as the largest labor uprising in U.S. history. After several deaths on both sides, the U.S. Army arrived and put an end to the workers' uprising. Hundreds of the rebellious workers faced trials and sentencing for murder and treason. Throughout the region, companies—often backed by the state—attempted to squelch the union movement in the 1920s.[39]

During the Depression the labor movement saw resurgence. Companies lowered production and cut hours until many men could work only a handful of days in two-week periods. To make matters worse, a drought plagued the region, and deaths from malnutrition began to climb. As the Kentucky director from the American Red Cross described it, "The picture of distress . . . in the eastern part of our state is almost unbelievable. . . . There is a growing army of itinerants traveling on foot."[40] Yet the Red Cross, unwilling to engage in industrial disputes and influenced by coal owners, provided aid only to victims of the drought (who were farmers) and not to miners.[41]

Hundreds of miners in eastern Kentucky (and across the region) turned to the United Mine Workers of America in the winter and spring of 1931. They went on strike, forcing some mines to shut down, and garnered union oaths from over eight thousand workers. Coal operators responded harshly, spying on and discharging pro-union miners, evicting them from their homes, and directing police to harass them. In Harlan County, Sheriff J. H. Blair deputized company officials to aid his campaign against the union and promised to shoot to kill if he believed his men were threatened. Mining families fled to Evarts (one of the few towns not owned by a coal company), and the union set up headquarters there. Without aid from either the cash-strapped UMWA or local relief organizations, the situation became dire. A rash of lootings broke out during one week in April, as thieves took food from surrounding grocery stores and commissaries. And on May 5, a gunfight broke out between mine workers and company guards. Known as the Battle of Evarts, the skirmish left a striker, a commissary store clerk, and two police officers dead. The National Guard arrived to quell the violence, and the UMWA retreated. Yet the drive of union miners only increased, with over five thousand workers going on strike after the Battle of Evarts.[42]

Some miners and their families looked to the communist-backed National Miners' Union (NMU), as they sought outside support and some way out of the nightmare of the Depression. One of the "dual unions" of the period, the NMU was part of the Trade Union Unity League, which offered an alternative to the more conservative UMWA. While the NMU never grew to be very large, coal operators acted swiftly and violently to put down what they perceived to be a threat by radicals. Following weeks of more arrests and the murder of Harry Simms, a young Jewish union organizer from Massachusetts, and the brutal assault of numerous black and white pro-union miners, the NMU also left the region defeated.[43]

In the wake of hunger, violence, and repression, women spoke out and, notably, sang out. Florence Reece, Aunt Molly Jackson, and Sarah Ogan Gunning, all relatives of miners, composed songs that described life in the coalfields. Many of their songs rallied the working-class community, and they also exposed women's particular hardships. Perhaps no one described women's lives in the coalfields more forcefully than Mary Magdalene Garland, known as Aunt Molly Jackson. A balladeer, midwife, and labor organizer from Bell County, Kentucky, Aunt Molly Jackson spoke at a public hearing in 1932. She exposed the company's attacks on pro-union miners in the protracted labor struggles of the early 1930s and described the impact of the Depression on the region. She testified that, weekly, three to seven children died of cholera and famine. She also chided the Red Cross for denying food to people based on union politics. Other women described hunger, the inability to feed and clothe children, and the stress of living under repression.[44] The stories that women circulated became part of Aunt Molly Jackson's lyrics. In "Hungry Ragged Blues," she described a scene where husbands labored all day but were denied pay: "All the women in the coal camps are a-sitting with bowed-down heads / Ragged and barefooted, the children a-crying for bread."[45]

Franklin D. Roosevelt's election to the presidency signaled positive change for many coalmining families. In 1933, Roosevelt's New Deal ushered in a new era of labor relations in the coalfields, with the expansion of state-managed capitalism. The Appalachian Agreements brokered by representatives of miners and coal operators at the White House led to a period of relative peace. The 1933 agreements set in motion a series of five wage agreements over the course of the 1930s up to 1941; blunted the southern wage advantage; and provided for an eight-hour day, a structured grievance procedure, and minimum age requirements.[46] They also prohibited the coal industry from requiring that miners live in company homes or receive payment in scrip that could be used only at company stores. Along with the Appalachian Agreements, the National Industrial Recovery Act provided protections for union workers across the nation.[47] The staunchest antiunion holdouts in the period of "Bloody Harlan," even Harlan County coal operators eventually capitulated.

World War II, Migration, and Lost Promises

War mobilization had a profound impact on the coalfields. An out-migration that had begun in the 1920s sped up as war industries attracted workers from Appalachia and the Deep South. In the early 1940s, the nation saw the greatest spatial reorganization in its history as World War II military production led to expanded labor opportunities in the nation's cities. No study of southern migration has explored the migration of young women, specifically. But as war industries opened the factory gates to them, young women from the South and Appalachia migrated to cities such as Baltimore, Cincinnati, and Detroit to work in factories.[48]

Many young women from Appalachia followed these patterns, finding opportunities outside of the mountains before returning home where they married and had children. Edith Easterling made the long trip to Ypsilanti, Michigan, to work in the war industries with a girlfriend. The young women soon found jobs as riveters at an airplane factory. Easterling loved the work and the freedom of life in a city. After she was married with children, she told stories about being able to buy lipstick at a dime-store for the first time. She also kept relics from that past: a reprint of Da Vinci's "Last Supper" and a flower pot that she had coveted so much that she took it from someone's stoop. (She soon felt horrible about taking the pot but kept it to remind herself that she was never going to steal again.)[49] Many others like her proved mobile and willing to explore new environments, countering the idea that people from the mountains were isolated or culturally backward.

In the late 1940s the coalfields were characterized by the expansion of highways and other infrastructure, a stabilized middle-class population, and an influx of goods. However, the war and the advancements in technology that it fostered ushered in the beginning of wide-scale mechanization of mines and brought an end to hand-loading, thus decreasing the number of people required to work in industry. Out-migration of black and white workers surged once again throughout the coalfields.[50] Moreover, the developments that accompanied militarization were not evenly distributed. Well into the 1960s, areas outside of the county seats or beyond the largest coal camps lagged behind in their access to electricity, plumbing, and paved roads. "Growth without development" characterized the Appalachian South, and when the regional economy declined, there was little to protect the previous gains.[51] Many in Appalachia thus experienced worsening economic conditions in the years after the war, setting it apart from much of the rest of the nation.

The decline in industrial jobs, especially those that were unionized, had a ripple effect in Appalachian communities. Since the onset of the New Deal, workers and caregivers had witnessed the expansion of social welfare that included both public and private policies and programs.[52] This welfare regime relieved some of the burdens of living and working in the coalfields, but it was founded upon fragile contracts. In 1946, the UMWA set up a Welfare and Retirement Fund, a private social welfare system aimed at filling in gaps in the New Deal by providing quality health care and retirement to miners. The fund provided the most comprehensive employee health plan in the nation, covering thousands of miners and their dependents.[53] After staff members documented dire conditions throughout Appalachia—from filthy, out-of-date hospitals to miners who were paralyzed and had never received adequate medical care—the fund built a chain of hospitals and sponsored a variety of health programs in the region.[54]

But the plan depended on steady union membership. As the union faced tumultuous years and a declining membership in the 1950s, the UMWA Welfare and Retirement Fund began to decrease benefits, first retracting programs for widows and dependents, then scaling back health programs, and, finally, threatening to close hospitals. Miners and widows protested the changes immediately. They called on the federal government to force the union to fulfill its responsibility to workers, and in 1962 they began a series of protests called the "roving pickets." They rallied at the mines that had defaulted on payments and sometimes engaged in destructive behavior, setting ablaze or bombing operators' property.[55]

Women brought important insight to the roving pickets of the early 1960s, reminding the public that their own fates were intimately bound with working men's. In 1962, midwife and union activist Frances "Granny" Hager helped to found the Appalachian Committee for Full Employment and led the band of roving pickets. Like many women who lived through the 1930s labor struggles, she understood the sacrifices working people had made to organize a union. She also recalled how coal operators crippled the labor movement by threatening to shut down unless workers would take cuts in pay and benefits. Hager explained, "Naturally the men would take a cut. First thing they knew, they were down to working for nothing. They were working for seven, eight dollars a day. And that's the way the coal operators busted the union and got the men to work for nothing."[56]

Women also joined and led other grassroots movements that sprang up in the early 1960s, most notably the fight against surface mining (also known as strip mining). The practice of stripping topsoil to get to coal seams underneath had become a cheap and easy way for industry to secure coal in the 1960s. Kentucky's state legislature had done little to regulate the practice, despite the destruction it caused. Strip mining was possible on private lands only because farmers at the turn of the century had sold mineral rights to industry under broad form deeds. With new technologies at midcentury, coal companies were able to reach low-lying coal seams. Landowners soon dealt with a shocking reality that the law did little to protect them or their land from strip and auger mining. Surface-mining operations wreaked havoc on the landscape, uprooting trees and disturbing stones that slid down hillsides into creeks and onto farmland, the mine waste often polluting waterways and causing floods.[57]

Protests soon erupted over the practice and what it signified: the coal industry's right to profit regardless of the disasters it unleashed on the land and in people's lives. Ollie "Widow" Combs became a folk hero in the burgeoning movement. In 1965, days after her neighbor armed himself and guarded against strip miners, she sat in front of a bulldozer and refused to move, hoping to protect her twenty-acre farm. Police arrested her and carried her away, and she spent Thanksgiving in jail. The actions of Combs and others led to the formation of the Appalachian Group to Save the Land and People. Over the next several years numerous communities set up their own chapters, and the anti–strip mining campaign became part of a web of activism that exposed the coal industry's abuses of the land and people of Appalachia.[58]

Political Imagery of Appalachia

In the early 1960s, poverty in the region captured the nation's attention as writers and journalists described shocking levels of need. Kentucky lawyer and writer Harry Caudill became the voice of the mountains. He offered a disturbing portrait of eastern Kentucky, where industry had plundered the coal and timber riches of the mountains and left the inhabitants of the region poor and dependent. His 1963 book *Night Comes to the Cumberlands* paired easily with Michael Harrington's best-selling *The Other America*, which included descriptions of impoverished whites in Appalachia and charged that American poverty had become invisible in the era of postwar affluence. Following the publications of these books, journalists flocked to the mountains. *New York Times* writer Homer Bigart was among them, and his series on Appalachian poverty, along with Caudill's and Harrington's books, caught the attention of President Kennedy and helped to plant seeds for the antipoverty programs that Johnson expanded once he took office.[59]

A series of events in 1963—increased unemployment, severe flooding that displaced twenty-five thousand people, and labor unrest—had put pressure on the Kennedy administration to respond to the growing crisis in

Appalachia. Kennedy soon met with the Council of Appalachian Governors, and the group formed the President's Appalachian Regional Commission (PARC), a joint federal-state organization that would coordinate efforts to tackle poverty and develop the distressed region's economy. Within a day of Kennedy's assassination, the newly sworn-in President Lyndon Johnson learned of Kennedy's plans to provide job training, development programs, and other forms of poverty relief to the Appalachian states. A believer in the government's ability to produce positive change, Johnson soon announced publicly that he would continue the antipoverty initiative. During his State of the Union address on January 8, 1964, Johnson declared that his administration would lead an "unconditional war on poverty in America," setting in motion antipoverty measures that delivered federal resources to poor communities across the country.[60]

In the spring of 1964, Lyndon and Lady Bird Johnson headed to West Virginia and eastern Kentucky for a tour and media campaign to promote War on Poverty legislation. In the rural town of Inez, Kentucky, reporters captured Johnson's visit with Tom Fletcher, a white unemployed coalminer and sawmill worker who struggled to provide for his wife and eight children. The now iconic image shows Johnson crouched on the porch, with Fletcher and three of Fletcher's young sons surrounding him, representing two generations of men that Johnson targeted with his antipoverty programs.[61]

Speaking from Fletcher's porch, Johnson declared that he intended "to work every way I can, as long as I can, to wipe out poverty in the United States." He cited the high unemployment rate in Inez—three out of ten men could not find work—and stated that he did not "want men to sit idle because coalmines are idle." He wanted to help put men to work.[62]

The image of Fletcher and the president came to represent the War on Poverty in Appalachia. The White House likely selected the Fletcher family, and Tom Fletcher specifically, for this purpose as part of Johnson's campaign to win southern Democrats over to his policies. The image of Tom Fletcher, a white man who longed to provide a better life for his family, sidestepped issues of black civil rights and welfare for single mothers. Rather, it drew upon the myth of an independent mountaineer, with his intact, traditional, and white family. Fletcher was a hardworking father in a mythologized place who happened to be poor. For those seeking to demonize the War on Poverty, this image was of little use.[63]

Johnson once again summoned a mythic Appalachia when he signed the Appalachian Regional Development Act in 1965. It created the Appalachian Regional Commission, which would oversee economic development from highway construction to vocational training. In his speech after the signing of the legislation, Johnson drew upon the story of white settlers who conquered the Appalachian Ranges to find their way "to the promise and the plenty of a continent that is united." He stated that "no region has contributed more to the shaping of our history." As he gestured to this romanticized historical memory of Appalachia (one that obscured the history of settler-colonialism), Johnson also recognized the wealth disparity that had come to define parts of the region, where family poverty rates were double the national average. Affirming his commitment to "human dignity and decency," he called on state and local governments to implement legislation to ease poverty in "this old and this honored region."[64]

The press kit for the Appalachian War on Poverty sent powerful political and cultural messages to Americans. By using the idea of Appalachia as a white enclave, represented in residents like Fletcher, Johnson and his aides spotlighted white men and mitigated charges that the War on Poverty would disproportionately target and serve African Americans. To do so meant ignoring that Appalachia's diverse population included African Americans, Native Americans, and recent European immigrants. As one member of a War on Poverty task force explained, "We were concerned that the public would think that this was a program for black kids, for ghetto kids. So we emphasized in all our speeches that there were hundreds of thousands of young people trapped in the hollows of Appalachia or in other rural areas, and that this was not just a black program; it was a white and black program."[65] Saturated in gender, the imagery of Fletcher and his family also indicated that the War on Poverty would focus on breadwinner men as the central beneficiaries.

Beginning the War on Poverty in Appalachia

Federal antipoverty programs in Appalachia operated on two planes, often in contradiction with one another. The first was solidly oriented toward market gains and concomitant job growth. The Appalachian Act promised, in the words of Kentucky and West Virginia senators, "to assist local bodies in the development of the basic resources and facilities on which economic growth depends" and to serve the national interest "by offering opportunity to those of different generations who want to work toward our national goals and continue to live in this great region."[66] Underlying this act were widely held beliefs that without new roads, highways, water systems, vocational schools, and overall infrastructure development, industries would not succeed in the region and Appalachian residents would need to move to cities or continue to face poverty and a depressed economy. The Appalachian Act would create opportunity for breadwinners like Fletcher, but, as importantly, it would expand opportunities for capital to continue its extraction of labor and resources.

The second plane of the War on Poverty—the Economic Opportunity Act (EOA)—promised a democratizing effect, and thus was often in tension with the development ethos. Signed by Johnson in 1964, the Economic Opportunity Act addressed more immediate concerns than the Appalachian Act, such as access to health care, food, water, and education, and it invited local people to participate in solving problems. The signature legislation of the War on Poverty, the EOA employed a "language of opportunity," opening the way for poor and working-class people, especially women, to take on roles in community organizations and direct resources in ways that they saw fit.[67] In particular, they took advantage of federal resources offered by the Office of Economic Opportunity (OEO). It mandated that Community Action Agencies (CAAs) should be "developed, conducted, and administered with the maximum feasible participation of residents of the areas and members of the groups served."[68] Local activists took "maximum feasible participation" seriously, and their efforts helped to produce community-led, democratic movements.

Developed under Title II of the Economic Opportunity Act, Community Action Programs (CAPs) made decisions about funding and brought together stakeholders across multicounty regions, including private and public nonprofit organizations committed to antipoverty efforts. As the organizations that administered resources, CAPs often became the battlegrounds where power struggles unfolded. They would prove to be the most controversial elements of the War on Poverty. As historian Susan Youngblood Ashmore explains, before the Economic Opportunity Act passed, members of the bill's task force worried about how well CAPs could function in the segregated South. If local, white-controlled governments administered the CAP grants, they could conceivably block the participation of African Americans. Foreseeing challenges, the task force built in separate funding streams for CAAs, private or nonprofit organizations that could operate independently of local power brokers. They also included a clause calling for the "maximum feasible participation of the poor" in CAP-funded programs. By providing funding to organizations that operated outside of a local government's purview, the bill's writers hoped to prevent segregationist politicians in the South from hijacking antipoverty programs and blocking African Americans' access to federal grants.[69]

To the task force, southern segregationists were the most direct threat to the idea of community action. But the bill's designers also understood that middle-class professionals and politicians often preferred to "do it for the poor and to the poor, but not with the poor."[70] This was especially true in Appalachia, where a patronage system continued to function: white middle-class elites controlled school boards and the courts, and many were affiliated with the coal industry. In many eastern Kentucky counties, tensions arose along class and urban/rural lines. By implementing the idea of "maximum feasible participation," policy makers spurred debates in many Appalachian communities about the role of poor people in designing and implementing antipoverty programs across all levels of community and government.

The OEO antipoverty programs drew upon, but ultimately stood apart from, older social reform organizations in Appalachia, where there was a long history of progressive reform. In the same decades that industry roared through the region, Protestant churches in the Northeast funded orphanages, schools, churches, and missions. Hand-in-glove with the missionary movement, social reformers established antipoverty networks in the Mountain South in the 1920s. These early efforts proved fraught. They brought needed resources like education and health care, but they also produced and reproduced myths about the region and fed into culture-of-poverty explanations of class inequality, which looked to behavioral rather than structural patterns to understand poverty.[71]

Chief among the early OEO-funded programs, the Council of the Southern Mountain Workers was founded in 1913 after missionary teachers John C. Campbell and Olive Dame Campbell of Massachusetts toured the region and concluded that missionaries and reformers needed a venue where they could share ideas about how to bring greater prosperity to the hills. In the first several decades of its existence, the Council primarily organized an annual conference where college educators and administrators, members of missionary societies, and heads of settlement schools came together to hear lectures on current social topics. After the organization nearly collapsed financially, Perley F. Ayer, a rural sociologist who had taught at Berea College in Kentucky, became the executive director in 1951. He transformed the Council, which took on a new name, the Council of the Southern Mountains (CSM). By the 1960s, it was the largest social reform organization in the Mountain South. With its deep roots in the region, it was an obvious choice to house and direct antipoverty programs.[72]

By the mid-1960s, the Council received funding primarily from federal agencies, including the OEO, as well as philanthropic organizations like the Ford Foundation. It was unique compared to many OEO-sponsored programs in that it coordinated with organizations across the Appalachian South and offered a more holistic view of the region than those situated in counties or controlled by local governments. Moreover, despite the attempt by policy makers to prevent local powerbrokers from controlling Community Action Programs, OEO staff observed that agencies in the region were "completely controlled by the influential power structure" and lacked representation of poor people. They saw the Council's structure as truer to the policy goals of democratic participation.[73] The Council soon oversaw four program areas in Appalachia, two of which related directly to the War on Poverty: a community action training program to provide technical assistance to antipoverty groups, and a service program, called the Appalachian Volunteers (AV). The latter also helped to implement the OEO's Volunteers in Service to America (VISTA) program in the region. The AV and VISTA workers stood at the center of community organizing in many Appalachian communities in the 1960s.

The Council had founded the Appalachian Volunteers in 1963 and expanded the program in the winter of 1964 with a grant from the Area Redevelopment Administration, a federal program that sought to stimulate job growth in distressed areas. Several hundred students from nearby colleges and universities spent their winter break in eastern Kentucky communities to repair school buildings, restore damaged homes, and organize recreational programs for children. Late that same year, Richard Boone, one of President Johnson's aides who took a keen interest in the Appalachian region, extended a demonstration grant to foster the expansion of the Appalachian Volunteers program.[74] The following summer, 150 college students lived in eastern Kentucky communities, where they developed education programs for children and community projects with adults.[75] As the Appalachian Volunteers continued to expand, it often became the first OEO-funded program locals encountered.[76]

Key to the Appalachian Volunteers' expansion was a partnership with the OEO program VISTA. Referred to by many as the "domestic Peace Corps" due to its focus on recruiting college students into community service, the program's roots lay in the Committee on Juvenile Delinquency and the President's Task Force on a National Service Program during Kennedy's presidency.[77] The Council of the Southern Mountains and the Appalachian Volunteers worked closely with VISTA to train volunteers as part of VISTA's rural project and then to place them in eastern Kentucky communities.[78]

By late 1965 and early 1966, the Appalachian Volunteers spread across the Mountain South, primarily in eastern Kentucky and West Virginia but with pockets in the mountains of Virginia and Tennessee, too. The staff of the AV, comprised of white, college-educated men, directed the volunteers, men and women from across the country, mostly in their late teens and early twenties.

Many of the volunteers were energized by Kennedy's calls to serve their country; others were inspired by the activism of young people in the civil rights movement; and a smaller number were from the region and wanted to do something positive for their communities. Full of idealism, they entered communities with the mandate to help them make improvements, usually in the form of building and repairing schools, starting adult educational programs, establishing tutoring programs, and petitioning school boards for more resources.[79]

The Appalachian Volunteers and the Council of the Southern Mountains overwhelmingly focused on white communities in Appalachia. Although African Americans made up only about 2 percent of the population in eastern Kentucky between 1960 and 1970, they were the poorest residents.[80] As historian William Turner has documented, across Appalachia the median income for blacks was about half of the median income for whites. The welfare rates in mountain areas of Kentucky were nearly 16 percent for all races, but nearly 21 percent for black Appalachians.[81] These numbers point to the particular struggles of black Appalachians, who faced racial discrimination in an economically depressed region. But they also suggest the complicated relationship between race and poverty in Appalachia. Poverty was worse for black people, but poor whites made up the overwhelming majority of the poor population in Appalachia, mitigating easy associations between black Appalachians and poverty. The outcome, however, too often rendered black people invisible in policy debates in Appalachia.[82]

Some AV and VISTA workers sought to build relationships with black families and communities, for instance in Mingo County, West Virginia, where antipoverty workers organized alongside African American residents. But throughout the region, volunteers faced specific challenges and often operated with blind spots. Partly it was a problem of imagination: from Johnson's speeches down to regional reports and programs, policy makers and antipoverty workers characterized Appalachia as a region made up of white mountaineers and thus focused antipoverty efforts in white communities. To compound matters, regional organizations faced particular challenges when they attempted to send resources into black communities. For instance, when white Appalachian Volunteers lived with black families, they experienced pushback from whites in the community. And the organization primarily recruited white antipoverty workers, making it difficult to build alliances in black communities.[83] The end result was that antipoverty organizations reinforced the idea that Appalachia was a place of whiteness in general and white poverty in particular.

The Appalachian Volunteers and Community Action

When antipoverty workers arrived in mountain communities—where they lived and worked with locals—they met people who pushed for deeper change in their communities. While many valued educational and service projects, they also understood them as short-term fixes. Before long the Appalachian Volunteers and their community partners began to take up the challenge of community action, with a focus on changing policies and expanding citizen participation.

As the Appalachian Volunteers shifted from service projects (and an ethos of cooperation with local elites), they also confronted and challenged local power bases. Such conflicts led to irreparable rifts between the Council's older, more conservative leaders and the AV staff. Ideology, generational divides, and differences over tactics soon led the Appalachian Volunteers to break from the Council and relocate from the college town of Berea, Kentucky, to Bristol, Tennessee, in order to be closer to the mountain communities in which they worked. The OEO continued to support the AV, which expanded its training of VISTA workers in the summer of 1966, supervising five hundred people.[84]

Following the break with the Council, the Appalachian Volunteers underwent a transformation. Its staff continued short-term, local projects, but the organization also began to take up a more complex range of issues, often at the behest of local people. This transformation was underway during a meeting in August 1966, when several hundred representatives from communities in Kentucky, West Virginia, and southwestern Virginia joined the Appalachian Community Meeting in Washington, D.C. There, they argued for an expansion of the grassroots war on poverty in Appalachia. Appalachian Volunteers and community partners discussed "the hopes and frustrations, the opinions and suggestions of the people of the Appalachian South . . . as well as a shared experience of poverty and a heritage of economic and political exploitation." In meetings with the OEO and the Appalachian Regional Commission, they presented research on environmental destruction, welfare, and unemployment. They also called for more funding for community action agencies (which were more likely than Community Action Programs to be led by poor people). Finally, they demanded more than nominal representation on CAP boards; they desired "the most powerful kind of local control: financial."[85]

At the close of the D.C. trip, participants convened a community meeting at the Hawthorne School, a progressive, experimental high school, which had provided lodging to the Appalachian group. As one participant recalled, "scores" of local people reflected on their lives, on poverty, and on politics in Appalachia. The meeting was one step in a "give-and-take process" that pushed the Appalachian Volunteers to take up the mandate of community action more forcefully.[86]

Over the next several years, the Appalachian Volunteers worked with local groups to organize campaigns on a host of topics: anti–strip mining campaigns, welfare rights protests, poor people's marches, rights for miners, and campaigns for health care, among others.[87] AV workers helped to establish an independent press, community health centers, legal aid societies, and various community groups that addressed particular concerns of local citizens. They also disseminated information about President Johnson's Great Society programs, the spate of legislation that focused on eliminating poverty and racial injustice, reforming health care and education, and expanding the social safety net in the form of programs such as food stamps, Medicaid, and Medicare.

Local women were particularly well positioned to take advantage of federal resources that flowed into their communities. Drawing on their historic positions as caregivers and upon a collective knowledge of the structural barriers in the coalfields, they were well suited to implement new policies in their communities. Those who already provided community leadership leapt at the chance to join more formal government organizations. For many others, the War on Poverty provided a foundation for a life of activism. Having grown up in the coalfields, they knew intimately how industrial violence and poverty could shake the land, body, and spirit, and they infused antipoverty programs with that knowledge. They are the subjects of the following chapters.

2 "I Was Always Interested in People's Welfare"

Bringing the War on Poverty to Kentucky

A one-lane road switches back and forth up the ridge, and from the top—the head of the hollow—one can peer down into a stretch called Poor Bottom. Clapboard houses with large front porches line the Marrowbone Creek. Tidy gardens grow in front yards, the sunniest spots in the hollow. Behind the houses, the ridge rises up, a forested wall. Chickens peck in some yards, cats lounge on porches, and dogs howl when cars approach. Around a gooseneck bend in the narrow road, the old one-room schoolhouse sits. Further down, on one steep hill, the manicured cemetery stretches up toward the sky—an ancestral plot, kept clear of the brambles and ever-encroaching forest. Before long, the road straightens out. On the right, a gnarled crab apple tree, heavy with fruit, extends its branches across the yard of a simple, red brick house. It marks the home of Edith Easterling—daughter of these hills—who lives with her retired coalminer husband, Jake.

This is where Edith welcomed the man representing the federal War on Poverty as he arrived one day in 1965. She had met him at the school where she worked as a cook. He had come to take a survey about the needs of the community in anticipation of the federal War on Poverty. Edith had no end of ideas about how antipoverty programs should be run and where they should focus their attention. She had long been a community advocate. The man did not think her ideas were feasible, and he told her as much, underestimating her knowledge of the place and ignoring her life's work there. But he did not throw her off course. By the end of the decade, she was considered by many to be a hero or a firebrand, depending on where one stood in relation to the War on Poverty.[1]

When the University of Kentucky man arrived at her house, he would have found a different picture of Appalachia than what appeared in *LIFE* and other glossy magazines, which portrayed only the starkest poverty and direst conditions in the region, often with a hint of nostalgia.[2] Gaunt and dirt-streaked faces, rags for clothes, and distended bellies did not describe the Easterling family, yet there they were in the middle of an Appalachian hollow. Edith was not wealthy, but she was not poor; she was solidly working class. And she and Jake worked hard so that their four children could live easier than they had. Prosperity could mean a comfortable home, but more and more it meant avoiding the coalmines that had crippled Jake, poisoned the bodies of hundreds of men, and decimated the landscape. The Easterlings were proud of the work that Jake had done, but they were not sanguine about the industry. Edith told an interviewer in the 1980s, "I couldn't sleep a wink if that boy of mine went" to the mines.[3] Missing from the portraits of Appalachia were people like Edith, whose dynamic political and community lives could not be captured in gratuitous portraits of poverty. Edith wanted as much as anybody to solve poverty, but she also saw the War on Poverty as an opportunity to change politics as usual.

Edith Easterling challenged the culture-of-poverty models that guided many policy makers in the mid–twentieth century. Drawing on social science

Figure 4. Edith and Jake Easterling inside their store, formerly the Marrowbone Folk School, Pike County, Kentucky. Courtesy of Phil Primack.

theories, they proposed that ending poverty required interrupting deeply entrenched behavioral patterns that poor families and communities reproduced in the next generation. In the 1965 policy report, *The Negro Family*, sociologist and White House advisor Daniel Patrick Moynihan diagnosed black communities with pathology, rooted in the practice of black women heading families (thus stunting male economic independence, in his view).[4]

Experts on Appalachia also employed the model, although in racially specific ways. They bound a heroic history of Anglo-Saxon mountain culture, forged during the eugenic calls for a pure white race in the early twentieth century, to the images of a fallen people—the shiftless hillbilly in popular accounts. For example, Jack Weller, a Presbyterian minister who served in West Virginia for years, outlined the problems of poverty in a best-selling book that became a "training manual" for many of the first Appalachian Volunteers and VISTA workers, although it was soon replaced by more historical accounts of the region. Weller argued that poverty in the region boiled down to the mountaineers' traits: their celebrated independence had become corrupted, leading to a fatalistic individualism that prevented them from pursuing the promises of modern American life.[5]

The War on Poverty in Appalachia, specifically OEO-funded programs, helped to usher in new critiques of the political economy in Appalachia. Edith Easterling, local activists, and their allies focused squarely on the antidemocratic practices of the coal industry and the politicians who made up the local power base. They countered arguments that so-called mountaineers possessed inherent traits that led to their impoverishment, putting a spotlight instead on powerful institutions. Edith worked in cooperation with the Appalachian Volunteers, eventually becoming one of the few female staff persons. In her position, she took the mandate of the Economic Opportunity Act—to make politics more democratic—to heart. Her work brought into focus the grave problems poor and working-class people faced in Appalachia: environmental destruction, a punitive welfare system, a lack of democratic spaces, and political elites who demanded working-class people's quiescence. With a pairing of local knowledge and federal resources, Edith Easterling helped to implement the grassroots war on poverty at the same time that she worked to redress the barriers and prejudices that structured so many lives in Appalachia.[6]

Biography of an Activist

Edith Coleman was born in 1925, in a hollow called Poor Bottom in the Marrowbone Creek community of Pike County, one of the heaviest coal-producing counties in the region.[7] The county seat, Pikeville, bustled by the early twentieth century, with a steamboat line, a railway station, schools, hotels, shops, and a warehouse district. It was home to a population of middle-class professionals and business elites. In the 1930s, the Roosevelt Administration designated it a Works Progress Administration site, making it one of the modern cities of the region.[8] In contrast, the rural reaches of Pike County were considered inaccessible. Locals navigated the region by identifying post offices, hollows, creeks, and forks of creeks, and they tended farms or worked in coalmines or other industries. Poor Bottom was a long twenty miles from Pikeville.

Edith's first months of life were cruel. When she was a baby, Edith's mother Ellie died. She was told that a mule kicked Ellie over a bank, leading to her death. Ellie left behind five-month-old Edith and five other children. Easterling's grandmother Vina Coleman assumed responsibility for the children for several years until Edith's father, Bev Coleman, married again and had a wife to help care for his children.

Vina Coleman was an early role model for Edith. By the time she was raising Edith and her siblings, Vina was a widow who owned her home and farm and received a Civil War widow's pension. According to family lore, Vina and her older Union veteran husband, Joseph, operated a boarding house for men with "bad diseases" and girls who had been thrown out of their homes because they were unmarried and pregnant. Easterling remembered, "My grandmother told me that there'd been many a time at 12 and 1 o'clock in the morning she'd be out on these ridges, a'coming on her horse with some girl that'd been run off. Maybe she'd find her under a cliff somewhere; maybe she'd hunted all day for her." After she picked up the girl, no doubt scared and confused, Vina housed her and nursed her through her pregnancy. Joseph treated the males and Vina the females, and the sexes lived on separate floors. Edith noted that because of seeing and hearing about her grandmother's work, "I was always interested in people and people's welfare."[9]

The family lore of Vina Coleman rescuing girls on horseback is only part of the story. As Edith would learn, her grandparents received a Civil War pension, buffering them and later Vina from economic insecurity. Edith's own ability to speak up to injustice, she argued, was rooted in her family's history as Union pensioners. Well before the start of the War on Poverty, or even the New Deal, Edith Easterling's grandparents understood social provisioning as a proper function of the federal government.[10]

The Colemans' history with the Bureau of Pensions within the Department of the Interior reveals a complicated tangle of family relationships and persistence on the part of the Colemans to prove that they were deserving and legitimate claimants. Edith's grandfather Joseph Coleman and his siblings navigated the bureau and secured Civil War pensions for numerous family members. Between 1863 and the 1910s, the bureau collected a file over 150 pages long, detailing the beneficiaries of Isaac Coleman, Edith's great-grandfather. He had fought in the 39th Regiment of the Kentucky Infantry in the United States Army with three of his adult sons, including Joseph. In the early 1900s, Isaac's four children, who were minors in 1863, petitioned the bureau for back payments. The bureau began a lengthy process of investigating the validity of their claims, during which officials recorded a deposition by Joseph Coleman, Edith's grandfather. Joseph had received a pension beginning in the 1870s. Sixty-seven years old at the time, he testified to the special examiner of the bureau: "I had not heard that the minors of Isaac Coleman had applied for pensions but I have often said that they were entitled to a pension." The bureau approved and paid claims to the children of Isaac Coleman in 1907.[11]

Joseph Coleman's statement indicates that he considered Civil War pensions an important function in the federal government's relationship to citizens. As historian Theda Skocpol argues, Civil War pensions accounted for the first widespread, de facto social provision in the United States, absorbing between one-fifth and one-third of the federal budget between the 1870s and 1910s. Veterans of the U.S. Army and their widows and children petitioned the bureau for public assistance without hesitation or the sense of shame that would accompany later forms of social provisioning.[12]

Joseph Coleman's pension allowed for wealth accumulation and proved crucial in shielding his family from economic distress well after his death. Joseph, who had received a pension since the 1870s, married Vina Jane Rose from Yancy County, North Carolina, in 1892, when Vina was about sixteen years old and Joseph was fifty-two. They had four children, three of whom survived into adulthood. The couple owned a two-story log home, a symbol of prosperity, and they operated a farm during the years in which many in the Mountain South were trading agricultural life for coal mining. Joseph also owned "shacks," as Edith called them, that he rented to workers. Joseph died in 1910, and by the following year Vina claimed a widow's pension for herself and one dependent child. As a widow, Vina continued to manage the farm with the help of her sons, and she rented out rooms to boarders for extra income.[13]

Vina's family leaned on her. Her son Theodore lived with her and worked on the farm. When her son Benjamin died in the mines, she took in his two children. And when Ellie Coleman died, Vina took in the six children of her son Bev. Among the eight grandchildren, three were still in diapers, yet Vina managed. Edith described Vina as an industrious woman who worked tirelessly. One night when Edith was old enough to help her grandmother with chores, one of the pigs got out, and a car hit and killed it. With Edith's help, Vina skinned the pig that night and prepared to cure it. Even in old age, Vina continued to work in her garden and help provide for her large extended family. Edith recalled that her grandmother often used the garden hoe as a walking cane, steadying herself on the way to the garden and, once there, using it to work the soil.[14]

In Edith's stories about her childhood, Vina Coleman is a hardworking woman who kept the children fed and clothed, acting as the mother to many of her grandchildren, and she is also an active citizen, whose stability in part came from her claims as a widow of a Union soldier. Edith heard stories about grandparents who understood that they had a relationship to the federal government, and that their lives were better for it. As they prospered, they "shared what they had." In explaining this family history to interviewees Edith laid out several themes: her understanding of citizenship from an early age, the centrality of a woman caregiver in her life, family, and community, and her interest in activism as a trait passed down to her. "I inherited [that] from my Grandma Coleman," she said.[15]

In her stories, she contrasts Vina Coleman and her father Bev, a foreman in the mines. Unlike Vina, he signaled his beliefs that women and men were fundamentally different. Edith believed that he didn't like his girl children because they couldn't work the "old rocky field." She sometimes described him as "mean-hearted" and at other times as "tender-hearted." He would sob in church services, but "when he'd get out of there he'd cuss out the blue moon." He was especially harsh with his children; the line between discipline and violence was thin. He used a leather strap on which he sharpened his razor to whip his children. Edith, who had witnessed her father beating her siblings, learned to stay out of his way.[16]

Prominent in her stories is a sense of a dynamic working-class and the intra-class (and even intra-family) tensions that she witnessed as a child: between foremen (like her father) and miners, workers and strikebreakers, labor and capital, "sorry families" and respected ones, those who were union and those who were antiunion. In the small community along Marrowbone Creek, families lived fairly close. Many of the men worked in the mines, and the children attended school together. Yet the community was segregated by class. Property-owning families like the Colemans lived on the outskirts of the town center of Lookout, Kentucky, the coal town where the train station and post office were located. Coalminers and their families lived in the company-owned, clapboard homes in the coal camp. Foremen and managers lived in larger homes in "bosstown," down the road from the coal camps. Many property-owning families looked down on the "coal camp kids": Bev Coleman referred to them as the "sorry families."[17]

As a child, Edith learned to distinguish between not having enough money for consumer goods and not having basic life necessities. She remembered that the difference between her house and the poorest people's homes was that her family's home was painted, it had weather boarding, and it was slightly bigger than the coal camp houses. Eventually, her father was able to afford a refrigerator and a washing machine, too. But there were also similarities between the families. None of them had running water or indoor plumbing. Few of the children went to school beyond the eighth grade because their families could not afford to send them. Edith understood that her family had more, but she also knew that her family struggled. When she was a child she thought her family "was poor as church mice." Looking back she observed, "We lived hard; we lived like vagrants, almost." But she came to understand that children who lived in shacks perceived her as living lavishly. She remembered: "I had this boy to tell me one time he didn't want me to come into his house. He said, 'I hated to see you come so bad because you'd see what we had to eat.' And see, I wasn't thinking what they had to eat. And I ask him, 'Why?' And he said, 'Well, you've always had so damn much and we had so little.'"[18]

This class stratification made a deep impression on Edith. She remembered a time when she was staying with her grandmother and a neighbor snuck into her kitchen and ate lard out of a bucket because he was so hungry. When her grandmother found him, she fixed him something to eat and sent food for his wife and children. "I thought about that so much," Edith mused.[19]

Edith also recognized the wider class dimensions of Appalachia, especially the gap between rural and urban Appalachia. She knew that there were "people raised with a silver spoon [who] looked down on us."[20] Even if the Colemans had more than others, they were still people from the hollows, and coming from the rural outskirts of the county seat carried with it a stigma. After becoming a community activist, Edith confronted such divisions between town and country head-on. For instance, in a meeting with a school superintendent, Edith argued for a new road so that rural children could ride buses to school. The superintendent fired back that if families chose to live in hollows, then they deserved to walk in the mud.[21]

Stories of the labor movement added a layer of moral struggle to her understanding of class dynamics. She came from a family split on the value of unions and thus understood the psychological complexity of working-class people, but also the stakes of the union in the coalfields. In 1933, workers at the Henry Clay Mine, where Bev Coleman worked, attempted to organize under the UMWA, and the company promptly began to fire miners. The mine owners soon closed down the mine rather than honor a union contract. But before the shutdown, one miner was shot and killed, another was wounded, and many others were arrested during a gun battle between pro-union workers and company guards.[22]

Bev Coleman did not support the union. As a foreman, he profited by working the miners hard (he stayed at the mines 12–15 hours a day himself), and the company rewarded him for his commitment to driving the men under him to produce as much coal as possible. Edith remembered watching him crawl out of the window and sneak to work during strikes. Within her own family there were pro-union miners, and she watched as her family split along labor lines. One of her uncles lost his job and "everything he had" because he supported the UMWA. As an adult, Edith was haunted by memories of sitting on the front porch and seeing the big spotlights that the company shone into the woods as they searched for pro-union workers who were hiding out. Edith was the same age as the daughter of the man who had been murdered during the labor conflict, and though she was too young to understand what had happened at the time, she later reflected: "It was a sad time. It was hard on the children. [We] didn't know what was happening. Times was hard."[23] Edith came to believe that the mining operators' harassment of union workers was symptomatic of a larger imbalance of power in the coalfields.

In 1943, Edith had returned home after working in a munitions factory in Michigan. Perhaps in an impulsive move, she quickly married a local man who had been in the Navy. "There wasn't much progression to it," she demurred. As the story goes, she married in order to get out of her father's home and to escape a whipping for not doing chores. The marriage was short-lived; her husband was soon hospitalized for mental illness. While he was gone, Edith met Jake Easterling when she was on a walk with her friends, and he offered to take a picture of the group of young women. She soon got to know Jake, and she waited for her husband to return home so that she could get a divorce. In 1945, Edith married Jake, a pick-and-shovel coalminer, over the protests of her father. Bev Coleman had long looked down on people like Jake, who had grown up in the coal camps. Jake had worked in the mines since he was sixteen, and his knee had been mashed in a work accident, causing him to limp. Bev Coleman worried about his ability to provide for his daughter. "I can remember Poppy said to me, well, if you marry him, you'll end up in the coal camp," Edith recalled.[24]

Edith did not share her father's bias, and she made a home for herself and Jake in their coal camp house in Lookout, just down the road from Poor Bottom, where they moved the day following their courthouse wedding. The company would withdraw $10 a month from Jake's paycheck to cover rent.

Jake's brother, who was in the army, sent the newlyweds $150, and with it they bought all the used furniture they needed to start a home together: "two iron beds, a cook stove, a table, a kitchen cabinet, and a rug for the kitchen." Edith replicated American consumer goods using resources available to her, styling her home to look like the kitchens that appeared in glossy American magazines. She used butcher paper to create window blinds, and she scavenged tin boxes, covered them with feed-sack skirts, and used them as kitchen "counters." She taught herself to crochet, and she made three dresses—pink, white, and purple—for her baby girl Sue Ella.[25]

Jake and Edith came to share a belief in the power of unions and a deep sense of working-class solidarity. Jake had been active in the UMWA since the 1930s. As a person who had suffered the physical tolls of working in the mines, he knew as well as anyone the importance of the union for securing safety measures, health benefits, and good wages. For people like Edith and Jake, the relationship between antipoverty programs and labor unions was not difficult to fathom. Both could improve the conditions of people's lives. Union families like the Easterlings welcomed organizers and poverty programs, and the Easterlings were one of many local families who opened their homes to young organizers who eventually migrated to Appalachia to work in poverty programs in the 1960s.[26]

Even before the War on Poverty, Edith had an abiding interest in local politics and had long found ways to support her neighbors and improve her community. After living in a coal camp for about four years, Edith and Jake moved to "the backside of town," where Edith had grown up, and built a house on her father's farm in Cow Bell Hollow. There they raised their four children. Although Edith and Jake constantly struggled to bring in an adequate income, they had more stability than many others in eastern Kentucky: they had each other, and they had a family member with land. These slight advantages do not fully explain Edith's early forms of community organizing, especially in a sex-segregated community where women lacked access to the majority of wage work and political positions. Still, she found ways to be involved. Easterling was an active member of the Parent and Teacher's Association and served a term as its president. She was the chairman of the Republican Party in her district in the early 1960s, following in her father's and grandfather's political tradition. Her candidate, Thomas Ratliff, won a seat as Commonwealth Attorney in 1963, and for her work she was awarded a patronage position in the school, as a cook. (Ratliff eventually turned on Easterling as she got more involved in the War on Poverty). Sue Ella Kobak, Edith's firstborn, recalled that Edith "knew everybody's business" and "knew every property line in our part of the county." Sue Ella also recognized that her mother was different from other women, but that she managed to find ways to adjust so that she did not appear *too* different.[27]

Thinking back on her mother's work in the community, Sue Ella called her "the unofficial social worker." Edith often read letters to illiterate neighbors, and when neighbors and kin were eligible for Social Security benefits, she helped them fill out the paperwork. Even when family members moved on to northern industrial towns to find work, she kept in touch and notified them when they were eligible for veteran's benefits from the state of Kentucky. She followed in the tradition of her grandfather who, many years earlier, argued for the fair distribution of entitlements to the children of Union soldiers. Easterling also drove people to polling places during elections and provided them with sample ballots. When the polio vaccine became available, Edith and Sue Ella were the first in their community to receive the vaccine. The health department called on Edith to visit families to assure them that the vaccine was safe, and to convince them that they should have their children vaccinated.[28]

For Edith, the antipoverty programs were an extension of her volunteer and outreach work. As she saw it, "it was normal" to be involved. She asserted, "I was pretty active in the community. I wasn't doing anything that I shouldn't have done."[29] By the time federal antipoverty resources reached eastern Kentucky, Edith had decades of experience in community work and a keen understanding of social welfare.

Joining the War on Poverty

Sue Ella resembles her mother Edith in many ways. Both have high cheekbones and broad shoulders; both are known for being resolute when they make decisions and take political stances. While her mother was one of many middle-aged mothers to join the War on Poverty, Sue Ella represents a generation of Appalachians who saw the federal programs as an opportunity to join the wave of youth movements across the country. While many of the youth who got involved were from outside the region, a significant number were from mountain communities.[30]

Born in 1945, Sue Ella was a bright child who liked to read. But she always felt different when she was growing up in Poor Bottom. She was not good at hiding her intelligence, and girls and women who were smart—and revealed that they were smart—threatened traditional family and community values. Those values reflected the fundamentalist Christianity that was common in the mountains. Although the Easterlings were people of faith and attended church, they were not doctrinaire. For instance, even though her Regular Baptist church was opposed to Sunday school (the classes offered to children before regular church services), Edith sometimes let her children attend classes at another church because it gave them something to do. Edith also pushed her oldest daughter to be a high achiever. Sue Ella had been born with a dislocated hip that had not been corrected, so she walked with a limp. Fearing that her daughter would not be able to count on the financial stability provided by a husband and marriage, Edith urged Sue Ella to seek an education and career.[31] Perhaps Edith was also pushing her to achieve what had not been available to her. Sue Ella felt that her mother never had an "outlet" where she could explore her intellectual capabilities.[32]

Sue Ella entered Morehead State University in Morehead, Kentucky, the same year that President Johnson announced the War on Poverty. She hoped that an education would pave the way for a more adventurous life, what she called her "path to the yellow Corvette." Her plan was to go to college, move to Ohio, become a teacher, and buy a nice home and a fancy car. Her most important college experiences, however, took her quickly from consumer desires to a deeper analysis of where she came from and the meaning of poverty in Appalachia. Like many college students in the 1960s, Sue Ella began to think critically about democracy and the role of government in Americans' lives, and she brought to that analysis her own experience of growing up in the coalfields.

When Sue Ella was a child, her mother tried to protect her from the realities of class disparity. Edith had told her that the world portrayed by television programs—the clothing, furniture, houses—did not reflect reality for anybody. Edith reassured her daughter: "That was what we wanted but that's not what anybody had." Sue Ella remembered, "It wasn't until I went to college that I found out that she had lied to me." She continued, "[I] didn't know I was poor until I went to college and saw all these girls wearing all these clothes and I had no idea that people had that." Sue Ella had fifty dollars, an umbrella, and a suitcase full of secondhand clothes.[33]

At her freshman orientation in 1964, Sue Ella heard Bill Wells, a staff person for the Appalachian Volunteers, speak about the mission of the program. Late that year, Sargent Shriver and the Office of Economic Opportunity committed the first substantial grant of nearly $300,000 to the Appalachian Volunteers.[34] The Council of the Southern Mountains opened four AV offices in eastern Kentucky, including one in Morehead. Curious about what she heard in Wells's speech, Sue Ella attended the first AV meeting on her campus, and she became a committed member for her four years of college. When she started the program, she mostly worked as a tutor and helped to repair one-room school buildings in Elliot and Carter Counties. It was not long before she saw the miserable conditions in Appalachian schools as connected to larger problems, such as a lack of political representation for the poor.[35]

Her participation in the Appalachian Volunteers also connected Sue Ella to the burgeoning youth movements of the 1960s. She coedited an underground, radical newspaper at Morehead, and she began to educate herself on the major social issues of the day. She soon became familiar with efforts within the civil rights movement to build interracial coalitions, led in part by the Highlander Research and Education Center as well as progressive white college students.

In the spring and summer of 1964, Myles Horton, the cofounder of Highlander, recruited students from the white student project of the Student Nonviolent Coordinating Committee (SNCC) for a series of workshops. In the 1930s, Highlander had promoted labor organizing, which had brought its staff into contact with miners and the UMWA. By the 1950s, Highlander had shifted its focus to the civil rights movement and began providing a space for civil rights activists to meet. By the mid-1960s, as the movement evolved, Highlander's staff began to consider a next phase in social justice organizing, and they turned their attention to antipoverty activism and working-class movements in the Appalachian South.[36] The War on Poverty offered a line into those communities and the opportunity to build on SNCC's effective civil rights campaigns in the Deep South, where black and white youths focused on community organizing through education programs and voting rights campaigns. Horton drew explicit links between the antipoverty programs and the civil rights movement. He asserted, "It is encouraging to find Southern students concerned with the problems of white people in underdeveloped areas of the South as well as with the problems of civil rights. The war on poverty and the struggle for civil rights cannot be separated."[37] Once they joined community action campaigns as part of the War on Poverty, many local and outsider white activists, including Sue Ella and Edith Easterling, sojourned to the Highlander Center to strategize and participate in workshops.

Sue Ella also became acquainted with the Southern Student Organizing Committee (SSOC), made up of progressive white students from fifteen southern college campuses. SSOC members determined "to build together a New South which brings democracy and justice for all its people." They outlined as some of their goals "the rise of full and equal opportunity for all" and "an end to personal poverty and deprivation."[38] SSOC organizers networked with AV leadership about how they could contribute to the antipoverty programs in Appalachia.[39] Sue Ella and other Appalachian students developed a wing of SSOC to work on Appalachian campuses, calling it Appalachian Students Organizing Committee (ASOC).[40]

Along with fostering her connection to social justice movements, Sue Ella's work with the Appalachian Volunteers put her in touch with people who had access to resources that might be put to good use in her home community.[41] As she explained, the AV provided a "foundation" on which she designed her own political education.[42] Through the AV, Sue Ella met Thomas Rhodenbaugh, who worked in the program's central office. He was one among the young adults who found their way to Appalachia in the mid-1960s. Rhodenbaugh had attended Loyola University in Chicago, where he met Richard Boone, who would serve in Johnson's administration. Boone was one of the people behind the idea of "maximum feasible participation," and he had been an early AV supporter. During college, Rhodenbaugh had worked in programs for urban Appalachian migrants. Noting Rhodenbaugh's interest in Appalachian culture and problems, Boone helped put him in touch with Milton Ogle, the AV director, who soon gave him one of the first staff positions.[43]

By the time Sue Ella met Thomas Rhodenbaugh, she had already been thinking about her home community in Pike County and how the Appalachian Volunteers could be of service there. She also saw the chance for her mother—a consummate political and community worker—to get involved. She soon invited Rhodenbaugh to Poor Bottom to meet Edith. In the spring of 1966, the Appalachian Volunteers sent fieldman (or supervisor) Joe Mulloy to Pike County, to start community organizing with a focus on the Marrowbone Creek community near Lookout, Kentucky, where about 6000 people lived in the mid-1960s.[44]

Mulloy had been working with the Appalachian Volunteers since the fall of 1964, when he was a student at the University of Kentucky. A recruiter's compelling lecture led him to sign up, but he had already felt the desire "to be involved in change that was happening all over the country." President Kennedy's inaugural address calling for Americans to serve their country motivated him. And in the summer of 1964 he had followed the news of Freedom Summer in Mississippi closely, inspired by the young civil rights activists. It was a time of "turmoil and change," he recalled, and the Appalachian Volunteers seemed like his opportunity to join the waves of activism.[45]

In the summer of 1966, Edith worked with Joe to place AV workers in Marrowbone Creek. She headed a local committee that sponsored volunteers and helped place them in the homes of local families, who would be paid for room and board and could help direct the students' work, by having them tutor children in the household or start recreational programs in the community. Edith and Jake also housed two summer workers.[46]

Edith's involvement with the Appalachian Volunteers almost immediately put her in the crosshairs of local elites—she lost her job as a cook in the school system because she had become an "outspoken person."[47] The AV then hired her as an intern, for which she was paid a salary of $300 a month. AV interns were the community counterparts to the student volunteers, many of whom were VISTA workers placed with the AV. The AV leadership identified local people who exhibited "leadership potential" and would help the organization live up to the goals of community participation as laid out by the OEO.[48]

At the end of the summer, Joe Mulloy reported, "Marrowbone Creek is an excellent example of the community development process." When he arrived, the Appalachian Volunteers had initially planned to work with a local development group, but it had turned out to be controlled by middle-class people who did not represent the views of the majority of working-class and poor people. Because the group was not "representative," he and his staff began coordinating new community groups, including one in which Edith would figure prominently. He summarized the summer activities as paving "the way toward positive and democratic community action."[49]

Community Organizing and the Marrowbone Folk School

By the spring of 1967, grassroots community activism was fully underway, and Edith Easterling stood at the center of much of the action. As an AV intern, Edith fundraised for a community center, collected books for a local library, and helped parents of young children access Head Start funding for school clothing. She also continued to foster alliances between the community and the Appalachian Volunteers and other activists. Edith and Jake hosted gatherings for AV and VISTA workers—most of them college students from across the country. Edith feared that some of the young people—whom she believed were emblematic of the counterculture—would not be welcomed into the community. She took it upon herself to bring them to her house, feed them, and show them around. In the space of the Easterlings' home, they would sit around and play music, and sometimes they would talk through the night. She also welcomed cultural workers and civil rights activists interested in progressive activism in the mountains. For instance, activists and folksingers Guy and Candie Carawan from the Highlander Center, who lived in Pike County briefly, were among the guests at the Easterlings' home.[50] With Edith they organized jamborees, or the problem-solving meetings that included "singing, dancing, and clapping together." According to Edith, such events helped to build community trust.[51]

Edith also mediated cultural differences between locals and young activists and allayed fears of older locals who were uncertain about some of the outsider youth. She recalled that some of the locals, who lived by conservative religious values, called her when volunteers "paired off." "It was little petty stuff," Edith explained, as she laughed off stories about the young people who sneaked off into the woods for trysts. Before long, Sue Ella fell in love with one of the VISTAs who was working with the Appalachian Volunteers. John Kobak had dropped out of Harvard University to join the Appalachian Volunteers, and he soon endeared himself to Edith and then started dating her daughter. Although he was from a well-off family, he wore "cut-off britches" and went barefoot, and some of the locals found his dress offensive. But Edith saw past John's "raggedy" clothes. She knew that he focused his attention on the poorest, most destitute families. He always had a passel of boys following him around, and anytime his parents sent him money, he passed it on to the families with whom he worked.[52]

She was especially fond of Joe Mulloy, in whom she found a trusted ally. She remembered that, while some of the other antipoverty workers were interested in socializing and "chasing girls," Mulloy took his job seriously and made attempts to get to know older people in the community. She trusted and often relied on him. "He was like my kid," she recalled.[53]

In the spring of 1967, the Appalachian Volunteers promoted Edith to the position of administrative assistant for Pike County, for which she received a substantial raise. One of her jobs that summer was to edit a local newspaper, spreading news of antipoverty programs and explaining their impetus. The paper notified community members of the work of local people and volunteers, who tackled a series of needs: they petitioned the state to pave the main road in Marrowbone Creek, assisted people in navigating the local welfare and food stamp programs, and organized a teen club and recreational programs for local kids.[54]

Easterling and Mulloy also put energy into building and promoting a community center, the Marrowbone Folk School. AV workers and community partners had identified the need for community meeting spaces in Pike County. Early reports by the Appalachian Volunteers across eastern Kentucky noted that they held community meetings and workshops wherever they could secure space: schoolhouses, churches, barns, empty garages, and abandoned stores and houses.[55] AV workers soon began to discuss the creation of community centers where members could gather, discuss the future of their community, and build fruitful alliances. When it first began, the Marrowbone Folk School was located in a rented building, and Joe Mulloy sought to purchase a permanent building situated in the community.

The school's mission was similar to that of the Highlander Center in Tennessee: it promoted community knowledge as the foundation for successful social movements. In fact, Easterling's involvement in the Marrowbone Folk

School led to a long relationship with Highlander and its staff members. Myles Horton visited Marrowbone on several occasions, and Easterling served on Highlander's board of directors.

The school's organizers cast the Marrowbone Folk School as an alternative to the coal industry, which too easily tossed aside workers. In promotional material, they described how, in the years during and after the Second World War, the Marrowbone Creek area had been booming, "Coal was King," and employable men could find jobs. By the mid-1960s, all but the smallest mines had shut down and "suddenly miners and their families were caught in the vice like grip of poverty." Nothing was left "except the people."[56] And the people—poor and working-class—would be the focus of the school. "I feel like a chance is all they need," Edith declared.[57]

After incorporating the Marrowbone Folk School in June 1967, the organizers compiled a pamphlet to garner support for a "nonprofit education institution" that "seeks to concern itself with the massive social, economic, and political problems of the poor class of people in the Appalachian South." The school would help to dispel the myth that poor people and mountain people were ignorant and apolitical, contending that "the Marrowbone Folk School will prove that this is a lie. It will show that when given the opportunity and right information the poor people can and will speak out and come up with their own solutions." It promoted experience over formal education, stating that the people who lived in poverty and struggled to survive knew more about how to solve the problems of poverty than "most of the high salaried poverty warriors." Over the next several years, with Easterling at the helm, the school hosted workshops, jamborees, and health clinics, and it also included a library and study center. The school also aimed to preserve mountain culture, offering classes on traditional music and crafts to visitors. Organizers held evening square dance and teaching sessions for banjo and fiddle, and they published ballads that spoke to the ongoing struggles in the mountains.[58]

Poverty, Politics, and Campaigns to Stop Strip Mining

Along with organizing in her immediate community, Edith Easterling joined AV workers in addressing an issue that had arisen as one of the most important across the Mountain South: surface mining. Nothing symbolized the outsize power of the coal industry—and the powerlessness of poor and working-class people—more than its extraction of minerals at any and all cost. Following the lead of local citizens who identified strip mining as a major concern of poor people, the Appalachian Volunteers' central office had begun coordinating with the grassroots organization Appalachian Group to Save the Land and People. Together they printed pamphlets that educated communities on the destructive practice of surface mining and how the coal industry profited from the practice.[59]

By the late 1950s, residents of eastern Kentucky had begun petitioning legislators to regulate, if not totally ban, strip mining. They often garnered hundreds of signatures. Facing policy makers who were unwilling to take effective measures to protect their land and homes, residents ramped up their activism. In 1965 "Uncle" Dan Gibson and Ollie "Widow" Combs had taken courageous stands against strip mining, inspiring the formation of Appalachian Group to Save the Land and People (AGSLP) chapters across the region. Pike County residents built on these efforts.[60]

In the spring of 1967, Pike County resident and farmer Jink Ray denied strip miners access to his land, and he found backing in AV Joe Mulloy and his wife Karen Mulloy, who had come to Pike County as a VISTA worker. Joe started attending meetings of the AGSLP, and he invited Easterling to go with him. Easterling described people's frustrations over strip mining: "It was one of those things that you didn't like, but you didn't know what to do about it."[61] Mulloy and Easterling learned of a conference in Owensboro, Kentucky, where representatives from the Kentucky Coal Association, the Department of Reclamation, and the Department of Natural Resources planned to meet with Governor Edward T. Breathitt. They and other activists decided to insert themselves into the conference where they could make a case for outlawing surface mining. A group of more than 200 people attended the meeting, hoping to counter the coal operators, who were, as Easterling summed up, "showing the governor what a good program strip mining was."[62]

When the eastern Kentucky group arrived, they began distributing pamphlets with information about strip mining, which explained that, while strip mine operators promised jobs, they were in fact ruining the land and the economy. Organizers of the conference deemed the activists disruptive and asked them to wait on the lawn, where the governor would eventually speak to them. The protestors went outside and sang protest ballads and civil rights hymns. "We was singing so big," Easterling remembered, that people in Owensboro began to stop and listen to them. When Governor Breathitt finally came out, he promised that he would investigate surface mining and keep strip miners off of Jink Ray's property. Days later he revoked Puritan Coal Company's permit to mine on Ray's land.[63]

Just over a week after this seeming victory, local officials in Pike County made plans to root out radicals and quell the grassroots movement in eastern Kentucky. Commonwealth attorney Thomas Ratliff, one of a handful of Pike County millionaires, was among the ringleaders. At the time he was also planning his run for lieutenant governor on the Republican ticket. Ratliff was a coal operator before and after his stint as commonwealth attorney, and he was a cofounder of the Independent Coal Operators' Association. He had never hidden his antipathy toward the Appalachian Volunteers. Edith had campaigned for Ratliff when he ran for commonwealth attorney and invited him to the Marrowbone Folk School for a tour when it opened. He allegedly responded, "Edith, I like you as a person but I hate these damn poverty programs. I'll get rid of them if I can, including yours."[64] Ratliff met with the county sheriff, coal operators, the president of the Chamber of Commerce, and the director of the Big Sandy Community Action Program, Harry Eastburn (who had long questioned the need for the Appalachian Volunteers). Together they considered the best way to shut down the AV program, which they saw as fomenting unrest.[65]

On the evening of August 11, 1967, Margaret McSurely noticed police officers in her backyard. Margaret had worked for SNCC before heading to the mountains to organize with her husband, Alan "Al" McSurely, as part of a push by the leftist Southern Conference Education Fund (SCEF) to organize working-class whites. An outspoken and at times iconoclastic activist, Al had worked briefly for the Appalachian Volunteers before being fired due to his controversial political views. He remained in Pike County, determined to expose the coal industry and its political hacks as oppressors. He and Margaret soon met the Mulloys, and together they began holding meetings with locals to discuss strip mining. Not long after Margaret spotted officers in her yard, Sheriff Perry Justice knocked on the door and notified Al that he had a warrant for his arrest on the charge of sedition. About twenty men then followed him into the house, and they began a search, following Ratliff's lead. When Ratliff found a document that referenced Margaret's former employment with SNCC, he decided that she, too, should be arrested and drew up a warrant. Later that evening, they also arrested Joe Mulloy on the same charge.[66]

Ratliff claimed that the search resulted in a "truck load of communistic literature." The cache included "instructions on how to use weapons and how to fight guerilla wars" and a "'white paper' on how to 'take over Pike County from the power structure and put it in the hands of the poor.'" He reported to the FBI that he "found works by and about Lenin, Marx, Mao Tse-Tung, Castro and other communist leaders. Others dealt with Russian short stories, socialist thought, and the Berkeley revolt." All of this material, he maintained, "points to just one objective, to stir up dissension and create turmoil among our people." He believed that the Marrowbone Folk School was "an indoctrination school." As evidence, he pointed to the fact that its staff had "helped boys into the Neighborhood Youth Corps" (an OEO educational and jobs training program), and "they have taken some young people to civil rights meetings in Chicago and other places."[67]

The McSurelys' relationship to civil rights activists Carl and Anne Braden provided ready fodder for Ratliff and his associates. Carl Braden, who directed SCEF with Anne in Louisville, had been charged with sedition in the 1950s after the couple helped to purchase a house for an African American family in an all-white neighborhood. It took more imagination to infer that Mulloy was a communist. Robert Holcomb, president of the Pike County Chamber of Commerce and the Independent Coal Operators Association, declared that Mulloy—who was clean-shaven—had a beard "patterned after Raul Castro" as well as a poster of Castro displayed in his home.

Ratliff sent a deputy to Edith's home and requested that she meet with him to discuss the charges. She agreed to meet him, but she refused to ride in the police car. At the meeting Ratliff described the books and posters that the police had confiscated, claiming that they revealed plans for a communist-inspired insurrection. But Edith knew better. "The police took everything and anything from the McSurely's [house] so they could fill up the pick-up truck and say they had a truck load of Communist stuff," she recalled. When Edith challenged Ratliff, he rebutted that Edith had been brainwashed by the young activists. He also took the opportunity to call her a "nigger-lover" and to chide her for her support of labor unions.[68] Easterling's unwillingness to buy the charges against Mulloy and the McSurelys must have rattled Ratliff, who seemed confident that the story would be unquestioned by locals.

Ratliff was in fact the mastermind behind the story of a communist plot, although he claimed publicly that he was as surprised as anybody to discover such activity in Pike County.[69] He was in frequent contact with the FBI, on a search for any evidence that could be construed as subversive. Moreover, FBI documents indicate that he was well aware that his charges of sedition would not hold up in court: the Supreme Court had overturned state antisedition laws in the late 1950s. But the innocence or guilt of the activists was beside the point. He believed that "his primary objective of ridding Pike County of antipoverty workers would be accomplished."[70]

In September, a grand jury in Pike County indicted Joe Mulloy, Al and Margaret McSurely, and Carl and Anne Braden (who had traveled to Pike County following the arrests) for "advocating criminal syndicalism or sedition." The grand jury concluded that the defendants were part of "a well financed" campaign to spread "communistic theory" and to promote the takeover of the local government. Communist organizers, they concluded, had infiltrated antipoverty programs, including the Appalachian Volunteers. They had begun to "promote their beliefs among our school children," and they had plans to infiltrate churches and labor unions as well. Their goal was to organize armed groups—"Red Guards"—through which they would enact their coup in Pike County. The remedy to this nightmarish situation was straightforward from the grand jury's perspective, although it hardly matched the severity of the charges: the jury called for an end to the AV program in Pike County and advised that the organization's federal grants be terminated.[71]

Over the next weeks and months, even as the Kentucky courts deemed the state's sedition law unconstitutional and the charges against the organizers were dropped, rumors circulated about Edith Easterling's political alignments. She faced the consequences of rumor and gossip that she was a communist sympathizer on a very personal level. People shone lights in the Easterlings' home at night and made threatening phone calls. Some of Edith's friends quit speaking to her. She and Jake belonged to a Regular Baptist church but soon stopped attending because of the gossip circulating among members of the congregation. The church body soon revoked the Easterling's membership. Some people told Edith to her face that she had changed for the worse. When she had visited Joe Mulloy and the McSurelys in jail, the jailer told her that it was sad to see a woman from one of the finest families of Pike County become one of the sorriest, and similar sentiments appeared in newspaper articles.[72]

A day after Joe Mulloy's arrest, the Louisville draft board revoked his 2-A deferment and requested that he report to his draft board. Mulloy decided to resist. On the heels of the sedition charges and negative attention in the media, the AV director Milton Ogle planned a staff vote on whether to retain Mulloy on the staff or to fire him. Easterling made one of her most difficult decisions as an antipoverty worker and voted to fire Mulloy. In a memo to the AV staff she explained her decision: "I feel like we the people need the help that we get from the AVs and we could not work in Pike County if Joe stayed on here." She continued that Mulloy had contributed greatly to the programs in Pike County, but the work would "all go down if Joe stays." Easterling reported that the day news came out that Mulloy was resisting the draft, someone shot a bullet through a window at the Marrowbone Folk School. Easterling concluded her letter: "My feelings for Joe is as great as the feelings I have for my daughter, Sue, and I know Sue would take the same stand that Joe took but I would also vote against Sue if she took the stand and helt [*sic*] the position Joe does. I admire Joe for his bravery and it does take bravery to do a thing he has done. He was brave in my book when [he] helped stop the bulldozer on the Jink Ray Farm. But this is a different kind of bravery I gess [*sic*]."[73]

Easterling realized that Mulloy's position on the Vietnam War and his draft resistance could be more divisive in Pike County than his position on strip mining. Working-class people who knew that strip mining could hurt their livelihoods and destroy their homes allied with outsider activists. But those relationships were always tenuous, and the politics of the Vietnam War strained them more than other issues. Regardless of Easterling's own stance on the war (she came to oppose it), she knew that young men in eastern Kentucky, with fewer educational and work opportunities than middle-class men, had little chance of receiving draft deferments. And many men in Kentucky prided themselves on their patriotism and saw the military as a valid route to gainful and honorable employment. Prior to Mulloy's draft resistance, several male employees of the Appalachian Volunteers had requested and been granted occupational deferment or conscientious objector status.[74] Those deferments were not always received well in eastern Kentucky communities. One local AV recalled that older men in her community considered the outsider men, despite their legal deferments, "draft dodgers."[75]

Easterling's decision reflected her core principles that antipoverty workers had a responsibility to do what was best for the community. In this instance, Mulloy's antiwar stance seemed to threaten the work of the Marrowbone Folk School. Following Mulloy's firing, Edith became the new "fieldman" for Pike County, and she continued her work with the Marrowbone Folk School. The Appalachian Volunteers had planned to help purchase a permanent building for the school but were unable to secure a site due to backlash.[76] The Easterlings offered up their own land, and Jake Easterling began building the structure, a 30-by-50 block building, with the help of AV workers and anyone else who wanted to lend a hand.[77]

As the Easterlings built the community center, state officials and politicians continued to use the sedition arrests to make a case to the federal OEO office that the Appalachian Volunteers should be dismantled. Governor Breathitt was not opposed to the War on Poverty but was a greater champion of the development ethos promoted by the Appalachian Regional Commission. He wrote to the director of the federal OEO, Sargent Shriver, that he was "concerned over mounting damage to the entire antipoverty program" by some Appalachian Volunteers, who in his opinion were not supervised to a satisfactory degree. He pleaded with Shriver to refuse further federal funding to the organization. Shriver reassured Breathitt that the OEO was taking action. The office had decided not to renew the summer project for the following year and to cancel an upcoming training session with the Appalachian Volunteers. But Shriver would not promise to defund the program completely.[78]

Shriver and the federal OEO hesitated to abandon the Appalachian Volunteers. By 1967, the office had poured thousands of dollars into the program, which had sixty full-time employees in the field. Their own investigations revealed no violations of federal, state, or local laws by AV staff or VISTA workers in eastern Kentucky. Moreover, federal officials suggested their understanding of local political dynamics. For instance, they noted that one Kentucky Congressman, who was a vociferous opponent of the AV program, "likely" opposed it because it threatened the continuation of barely regulated surface mining. He was also upset that Peggy Terry, a prominent welfare rights activist from Chicago, had given a speech in his district at the invitation of someone affiliated with the Appalachian Volunteers. He saw her speech as another sign of radicalization and, in his opinion, it warranted an FBI investigation and withdrawal of all federal support for Appalachian Volunteers and VISTA.[79]

The Kentucky Office of Economic Opportunity also weighed in on the matter and, like Governor Breathitt, argued for defunding the Appalachian Volunteers. Following the sedition arrests, the director, Al Whitehouse, made a statement on the AVs and garnered signatures from eighteen of the twenty-four Community Action Program directors in Kentucky. He did not explicitly address the sedition charges but, rather, argued that the Appalachian Volunteers caused confusion and undermined the authority of Community Action Programs. He suggested that the AV program did not do enough to "unite the entire community—the rich—the just well-to-do—and the poor," and instead created conflict between those segments of society. Federal OEO officials responded internally that the statement was a "piece of pompous arrogance." Some viewed Whitehouse, as well as several CAP directors in eastern Kentucky, as obstacles to achieving the mandates of the OEO—in particular the involvement of poor people.[80] OEO officials' skepticism of Kentucky politicians' motives and their investment in the Appalachian Volunteers helped to buffer the organization for the time being.

Poor People's Rights in Eastern Kentucky

Edith Easterling continued her work despite the onslaught of attacks. In her new role as fieldman, she began to explore the development of welfare rights campaigns in the region. Appalachian Volunteers frequently addressed problems facing recipients of public assistance, from Aid to Families with Dependent Children (AFDC) to Social Security and food stamps. Many people resided in rural and isolated communities, had no cars or access to public transportation, and found it difficult to travel to the county seat where most welfare offices were located. Moreover, the rules and requirements often negated the benefits of receiving aid and placed a disproportionate burden on recipients to prove they were not committing fraud. The initial registration often took hours of waiting for a detailed interview, and the office required personal interviews every month to ensure that recipients were still in need of aid. As one report concluded, the procedure implied "a deep suspicion of the people the program was intended to help," and social workers too often failed to acknowledge that small shifts in income were often temporary and rarely led to financial stability.[81]

From the time she was an AV intern, Edith Easterling helped people who qualified for public assistance but were unsure about the process. She accompanied people to the welfare office and offered advice to those confused about their rights. Welfare administrators came to know who she was and sometimes accused her of duplicating their work. But she saw herself in an advocacy role, helping her neighbors navigate a complex bureaucracy.[82]

Among the earliest workshops Easterling organized at the Marrowbone Folk School was a "Food Stamp Meeting." The school offered to provide transportation to anyone who wanted to attend and learn more about the food stamp program and who qualified to receive food stamps.[83] When the school relocated to its permanent building, the open house included information sessions on school lunch programs and welfare rights.[84]

The Marrowbone Folk School's programming reflected the turn to more militant calls for welfare as a citizenship right. As part of that move, Easterling worked to ensure that public assistance programs served the people who needed them. Two events provided a backdrop to the school's budding emphasis on poor people's rights: Senator Robert F. Kennedy's "hunger hearings" in eastern Kentucky, and the Poor People's Campaign led by the Southern Christian Leadership Conference (SCLC).

In February 1968, citizens and activists testified before Senator Robert F. Kennedy and Congressman Carl D. Perkins during Kennedy's "hunger hearings." Kennedy's tour started in Mississippi after civil rights activists took him to the Delta, where he saw firsthand the dire conditions in which many black Mississippians lived. A project of the Senate Subcommittee on Employment, Manpower, and Poverty and funded by the Citizens' Crusade Against Poverty, the subsequent hearings were part of liberal Democrats' efforts to expose hunger in America and document the progress of antipoverty programs, with an eye toward expansion. The hearings ended in eastern Kentucky, where Kennedy visited five communities. Dozens of local people testified and many more filed into meeting halls and one room schools to witness the events.

Edith and Jake Easterling attended the hearing in Fleming-Neon, Kentucky, where people packed into the school gymnasium. Outside the school, John Kobak and other VISTAs accompanied a group of high school students from Dickenson County, Virginia, and Harlan County for a demonstration. They wore paper bags over their heads and carried signs that stated "Poor Power," "Don't Give Us Promises! Give Us Education, Jobs," and "Stop Strip Mining

Now!"[85] As Kennedy passed by the young protesters, he stopped and spoke with them, inviting them into the meeting, where one of the students would testify.

Many of the most moving testimonies at the public hearings came from women, many of whom relied on public assistance to care for their families. For instance, Gussie Davis, a white woman from Pike County, made a case for expansion and better implementation of public assistance programs. She spelled out the burdens of caregiving, how the vital labor she performed was nearly impossible with the budget she cobbled together. Davis began her testimony: "I'm a welfare recipient. I practically raised my family on welfare. I raised nine children." At the time of the testimony, Davis had an eleven-year-old child and a twenty-three-year-old son with "busted nerves" living at home. She ticked off her monthly expenses: "I only get $101.60; I get $39 welfare and $61 social security and I have to pay $20 a month house rent and pay $15 and sometimes a little more for power bill." By the time she bought coal to heat her house, paid for her child's school lunches, and paid for transportation to the distant food stamp office (which ate up the cost of the stamps themselves), she could not make ends meet.

In Davis's and many other testimonies, food assistance was one of the primary focuses. The Food Stamp Act of 1964 revived and amended the 1930s food stamp program, which had ended after World War II (though the Department of Agriculture continued a food distribution program in many poor and distressed areas). One of the biggest complaints about the new system was that many people could not afford food stamps, or at least enough stamps to supply a family for an entire month. According to the 1964 act, families were to pay the amount they normally allotted to food purchases, and the food stamps would supplement their allowance. While the law gave state and local governments some room to provide food stamps to extremely poor families, the loosely written guidelines led to many poor families being denied food stamps because they could not pay.[86]

Gussie Davis closed by saying that she was willing to work outside of her home but that raising nine children had taken a toll on her body, limiting her options. Her testimony provoked expressions of disbelief from Kennedy. "Can you really support your family and survive on this amount?" he queried. Davis responded, "No, I sure can't."[87]

The following spring and summer, poverty politics gained a national hearing during the SCLC's Poor People's Campaign, conceived by Martin Luther King Jr. He had called for an ambitious, multiracial movement that would use "militant nonviolent actions" to force the federal government to take more dramatic steps to end poverty.[88] Tapping into the mood of poor people across the nation, King made plans to mobilize a mass demonstration of the "poor and disinherited."[89] The Poor People's Campaign in Washington, D.C. would bring together the nation's poor and put pressure on government to act. But the campaign's "most striking militancy," writes historian Gordon Mantler, "came in the form of an aggressive inclusion and recruitment of nonblack minorities," including Appalachian whites.[90]

On May 25, 1968, the SCLC held a gathering called the Appalachian People's Meeting. Five hundred people from across Appalachia traveled to Charleston, West Virginia, where SCLC representative Andrew Young gave a rousing speech on the need for a multiracial antipoverty movement.[91] Four days after the meeting, a group of 190 Appalachians traveled to meet activists at Resurrection City in Washington, D.C., the site of the Poor People's Campaign, where they built an "Appalachian hollow." A month later, a larger delegation traveled to D.C., and they stayed at the Hawthorne School, where they had met before, about two miles from Resurrection City.[92] The Appalachian delegation shared meals and talked with groups from around the country, from migrant farm workers from the West Coast and Mexican Americans led by Chicano activist Reies López Tijerina to Native American groups and NAACP representatives.

For those who participated, the campaign was a powerful moment of unity across race and region. One press release from an Appalachian group announced their purpose in attending: "to let our Congressmen and Senators, our President, our people and the people of the world know that the poor people of Appalachia, white and black, are standing together with the poor people of the Mississippi delta, the poor people of the Indian reservations, the Mexican Americans, the Puerto Ricans, the grape pickers of California, the potato harvesters of Maine—we all stand together."[93] Appalachian representatives also joined the Committee of 100 of the Poor People's Campaign and distributed an "Economic Bill of Rights" drafted by civil rights activist Bayard Rustin.[94] It called for more involvement of poor people in controlling antipoverty programs and demanded programs that led to access to jobs with a living wage, adequate income, land, and capital.[95]

Resurrection City provided a chance for participants to compare their experiences and their political struggles across place. For instance, Chicano activists joined a group of Appalachians for a protest at the home of West Virginia Senator Robert Byrd, who had been a vocal critic of the Poor People's Campaign. For both the Chicano and Appalachian activists, access and rights to land motivated their activism: for Chicanos, land lost during the U.S-Mexican War; and for Appalachians, land lost to coal operators and strip mining. Two hundred people piled into buses and rode to Byrd's home, where they gathered in front to sing, picket, and pray in English and Spanish. After about an hour, a representative knocked on the door. Mrs. Byrd and a security guard answered, and the group unfurled a banner that stated "POOR PEOPLE ARE NOT FREE PEOPLE—GIVE US BACK OUR LAND RIGHTS" and included about one thousand signatures. Mrs. Byrd told the protesters that her husband was at his office and they could find him there, to which the group responded, "Let him come to us."[96]

Sue Ella Easterling was one among dozens of white Appalachians who joined the Poor People's Campaign in the summer of 1968. Although Edith did not travel to Washington, she was supportive of those who went. Sue Ella's boyfriend John Kobak stayed at the Appalachian tent at Resurrection City, while she stayed with a friend. During the days she hung out with activists or attended whatever demonstration was occurring that day. After ten days in D.C. she had to return to Morehead State for summer school in order to graduate at the end of the summer. As a home economics major (one of the few programs of study open to women at the time), she had to stay in a campus house, where she was supposed to learn how to manage a household. Instead, she used the resources at her disposal to recruit more students to the Poor People's Campaign. She fielded phone calls, and, using funds left over from the underground paper she edited, she helped send eight students to D.C. Sue Ella's activism drew the ire of her college's administration. Just before she graduated, the president called her to a meeting. She thought he wanted to congratulate her for recently earning a Ford Foundation grant, but instead he berated her and told her, "You'll graduate in spite of us."[97]

The Poor People's Campaign helped to raise the profile of the welfare rights movement, which had been gaining traction across the country. While the National Welfare Rights Organization (NWRO) had organized formally in 1966, the campaign in D.C. spotlighted it as the "respected powerbroker on welfare policy."[98] During and after the campaign, the NWRO spread the message of welfare rights to a broader audience than it had known before. Welfare rights campaigns soon surged throughout the Mountain South in the late 1960s, with Appalachian Volunteers and VISTAs spearheading the campaigns.

In the months following the Poor People's Campaign, the Marrowbone Folk School hosted several community workshops on welfare rights. In August 1968, Edith Easterling organized a workshop with National Welfare Rights Organization staff person Tim Sampson. A white activist, Sampson had volunteered in the farmworker's movement before becoming assistant director of the Poverty/Rights Action Center affiliated with the NWRO. He had worked closely with black activists and welfare rights leaders Johnnie Tillmon and George Wiley in the early stages of the organization.[99] Edith arranged for Sampson to meet with Appalachian Volunteers and other organizers and to have a separate meeting with a group of welfare recipients so that he could learn "what's happening." She requested that Sampson discuss changes in disability laws and how they might affect welfare recipients. She asked also that he provide examples of successful poor-white welfare rights groups and discuss "the National Welfare Rights Organization, especially the white-black issue that some of our people talked about after they had gone to your last convention." It is unclear what Easterling meant by the "white-black issue," for, other than one mention, the records from that meeting are silent about race relations. Instead, the meeting focused largely on the challenges of place and the particular needs of welfare recipients in a rural region. Her statement, however, suggests that she was aware of racist attitudes that might prevent interracial organizing, but she did not seem to believe they were insurmountable.[100]

At the meeting, Sampson built on the union tradition in Appalachia to make a case for welfare rights organizing. He posited that "the bond is the basic thing in common that all the people have, underlying and related to the issues." Sampson pushed the organizers to think about welfare broadly, especially in Appalachia where families often drew more than one kind of provision. The issue was not AFDC for mothers solely, but how to access aid in general, whether one was elderly, disabled, unemployed, or a single mother. At the same time, Sampson warned that organizers needed to acknowledge the different treatment of Social Security recipients, typically male, and AFDC recipients, typically female. He noted that welfare recipients "tend to be put down more severely" and that "fear of being cut or punished is often great." Sampson's visit to the Marrowbone Folk School and his emphasis on dignity, respect, and social bonds between poor people reflected the NWRO's position that the welfare rights movement would be most powerful if it was a broad-based, multiracial coalition.[101]

Sue Ella also connected to national (and international) poor people's movements, with the financial support of the Appalachian Volunteers. Not long after the NWRO representative visited Pike County, Sue Ella attended the International Conference on Social Welfare in Helsinki, Finland. There she joined a group of community workers, including Johnnie Tillmon of the NWRO, who called on the International Conference to include poor people in its decision making and to commit to a universal standard of "social welfare rights." Sue Ella brought Appalachia to the attention of new movements for welfare rights and represented the region on a national stage.[102]

By the late 1960s, welfare rights organizations began to organize throughout Appalachia, mobilized largely by antipoverty workers. For instance, Thelma Parker, a young white local who worked for the AV, helped to organize a welfare rights group in Harlan County. She had previously used federal resources to set up an affordable daycare center, and in her daily work she had witnessed the hurdles that poor people faced when they sought medical and financial assistance. Just before the formation of the local rights group, a welfare rights activist from Chicago visited Harlan County and gave a speech. The woman's message—that "you shouldn't look down on people drawing welfare"—resonated with Parker. As she remembers it, the local welfare rights group formed shortly after the Chicago woman's visit. Parker also attended the welfare rights meetings at the Marrowbone Folk School, and she became one of the primary organizers of the Kentucky Mountain Welfare Rights Organization. The group rented space in a garage where members could hold meetings, and they decided together what programs to operate.[103]

From the start, the Harlan County group was integrated, drawing black and white recipients, including women, disabled miners, and elderly people. Jeanette Knowles, who worked closely with Parker, described the welfare rights movement in Harlan County as "a big net." She remembered, "A lot of people could fit into that net. . . . Welfare rights really collected a lot of people we met."[104] The group led a successful petition for a food stamp office located closer to where poor people lived; it successfully petitioned the county court to set aside $250 for textbooks for school children who could not afford to purchase them; it started a disability study in Harlan County, planned health fairs, and began work to establish a community health center. It also started a volunteer-run, used-clothing store, and, though it was short-lived, they ran a sewing co-op so that local women could supplement their incomes.[105] Welfare rights groups emerged throughout the region over the next few years, across eastern Kentucky, southwest Virginia, and West Virginia.

Using federal resources that flowed into their communities during the War on Poverty, local activists like Edith Easterling mounted campaigns to expand democratic participation in Appalachian communities and to make local and regional institutions responsive to the needs of poor and working-class people. Over the next several years Easterling and a cohort of Appalachian activists continued to press for land rights, organize welfare rights groups regionally, and spread a message of mountain people's power. But they did so in the face of internal conflicts and a concerted campaign of repression, each of which could have derailed their movement but which instead inspired them to think ever more deeply about the issues before them and to connect their efforts more tightly to national struggles.

3 "In the Eyes of the Poor, the Black, the Youth"

Poverty Politics in Appalachia

On the morning of December 3, 1968, Edith Easterling wore her new red dress to the Kentucky Un-American Activities Committee (KUAC) hearing. In later years, she laughed that she "never thought about the communists wearing the red." She was the only official employee of the Appalachian Volunteers who agreed to be questioned by KUAC, a Joint Legislative Committee backed by the governor and modeled after the House Un-American Activities Committee (HUAC).[1] She sat before a packed Pike County courthouse, where her family, residents of her community, and several AV staff members looked on. She summoned strength from the memory of her grandmother, who had always encouraged her to "speak what you believe" and never "let no man put you down. Because *you* are just as strong."[2]

Easterling had already witnessed attacks on organizers when her colleagues were arrested for sedition in Pike County. She did not stop her work in the aftermath, carrying on in the face of harassment and threats. Yet she soon faced an expanded backlash that further endangered antipoverty programs. The newly elected governor, Louie B. Nunn, rode a wave of declarations against Johnson's War on Poverty, which he saw as part of "big government," and he soon supported state-backed repression of antipoverty and civil rights organizing. KUAC was formed initially in response to urban uprisings in black neighborhoods in Louisville, Kentucky, and the perceived radicalization of black activists. But it soon engulfed other groups that appeared to be in alliance with left organizing or that challenged the status quo. For instance, the committee questioned Easterling about her relationships with civil rights activists who were perceived to be communists and attempted to prove that radicals funded the Marrowbone Folk School. The KUAC hearings, in fact, showed how anticommunism merged with and ultimately gave way to new calls for "law and order," repression of the black liberation movement, and an assault on antipoverty programs. The hearings and the broader political milieu of which they were part reveal how the backlash to movements for racial justice in Kentucky were also entangled with the repression of antipoverty movements in Appalachia. These assaults failed to dampen the resolve of Appalachian activists, however, and by the end of the decade they made another push to strengthen regional movements against poverty and injustice, drawing upon the language of poor people's campaigns across the nation.

The Conservative Response to Antipoverty Activism

In 1967, Kentuckians elected Louie B. Nunn governor, the first Republican leader of the Commonwealth in twenty years. Nunn's governorship was part of a national conservative response to Johnson's Great Society—legislation that promoted civil rights and expanded the social safety net—and the progressive social movements of the postwar era. In particular, Nunn vowed to use his power to bring an end to the Appalachian Volunteers in Kentucky, and the Green Amendment to the Economic Opportunity Act, which Congress passed in 1967, helped him in that endeavor. The amendment gave governors the reins in deciding which groups would be designated Community Action Agencies. The decision was significant because only groups with official designation could qualify for OEO funding. Along with taking advantage of this policy, Nunn mounted a political campaign to discredit antipoverty and civil rights activists and to associate them with communism.

Nunn's views on the War on Poverty were rooted in an ideology that renounced the "theory of big government and little people," which he linked back to the founding of New Deal programs. Nunn believed that antipoverty programs were detrimental to the national "soul." To him, public assistance represented a decline in the American work ethic and signaled that the average American was no "longer economically responsible for his own well-being or morally responsible for his own conduct."[3]

His ideology was rooted in his experiences as a judge in Barren County, Kentucky, in the 1950s. He contrasted what he witnessed as a judge to his own experience as a child during the Depression. In his memory, self-respecting members of his community—white and black—refused free food or any other handouts because "they were too proud." By the 1950s, social provisioning had expanded, and in his position at the county court, Nunn approved or denied relief for food, fuel, and medicine. He argued that too many people did not "properly utilize the funds that were sent to them" and did not know "how to budget." He saw people who had "lost their self respect," who had no "reason to be entitled to it other than an excuse of being hungry or cold or needing medication." The War on Poverty "encouraged more" of the behaviors that Nunn had come to detest.[4]

Nunn's argument that the government was too big and the morals of ordinary citizens too lax followed an oft-repeated refrain in the GOP by the 1960s. Yet his story of how, as a county judge, he knew who was deserving and who was undeserving, who was responsible, who budgeted appropriately, and who was using "excuse[s] of being hungry" in order to attain assistance, suggests that Nunn was frustrated at the loss of local control in deciding poor relief. As historian Karen Tani argues, by the 1940s, the Social Security Administration had ushered in a new era of centralization. In order for states to receive grants-in-aid, they had to follow federal regulations and oversee the implementation of poor relief in localities, thus stripping power away from the elites who thought they knew best what was good for the poor people in their vicinity. The centralization linked to the New Deal also gave rise to a "rights language" that empowered poor people and their advocates, or at the least led them to expect a certain measure of aid, which Nunn perceived as a lack of "self respect."[5] The War on Poverty only compounded Nunn's frustrations with a sea change that was decades in the making.

Governor Nunn promised to cut funding to the Appalachian Volunteers, but he also led a campaign to rid the state of progressive activists in general in the guise of the Kentucky Un-American Activities Committee (implemented by legislators, but appointed by him). KUAC reshaped anticommunism in an era of civil rights, antipoverty campaigns, and black liberation movements. Nunn did not "see any harm" in the committee. Years later, he reflected that the political hearings were "like the wind blowing in the trees": "rotten limbs would get blown off," but if there were no rotten limbs then "nothing will fall out."[6] The simplicity of the image belies the intent, however. The hearings targeted activists and built a campaign of lies, insinuation, and hearsay and played on white people's worst fears and racial biases.

KUAC continued a long history of anticommunism, especially as practiced by Congress's House Un-American Activities Committee, which formed in 1938 to investigate so-called subversive activities by U.S. citizens.[7] In the 1950s, southern segregationists targeted civil rights activists as subversives, using the anticommunist hysteria of the period to their advantage, often with the aid of J. Edgar Hoover's FBI. In 1954, Mississippi Senator James Eastland oversaw the first hearings of the Senate Internal Securities Sub-Committee (the Senate counterpart to the House Un-American Activities Committee) in the South, when he called white supporters of the civil rights movement before the committee for questioning.[8] Martin Luther King Jr. was famously branded a communist after attending the Highlander Folk School, run by Myles Horton, a white activist targeted by Eastland.[9]

In the same period in Kentucky, Louisville residents and white civil rights activists Anne and Carl Braden were arrested for sedition, and the whiff of that charge lingered around them for years. The Bradens worked for and eventually directed the Southern Conference Educational Fund (SCEF), a leading proponent of integration founded in 1946. Initially, authorities arrested the Bradens after they helped Andrew Wade, an African American veteran and his family, buy a home in an all-white neighborhood in Louisville. The arrest followed weeks of threats on the Bradens and the Wades, including a bombing of the Wades' home.[10]

The commonwealth's attorney, A. Scott Hamilton, argued in Carl Braden's trial that the sedition charges were more about the ideas that he espoused than the act of buying the home for Wade. Hamilton painted a picture of Braden as a ringleader who read communist literature widely and stirred up "racial trouble." The jury found Carl Braden guilty, sentenced him to prison for fifteen years, and charged a $5000 fine. He spent eight months in prison before the charge was overturned after the Supreme Court ruled state sedition laws invalid. Not long afterward, the House Un-American Activities Committee summoned the Bradens for questioning. The committee charged Carl with six citations of contempt when he refused to answer questions, and he was incarcerated for a year in the early 1960s. In 1963, authorities raided SCEF, charging that it was in violation of Louisiana's antisedition laws.[11]

Resolute in the face of such attacks, the Bradens accepted directorship of SCEF in the mid-1960s and moved its headquarters from Louisiana to Louisville, Kentucky. SCEF supported the southern freedom movement, trained organizers, published an underground newspaper, and supported interracial organizing efforts in Appalachia. The Bradens' association with some activists in the eastern part of the state would become a lightning rod for state officials in search of ways to rid the mountains of progressive organizations.

Although conservative politicians were often sloppy in lumping together any and every progressive organization in the 1960s, erasing ideological and tactical distinctions, it was nonetheless true that civil rights activists saw the grassroots war on poverty in Appalachia as an important site for building interracial alliances. The Highlander Center had begun training white civil rights workers to organize unemployed white workers in Appalachia as early as 1964. SCEF had also been a part of this turn to organizing working-class whites in the mountains. Long committed to integration, SCEF renewed its efforts when black civil rights organizers in SNCC—who began espousing black power—called on white organizers to mobilize white communities. With its long history of labor radicalism and working-class solidarity, eastern Kentucky seemed like a prime place to build progressive coalitions with working-class whites.[12]

SCEF worked with white activists from SNCC to devise a project that would distinguish it as a leftist political organization and as critical of liberal, Democratic economic policies. SCEF's Southern Mountain Project proposed to organize "jobless and underpaid whites and Negroes into integrated groups to improve their conditions" through "economic and political action." These groups would "no longer be divided when dealing with the people who own the land and the industries" and thus would be able to use their collective voices to gain power.[13] The project hobbled along as it tried to help activists recalibrate to a new environment, but antipoverty organizing in eastern Kentucky seemed to hold out new promises. In 1967, Anne Braden hired Al and Margaret McSurely to organize in Pike County.[14]

The backlash that emerged in Kentucky was a reaction to the policies of the War on Poverty, but it was also an attack on these new militant strands of the civil rights movement, which were intertwined with many antipoverty campaigns. During the backlash, SCEF, Highlander, and people affiliated with them became the "rotten limbs" in the words of Nunn. KUAC used them as a proxy to bring down anyone who might have ties to them.

The Hearings of the Kentucky Un-American Activities Committee

The initial target of KUAC was the black power movement in Louisville, Kentucky. In 1965, Stokely Carmichael and SNCC had begun political organizing in Lowndes County, Alabama. Although African Americans made up 80 percent of the population there, they had no political voice, with only one black person registered to vote. Community activists began calling for black political power, and Carmichael soon popularized the slogan "black power" following the violent attack on James Meredith during the Meredith March Against Fear. The idea that meaningful change would come only if black people had access to political institutions motivated black activists across the country.[15] In Louisville, community organizers called for black leadership in community action programs, black community control, and black power programs. They also organized a community center, held workshops on African American culture, developed black studies curriculum, and organized festivals celebrating African American art.[16]

Calls for black liberation put white politicians and city officials on edge, in part because they feared a link between these more militant movements and urban riots. In the spring of 1968, their fears of an uprising materialized, but only after city police fed into mounting tensions. Following an incident of police brutality—when an officer pulled over a local black man and assaulted him—local black and white activists led a rally in the primarily African American West End neighborhood and called for unity in the face of police abuse of power. Within minutes of the rally's conclusion, the city erupted in a riot after police bore down on the neighborhood and some onlookers threw bottles. The uprising culminated in the deaths of two African American youths and the arrests of more than a hundred people. A grand jury indicted six prominent black activists with conspiracy to disturb the peace and damage property. As the case slowly made its way through the judicial system, the state legislature passed a resolution forming KUAC.[17]

KUAC focused initially on the events in Louisville, but it soon took aim at the movement of Appalachian whites and their allies. The committee headed to the mountains in October and December. The same people who had been behind the sedition arrests of the McSurelys and Joe Mulloy in Pike County turned to KUAC to target antipoverty programs in eastern Kentucky. This time the Marrowbone Folk School was at the center of the controversy. Prior to the hearings, investigators visited Pike County, questioned affiliates of Edith Easterling, and scouted the Marrowbone Folk School for evidence that she and the school were involved in an un-American plot.[18]

State Senator W. Scott Miller, a Republican appointed chair of the committee, presided over the hearings. He introduced the October hearings, stating that the committee would "seek out and examine the facts concerning problems in the Appalachia region of the State concerning" safety, health, welfare, and security of the state, as well as "persons or groups creating strife among the citizens of the state."[19]

The backdrop throughout the hearings was the sedition case from the previous year. In fact, the committee called James Compton, a storeowner and landlord who claimed to have initiated the investigation of the McSurelys. The committee asked him to rehash the lurid details of the initial search and arrest. Compton, who had rented a house to the McSurelys, said that he had entered the home when the McSurelys were away. He found stacks of books on "the Communist line," posters of "colored and white mixed," black power slogans, and film clips about Cuba, which he reported to officials.[20]

Prompted by the committee's attorney, he and other witnesses insinuated ties between the Appalachian Volunteers and perceived radical groups. Local educator Charles Persinger charged that Joe Mulloy had worn bibbed overalls to a meeting. He concluded that Mulloy was either making fun of poor people, or he was wearing "the uniform of civil rights workers." Magistrate of the Marrowbone district Foster Bentley claimed that someone affiliated with the Appalachian Volunteers sang the civil rights anthem "We Shall Overcome," which to him was an example of how the AVs created trouble and confusion. Gracie Rowe had worked with the Appalachian Volunteers until she saw Sue Ella Easterling pass out pamphlets about the draft and the antiwar movement. She had liked the work but quit because she thought any American who did not support the war was suspect. Clara Jo Bowling was invited to attend a meeting at the Marrowbone Folk School, and while she was there she felt uncomfortable and testified that she believed "fully within [her] heart" that something other than the Appalachian Volunteers was organizing there, although she could not say what. The Pike County jailor who had been on duty the night of the McSurely and Mulloy arrests took the stand and told a murky story about a dinner he had with antipoverty workers, including Sue Ella, during which he came to believe "their cause was in sympathy with the communist way of life."[21]

The stated goal of the October hearings was to investigate several local conflicts, none of which, AV director Dave Walls noted, should have been taken up by a legislative committee.[22] One focus was a conflict over a planned water system in the Marrowbone district. Local elites believed that AV workers had stirred up trouble when they assisted the Pike County Citizens' Association (PCCA), a group supported by the Appalachian Volunteers. Led by the elderly Reverend James Hamilton, PCCA called for the middle-class controlled community development organization to adopt lower rates for poor people, offer local people training and jobs on water projects, and promise not to charge people living below the poverty line. Hamilton used his time before the committee to read into the record a report by the citizen's association that called for jobs, a health clinic, higher welfare payments, better roads, regulations on strip mining, and more responsive government.[23]

The committee, however, cared little for the citizen demands and was more interested in what Hamilton could tell them about activities of the Appalachian Volunteers. Hamilton attempted to dispel rumors, offering earnest answers that he believed the antipoverty workers were there to help improve local people's lives. Addressing many local officials' obsession with the garb of AV workers, he stated, "Regardless of what kind of clothes they wore, this was as nice a bunch of young boys and girls as I ever met in my community."[24]

The committee also investigated ties between Pikeville College and the Marrowbone Folk School. In previous months, conservative students had demonstrated at the small liberal arts college because they believed that the college was becoming "too liberal" under the leadership of the college president, Dr. Thomas Johns. Johns held forums on controversial topics, like surface mining and the Vietnam War. The forums indicated to some locals and students that Johns had hired faculty who "encouraged opposition to the draft, the Vietnam War, and the local established leadership."[25] The last straw was the college's collaboration with the Marrowbone Folk School and Edith Easterling. A student group from the college coordinated with the staff of the Marrowbone Folk School, despite a letter from Governor Nunn stipulating that the group, which received state funds, could not work with the Appalachian Volunteers. Rumors of a professor involved in a communist plot followed. In the face of the controversy, Dr. Johns held firm on protecting academic freedom.[26] The hearings, however, led to a swirl of rumors and threats, and he and his family soon left the region.

The committee subpoenaed AV staff, but because there were no official charges and the legality of KUAC was in question, the Appalachian Volunteers as an organization refused to participate.[27] No AV staff testified during the October hearings, but Edith Easterling chose to take the stand during the December hearings. A liberal, local lawyer and go-to for activists, Dan Jack Combs, represented Easterling. Before the examination began, the chair of the committee offered the statement: "It is not the intention of this Committee to attach any stigma of being un-American to a person because he has been subpoenaed to appear before the Committee."[28] Given the sedition arrests the year prior and the history of anticommunism in Kentucky in previous years, his remark was little comfort to the people summoned.

Easterling sat before a group of powerful, well-educated men who were surely not prepared to hear an Appalachian woman lambast politicians as corrupt, money-grubbing cowards, but that is exactly what she would do.[29] Early in her testimony she offered an admission: "I will confess we have done wrong—or I have done wrong. I voted for that dirty bunch in that courthouse. I am a Republican and I'll stay one but I have been treated the meanest by that bunch than I was ever treated in my life, and my family can back me up."[30]

When the committee's attorney, J. T. McCall, asked her about the purpose of the Appalachian Volunteers, Easterling offered a long statement that described her activities. But she also excoriated mountain "politicianers," as she called them. "Well, the purpose of the program is to help people and help them in a better understanding [of their rights]. There are people in our community that never heard of welfare or Social Security." She then charged the elites of Pike County of refusing to believe that poverty existed in the mountains. "They are not out there, they don't know, because they don't want to come out. They are not interested in poor people," she contended, except when they wanted votes. Only then do they "come out with their bag of money." In describing her and the AV workers' relationship to people in her community, she stated, "We want these people to feel important. We have got some people out in these hollows that can't read or write a word, but brother, they are smarter than a lot of them in the Courthouse." Addressing the local male authorities as Christian peers—by referring to them as "brother"—Easterling gestured to the moral questions at the heart of the hearings.[31]

While Easterling attempted to turn attention to the politicians leading the investigations, McCall sought to draw connections between Easterling and so-called subversives. He questioned Easterling about an article on the Marrowbone Folk School that appeared in the *Southern Patriot*, SCEF's newspaper, apparently using the article as proof that SCEF underwrote the building of the school. When pressed, Easterling said that "a lot of people helped out" but that "we [meaning her community] built the school." McCall also established that Easterling met the Bradens at the time of the sedition arrests, as though simply interacting with the Bradens was an indication of suspicious activity. McCall then questioned Easterling on her relationship to the Highlander Center. Easterling defanged the line of questioning:

EXAMINER: Mrs. Easterling, what, if any, connection is there between the Marrowbone Folk School and the Highlander Folk School in Tennessee?
EASTERLING: You asked me that yesterday and I told you [there] was none.
EXAMINER: As far as you know there is no connection between these schools?
EASTERLING: That's right.
EXAMINER: Have you ever taken trips to the Highlander Folk School?
EASTERLING: Mr. McCall, this is a free country. I have taken a lot of trips.
EXAMINER: Yes, ma'am, I am just trying to find out whether or not you—.
EASTERLING: I have been down to Tennessee. I've been in many parts of it.
EXAMINER: Have you been to the Highlander Folk School there?
EASTERLING: I have visited the Highlander.
EXAMINER: Do you know anybody that is associated with the Highlander Folk School? Has anybody from that school ever come to Marrowbone to your all's school?
EASTERLING: To visit, you mean?
EXAMINER: Yes, ma'am, or to teach any classes?
EASTERLING: Oh, I had Conrad Brown (director of Highlander) up the other day and took dinner with him.[32]

Throughout the questioning, Easterling deflected questions that insinuated that her relationships were compromised or that she had been exploited by radical activists. She took ownership of the Marrowbone Folk School and the ideas that circulated there, refusing to allow the examiner to paint her as an unwitting accomplice. She knew that there was nothing illegal about visiting the Highlander Center or sharing a meal with staff members.

Yet whenever she got an opening, she turned the hearing around and asked the officials what exactly they were doing to serve the people they represented. She sought to shame the politicians who attacked programs that helped poor people, and she positioned herself as a person genuinely concerned with the betterment of her community, unlike the "politicianers." When questioned about her reasons for joining the Appalachian Volunteers, she stated, in a long, passionate response: "I have always been concerned. I have always give to people and done without myself and I have hauled people to doctors and I have always been concerned with people which was less fortunate than I was." She proceeded to explain how the political elite gladly accepted state and federal funds as long as they controlled them, and she knew that if local people did not join the War on Poverty, then resources would never get to the people who needed them. When local people had some success, the political elites, in her view, "was mad about it. That's their game. If they can't get it theirself, they don't want nobody else to have it." She concluded, "I wish every poor and deserving person could get it that deserves it. Now, that's the way I feel. I don't want to steal nothing. . . . I would assure you that [if] some of Thomas Ratliff's clique was getting that [federal] money, he wouldn't be fighting it. That's just how it goes but his clique ain't getting it."[33]

Throughout the hearings, examiners treated Easterling with condescension and refused to recognize her politics—and her role in the Appalachian Volunteers—as valid, seeing her instead as a guileless woman tricked by communists. They pushed a narrative that dangerous outsiders were causing chaos in the mountains and ignored or downplayed local activists' involvement in community action. If they publicly acknowledged the grassroots activism of local people, their conspiracy theory about outside agitators would evaporate. By the time of the hearings, Edith had protested strip mining, organized a meeting with the National Welfare Rights Organization (the committee filed documents from that meeting as "evidence"), and held numerous political meetings with people from across the country. Yet the examiner never asked Easterling about her political activities (although she sometimes offered descriptions without prompting). Rather, he tied her to activists perceived to be radical and implied that her ideas were not her own, simultaneously downplaying her role in the War on Poverty and stripping her of political agency. The committee seemed unable to imagine that a working-class woman from the mountains could possess the presence of mind and the intellectual savvy to see through their hearings and expose the red-baiting tactics for what they were: conspiracies meant to detract from the grassroots war on poverty.

Toward the end of her testimony, the examiner mocked Easterling, asking, "I'm afraid to ask you this question but is there anything else you would like to tell the Committee today?" Easterling threw back the curtain of Kentucky politics and placed herself at the center of antipoverty work: "We don't have anything to hide. I am proud of the AVs. The AVs had brought something to Pike County that's never been here before, and I would lay my life down for anything—I am not ashamed that I am one of them and I think that when Governor Nunn or when you birds say they don't deserve this or they don't deserve that, brother, you ought to think of the poor people that lives out in the heads of these hollows that do go to bed hungry. That's what I think, brother."[34]

Reflecting on this episode years later, Easterling observed that the collective power of poor people threatened many local politicians. The series of events in 1967 and 1968 in Pikeville, from the sedition arrests to harassment of poverty workers to the KUAC hearings, revealed the lengths that local officials and the state would go to oust community organizers and quell protests by poor people in eastern Kentucky.[35]

As intended, the KUAC hearings strained the Appalachian Volunteers. Even though KUAC lost funding and its hearings led to no criminal charges, the AV's reputation was severely undermined. Although the OEO approved AV funds for the upcoming year, Governor Nunn refused to approve the grant, using authority provided him by the Green Amendment and following the recommendations of KUAC. He rejected the OEO funds on the basis that the AV staff had failed to spell out objectives in their application.[36] The succession of blows to community groups led to infighting and distrust. Some felt betrayed by Edith Easterling's decision to testify before KUAC. Others believed that she no longer worked in the interest of poor people. At the same time, AV staff failed to find alternative financial support, and in October the AV director, David Walls, laid off Easterling and planned for the closure of the organization.[37]

The KUAC hearings, internal struggles for power, and loss of Easterling's paid position strained relationships between outsiders and local people, even pushing Easterling to reconsider outsider activists' role in Appalachia. In its final months, the Appalachian Volunteers continued to employ Thomas Ramsay, an activist from California, and he served as fieldman in Pike County. To Easterling, the Appalachian Volunteers had chosen to keep an outsider instead of her in a staff position, which she believed was a sign that the organization no longer valued local people's opinions and leadership. To make matters worse, Ramsay had made suggestive comments to Edith, and when Jake learned of them, he threatened Ramsay. The red-baiting and then the rumors surrounding her run-ins with Ramsay must have taken a toll. Nonetheless, she refused to give up on her work with the Appalachian Volunteers and organized a letter-writing campaign in support of her position. The letters ranged from mothers who testified on behalf of Easterling's character to people from around the country who had visited the Marrowbone Folk School and thought highly of the community programs there.[38]

Scholars have often focused on the internal rifts that hobbled the Appalachian Volunteers and have not always considered them in the bigger picture of assaults on the War on Poverty, which were intertwined with attempts to turn the tide of the civil rights movement.[39] Internal conflicts were important, of course, and weak organizations could not withstand the external pressures. But equally important is the story of how the KUAC hearings began as part of a series of racist attacks on the civil rights movement and black activists that soon encompassed white Appalachian activists. KUAC relied heavily on the notion of a radicalized civil rights movement that sought to subvert so-called American values. Tying white activists to civil rights organizations, especially those that supported calls for black power, was often proof enough that antipoverty programs were subversive agents. The Appalachian Volunteers' detractors used those relationships to malign them, drawing upon racist narratives of outside agitators to attack community action in poor communities. The narrative of radical outsiders proved a powerful and believable narrative in much of the white South, providing cover for politicians who did not wish to address the material concerns or protest messages of working-class whites in the mountains. As one legislator put it, "This state has become a headquarters for subversion."[40] Summoning images of these dangerous outsiders, state officials argued that activists foisted their radical ideas on locals, who needed to be protected.

The opposite was true. The social movements in Kentucky—whether in Louisville or the mountains—grew from the grassroots. They threatened the status quo, which in turn reacted to protect its standing.

As a spokesperson for her community, Easterling brooked no argument that she and her co-organizers were "un-American," and she refused to engage in race- and red-baiting. Rather, she reset the terms of debates about the validity of the Appalachian War on Poverty, making a case instead for democratic participation. Even as she mourned the loss of the Appalachian Volunteers, she did not hesitate to defend the work they had done in eastern Kentucky, writing in 1969: "Interest has aroused, stones unturned, dander up, fever risen, and people speaking out on what they [believe] . . . Marrowbone Creek is going to be a better place to live. Thanks to the Appalachian Volunteer who come in and helped the people to get things started."[41]

Political elites sought to extinguish antipoverty activism in eastern Kentucky and across the state, causing great pain in the process; yet seeds of change had already been planted and were growing. In the months after Easterling left the Appalachian Volunteers, the Highlander Center invited her to join the board. She wrote a letter of acceptance on a "beautiful spring day," exclaiming that "it will be a pleasure to be on a fine Board like yours" and that she believed it was "a big opportunity for me, not what I can give but what I can learn." As a board member of the Highlander Center and later with the Council of the Southern Mountains, she continued her work, speaking out on behalf of poor and working-class people in the mountains and demanding that their voices be central in the remaining antipoverty organizations.[42] In the year after the KUAC hearings, she and dozens of other antipoverty activists proved that state-backed political repression would not stop them.

The Evolution of the Council of the Southern Mountains

By the late 1960s, many activists returned to the primary antipoverty organization in the region, the Council of the Southern Mountains (CSM), remaking it in the process. Since its inception, white, middle-class men and women—many affiliated with Berea College and settlement schools throughout the region—had directed and sat on the board of the CSM. Well into the 1960s, it often looked more like the progressive social reform agencies of the early twentieth century than a hotbed of social justice activism.

The War on Poverty, with its call for "maximum feasible participation," as well as grassroots political developments of the period, had already led to transformations within the organization, which continued to receive funding from the Office of Economic Opportunity for vocational and research programs. In the wake of antipoverty efforts, structural critiques of poverty eclipsed the culture-of-poverty models espoused by an older generation of social scientists and missionaries, some of whom had been leaders in the Council. For instance, along with supporting the Poor People's Campaign, by the late 1960s the CSM's annual conference included leftist and radical speakers whose interpretations of poverty were far removed from the social reformers of the past. In 1967, speakers debated A. Bayard Rustin's Freedom Budget, called for citizenship schools, and discussed the feasibility of a public, nonprofit coal industry.[43] Despite shifting views of some of its members and leaders, however, the CSM continued to be managed and directed by white, middle-class men.

In the summer of 1969, local activists seized the opportunity to remake the CSM and, in so doing, followed a broader national pattern of democratizing antipoverty organizations. A cadre of youth activists worked in coalition with poor and working-class Appalachians to demand majority representation of the poor on the CSM's board, which decided how resources were allocated to local organizations. Together, they fomented a campaign to overhaul the CSM's board and mission and to develop new "commissions," the groups under the CSM umbrella that oversaw planning and organizing on particular issues. Former commissions revolved around education, arts and the humanities, and education. New commissions addressed the needs of black Appalachians, women, and poor people, among other topics.[44]

Young activists were key to the evolution of the CSM. In the year leading up to the annual conference, Sue Ella Easterling, cochair of the CSM's Youth Commission, developed the idea and recruited participants for a free university. This "floating education system" would consist of a series of workshops and panels representing all the major issues of the day, and it would take place in conjunction with the annual CSM meeting. Influenced by training in community education she had received at the Highlander Center, which she had begun attending at age nineteen, Sue Ella outlined her goal to create a "curriculum and process of education that is meaningfully relevant to students of Appalachia."[45]

Sue Ella had become increasingly critical of the Appalachian Volunteer leadership. She believed they had not done enough to support local people in their efforts to transform regional politics. Moreover, while she did not explicitly voice a frustration with sexism at the time, she increasingly came to see how she was marginalized in the organization as a woman. Female student workers in the Appalachian Volunteers, called "Vistadollies" by the staff, remember that men made decisions, and women implemented them; women were the organizers on the ground. According to Edith Easterling, the men brought the money in and women did the work, but they were rarely rewarded with official staff or leadership positions. Among the young women, there was a sense that they were placed in certain communities based on the whims of male staff—for instance, women they found attractive or wanted to get to know better. They also knew that some prominent male leaders did not take "women's issues" seriously, even as they relied on the organizing efforts of women.[46]

While Sue Ella focused on developing local youth leadership, Myles Horton (one of the male leaders who could simultaneously support yet condescend to

Figure 5. Sue Ella Kobak, 1971. Courtesy of Sue Ella Kobak, from her personal collection.

young women) was on the conference committee. He met with other Council members and urged them to begin recruiting poor people from Appalachia to the conference. In the months leading up to the Fontana conference they ran workshops on "developing leadership" and "preparing" poor people in the Appalachian region for the conference. Highlander staff discussed the workshops as "part of plans to adapt the Citizenship School Program to Appalachian problems," and they saw the conference as a place "to develop an Appalachian social movement which can be made a part of the Poor People's Coalition."[47] Developed by black women to promote voter registration in black communities, citizenship schools had been fundamental to grassroots organizing in the civil rights movement of the Deep South. Highlander staff imagined a similar program in poor and working-class white communities in Appalachia.

Sue Ella's Free University proposal stressed similar themes, but even more forcefully connected the Appalachian Movement to the multiracial organizing that was happening in cities across the country. As the Youth Commission explained: "We the youth of Appalachia are dedicated to ending an exploitive system; a system that has as its intent the destruction of the culture, spirit, and riches of this region; an economic system which forces people off the land and which makes survival impossible for those left behind." The organizers hoped to "encourage a new awareness in the youth of Appalachia" and to foster in young people a "desire to gain an Appalachian identity that they can recognize with pride."[48] To achieve their goals, they would develop "political and social conscious" of young people, tell a "true Appalachian history," and foster interracial coalitions that brought together "all of those who are oppressed."[49]

In the year prior to the 1969 conference, Sue Ella had visited Jobs and Income Now (JOIN) in Uptown Chicago, led by Peggy Terry, a white working-class woman, and Dovie Thurman, a black working-class woman. An outgrowth of Students for a Democratic Society's (SDS) Economic Research and Action Project (ERAP), JOIN organized around welfare rights and poor people's needs, and it took on the issue of racism in working-class white communities.[50] When Sue Ella returned to eastern Kentucky, she wrote a hurried letter to Milton Ogle, the director of the AVs, who had funded her trip. Her eyes had been opened in Chicago. She explained, "I am sick, sick, sick of service-oriented projects that do nothing to help people realize what really affects their lives." She longed to make a bigger impact on the region than seemed possible with the federal antipoverty programs, which she had come to believe patched over problems more often than addressing them head on. She saw the Free University as a way for local youth to deepen their analysis of poverty in Appalachia.[51]

The Appalachian Free University workshops ran concurrent to the CSM annual conference in April 1969, at the mountain resort Fontana Village in the Smoky Mountains. The conference drew several hundred students, longtime Council members, and grassroots antipoverty activists. Organizers of the Free University arranged panels on such topics as civil rights, the draft, and women's liberation, and showed films, including one about the Black Panther Party and *Salt of the Earth*, which is about a strike in a Mexican American mining community. The majority of the panels focused on the Appalachian region, from politics and economics to labor history and what it meant to identify as Appalachian. The conference boasted well-known speakers, including civil rights lawyer Paul Kaufman and novelist Wilma Dykeman.[52]

In the run-up to the meeting, members of the Youth Commission had met with poor people's groups and discussed a plan to make their concerns central in the Council. They ultimately formed a voting bloc and pushed through an agenda. They amended the Council's bylaws to say that 51 percent of the board of commissioners must be poor people. They also established a Black Appalachian Commission, and they put forward resolutions opposing the war in Vietnam; called for a guaranteed income for all Americans; and demanded that federal military spending be rerouted into domestic programs.[53]

While the Youth Commission was clearly a part of an American youth movement culture, middle-aged poor and working-class people had different motivations for a takeover of the CSM. For them the Council provided access to resources to better serve communities. They also signaled a desire to have a seat at the table at one of the most influential institutions in the region.

Conference participant Mary Rice Farris offered one of the most insightful summaries of the 1969 meeting. A working-class African American woman from Berea, Kentucky, who had been employed by the Appalachian Volunteers before taking a job with a Community Action Program (CAP), Farris wrote: "We must recognize that the Council of the Southern Mountains has taken on a new look, a new approach, and has grown 10 feet tall in the eyes of the poor, the black, the youth, and other interested parties." She continued, "I feel that through their actions the Council has gained strength in a meaningful form. It has bridged the existing generation gap. It has condemned second-class citizenship and deepened its fellowship with all the people. I have confidence and hope that the Council now has a new opportunity to serve Appalachia in the coming years with eyes open to the future."[54] Farris's reference to the "future" was surely no coincidence. She understood deeply that the common perception of Appalachia as a white enclave and a place of nostalgia had hobbled progress in the region. And the Council's transformation signaled the possibility for new understandings of Appalachia.

Farris grew up in Berea, home of Berea College, where in 1855 the abolitionist John G. Fee organized an interracial community, in which freedmen and whites lived side by side. The experiment in interracial living, education, work, and worship was short-lived, however, as Kentucky's Day Law targeted Berea College, outlawing interracial education in 1904. Nonetheless, Farris absorbed the history of black self-determination and racial uplift. She also understood a history of loss. Her ancestors had enacted freedoms only to see them stripped away when they and future generations were denied access to education.[55]

As was so often the case, Farris was attracted to antipoverty programs because they allowed her to continue the community work she was already doing (much of it through her church), and it offered better pay than anything else available to her. Farris and her husband owned a farm, but they both sought wage work to make ends meet. Farris had worked as a "floating maid" at a hotel, a packager at a munitions factory (a job she lost after military cutbacks), and a cosmetics saleswoman. She was always on the lookout for "a better job" and found it in the Appalachian Volunteers. In her application, she stated, "Have all my life done political and community work around Berea and Madison County" and she needed "support to carry on the work I have been doing."[56]

A year prior to the CSM's annual conference she had confronted Congressman Carl D. Perkins, a celebrated Democrat representing the eastern Kentucky district, and Senator Robert F. Kennedy at the "hunger hearings," when the politicians visited Appalachian communities to document the successes and limitations of the War on Poverty. The only black woman to testify at the hearings, Farris discussed her work as an Appalachian Volunteer in a setting made up mostly of white people, who rarely considered the place of black Appalachians in policy decisions.

At one point in her testimony, Farris fired off a series of questions to Congressman Perkins: "[Why are we] spending $70 million dollars a day in Vietnam, plus loss of life, when [there] are millions of people in our area hungry, without homes and decent housing, or without clothing. And we would also like to know why the Negro is having to fight too for a decent place in society as a rightful citizen? Why we, as American Negroes, are having to fight and speak out for a right to take decent responsibility in this great nation?" Farris took the opportunity to challenge the idea that poverty and hunger could be separated from questions of political power and racial equality.[57]

Kennedy joked that Farris had "turned this hearing around," but Perkins, not amused, declined to address Farris's questions. He also refused to call her by her name, a courtesy he had extended to all of the white women who testified. He snapped, "Now, this lady here (referring to Farris). I do not have the answers to her questions, so that's it." But Farris did not back down. She accused Perkins of not doing enough to support poor people in Kentucky, prompting him to defend his policy decisions.[58]

Congressman Perkins, who had supported War on Poverty legislation, revealed how loathe some liberal whites were to confront systemic poverty in all of its complexity, especially when a working-class black woman was the messenger. As an African American woman and longtime community activist, Farris was especially well-positioned to expand the conversation from the particular (the material needs of her community) to the complex and systemic problems facing poor communities, from the war in Vietnam to widespread racism. Her frank questions unnerved Perkins and seemingly amused Kennedy. Her treatment by a white liberal politician, of course, was not unusual. White politicians had also mocked and discounted the knowledge of activists like Fannie Lou Hamer, Johnnie Tillmon, and other working-class black women who spoke out against poverty and racism.[59]

Albeit brief, the exchange between Farris and Perkins called into question the racial and gendered construction of the Mountain South. White policy makers rarely invited African American women (and men) to discuss poverty in Appalachia. In the performance of the hearings, Perkins attempted to erase the experiences and knowledge of a black, working-class woman who claimed Appalachia as home. He and other white politicians and pundits had long seen Appalachia as a white enclave, where the primary concern was class relations among whites, and usually as a conversation about white masculinity and manhood.[60] The Council takeover signaled a possible break in this old pattern, giving up the "old ways" according to Farris. She was hopeful that the major regional organization would no longer ignore the diversity of experiences in the region and that it would transform its goals based on those experiences.[61]

Other members were not so hopeful and would not accept the changes. One member, critical of the leaders of the takeover, charged that they had learned their tactics from "the movies on the Black Panthers and on the Columbia demonstrations." Another wrote that the event was "a mockery of due process."[62] In the year after the conference, director Loyal Jones, who had worked with the Council for twelve years, resigned. Jones had served as a bridge between the youth and older members, and he was universally admired. But the power grab at the conference unsettled him.[63] He argued that new members on the CSM board cared more about their "theories" than about working on the major issues confronting Appalachians. Middle-class professionals had long sought to address poverty by offering resources and educational programming. A new cadre of grassroots activists saw the Council as a way to build a broad-based, regional social justice movement. Yet from the perspective of Jones and others, the "far left" views of some members led to polarization. Pointing to developments in national politics, most notably the fracturing of the Democratic Party, Jones saw polarization as "a tactic and a fact in the present age" that, he predicted, would lead to the Council's failure.[64]

Many middle-class members also left the CSM, taking their resources and their connections to funding agencies with them. Years later, welfare rights activist Eula Hall discussed her own involvement in the takeover. She noted regrettably that she and other activists had not fully considered the effects on the organization as moderates left, taking with them their knowledge.[65] At the same time, they had not anticipated that those members would refuse to be allies or support the organization under its new leadership.

Jones and others emphasized the ideological divides within the new Council and mourned what they saw as an end to consensus politics. Yet, larger problems threatened the Council as Nixon's administration began dismantling the OEO, one of its major funders. Nixon appointed the junior congressman, Donald H. Rumsfeld, to serve as director of the OEO, despite the fact that Rumsfeld had voted against the Economic Opportunity Act. Rumsfeld presented himself as a careful administrator who would evaluate antipoverty programs and make scrupulous decisions about what to fund. In fact, Rumsfeld's primary task was to weaken organizations that the War on Poverty had emboldened to challenge the power of state and local agencies. A month before Loyal Jones resigned from the Council, he corresponded with Rumsfeld, pleading with him to maintain funding for the organization at least through another year. Jones argued that the director of the Mid-Atlantic Regional Office of the OEO had created a web of confusion before deciding without warning to terminate grants that Jones had previously been told would be renewed. Jones was unable to win Rumsfeld's sympathy. As Jones resigned from the Council, he announced to the board that a funding crisis loomed.[66]

For many Council members at the time, the political fractures and funding woes spelled disaster and decline, an end to the promises of the Great Society. The takeover of the Council took on symbolic significance, obscuring both the broader challenges that all antipoverty organizations faced as Nixon instructed his administrators to dismantle key programs of the War on Poverty and the ways in which antipoverty activism persisted in Appalachia.

In fact, in the decade after the 1969 conference, the issues represented at the conference rippled outward, especially those of economic power and welfare rights. With the changes in the Council's structure, more poor people and women entered leadership positions. And over the next decade, the CSM provided a clearinghouse for grassroots campaigns throughout Appalachia and proved an important resource for spreading news and connecting activists. To be sure, it never regained its status as the largest reform agency in the region, but it continued to provide an important network for regional activists.

The takeover signaled an evolution in the Council of the Southern Mountain's mission, from reform to an emphasis on an Appalachian identity that was not simply about cultural heritage, but about politics as well. New Council leaders announced a drive toward "Appalachian Self-Determination," an idea represented in the development of Appalachian studies programs.[67]

Drawing on the energy of the youth movement and the Appalachian Free University, in 1970 teachers, students, and activists began to develop a curriculum for Appalachian studies. At a Clinch Valley College conference in Wise, Virginia, activists titled the meeting "Tomorrow's People," a play on Jack Weller's statement that Appalachians were "yesterday's people." Attendees considered the best approaches to education in Appalachia and how to develop programs that acknowledged the diversity of mountain people and analyzed the economy and politics in the region. Sociologist and scholar activist Helen Matthews Lewis, who taught a seminar on Appalachia at the college, argued for educational institutions in the region to "see themselves as part of the Appalachian community." She believed that students "should become knowledgeable about Appalachian history and aware of themselves as Appalachians and as exploited people." Among the speakers, Edith Easterling argued for a stronger educational system that would provide students in secondary schools and colleges with the skills they needed to contribute to their communities. As things were, young people felt pressure to leave in order to pursue careers, lacking opportunities to invest in their home communities.[68]

Scholar activists at the forefront of Appalachian studies borrowed from new theories about imperialism and colonialism, especially the "internal colonialism model." This model explained poverty through a history of land and labor exploitation and the concentration of wealth in the hands of outside capitalists. Rather than attempting solely to solve the problems of poverty, they examined enormous issues in the capitalist system and charged that poverty in Appalachia was an effect of the unequal distribution of power and resources.[69]

New intellectual currents in the 1960s reflected the coalitional work of movements tied to the Poor People's Campaign and adopted a language of self-determination and justice. *Appalachian* offered a collective identity, one that countered the notion of individualistic, fatalistic poor people. It offered instead a sense of being one group among many seeking to transform society.

The politics surrounding Appalachian antipoverty movements in 1968 and 1969 have often been remembered as stories about white people and a supposedly race-neutral politics, divorced from broader national trends. Yet the Appalachian antipoverty campaigns, the political backlash to them, and the internal conflicts that roiled regional institutions were steeped in the racial politics of the era, from the attacks that KUAC made on the War on Poverty to the intellectual debates that circulated in the regional movement.

Despite conflicts that could have buried the movement, an undercurrent of progressive activism persisted into the 1970s, when a coalition of Appalachian welfare recipients, white and black, men and women, ushered in new campaigns for welfare rights.

• • •

As Edith Easterling looked ahead to the 1970s, her family faced personal tragedy. In 1969, doctors diagnosed John Kobak, then Sue Ella's husband, with a rare form of cancer in his leg. They believed that the cancer was related to a knee injury he had sustained during the Poor People's Campaign, when police officers attacked him and a group of activists demonstrating for fair housing. In December, doctors amputated his leg. He and Sue Ella were still hopeful about creating a life together in the Appalachian South. They moved to Dickenson County, Virginia, in the southwestern region of the state. John, who had finished his degree at Harvard after his stint with the Appalachian Volunteers, became a teacher, and Sue Ella worked in the local Head Start program. When John's cancer returned, he and Sue Ella were expecting a child. John died in November 1970, and his ashes were buried at the Easterling family plot in Poor Bottom. Sue Ella and John's baby, Zeke, was born the following April.[70] Sue Ella continued to work for several years as a teacher before heading to law school. In 1982, she received her law degree at the University of Kentucky, among the first generation of women to do so, and eventually began practicing law in Appalachian Virginia.

In 1971, Edith wrote to a friend that she was taking care of Jake, who had fallen ill. Not long after he was feeling better, her father had a stroke and needed assistance. "It takes so much of my time," she wrote. Twelve days before his death, she brought him to her home and cared for him and then stayed by his side at a nursing home in his final days.[71] Despite the many setbacks and tragedies, she did not stop organizing. She joined emerging welfare rights campaigns, participated in Highlander Center workshops, started a cooperative grocery store with Jake, joined the board of the Council of the Southern Mountains, and traveled around the country to meet other people fighting for democracy in their communities. She also led efforts to organize thirty neighbors to prevent the Hurricane Elkhorn Coal Company from strip mining on the ridge that rose up behind their community, an operation that potentially could have released water waste from an old mine, causing a devastating flood (a geologist confirmed the threat).[72] With or without the Appalachian Volunteers, she would continue the work that she had always done, but now with more tools at her disposal.

4 March for Survival

The Appalachian Welfare Rights Movement

At seventeen, Eula Riley believed that if only she could find a suitable husband, her life would improve. Born in 1927 in the community of Greasy Creek in Pike County, Kentucky, she had grown up with good-hearted parents in a caring but impoverished home. Her mother and father were tenant farmers, and her father a sometimes miner. Her family was "one of those poor mountain families that raised what you eat and eat it." She and her six siblings often stayed home from school to work in the cornfields or potato patch. They also gathered ginseng and sassafras bark, which they sold at the market in town. Her parents used the profits from selling herbs to buy the children shoes and clothes. Even then, the children never had more than one or two outfits at a time, and their shoes were often cheaply made and wore out quickly. "We never knew what it was to have good warm clothes or shoes," she mused.[1] Cold air and water, combined with the harsh lye soaps that were common at the time, dried and cracked their feet and hands. Some mornings, Eula had to roll cloth around her hands before she milked the cows so that she wouldn't get blood in the milk.

Eula's childhood was defined more by work than formal education. She went to school until she was fourteen, when she graduated from eighth grade. Because she had started late, she had only attended for five years. "I loved school. I hated the last day of school," she said wistfully. Eula was a good student who wanted desperately to go to high school. But there were no secondary schools in her community, and her family could not afford to send her to the high school in town. Reflecting back on that loss, Eula stated that when you are poor, a child, and cannot afford to go to school, "You want to be somebody, you want to make something out of yourself, and you ain't got a chance in the world."[2]

After a brief stint working in a canning factory in New York, Eula returned home to Pike County and began working as a domestic servant. Called "hired girls," young, white domestic servants in Appalachia usually worked in boarding houses or for wealthier women who were sick or pregnant and who lived in middle-class communities. Eula's first job was for a family that lived in a "real nice house." Among the family members was a daughter close to Eula's age, who offered a comparison of the different expectations of girls based on class status. The daughter of the house did not perform chores. Eula explained: "She stayed in the house, and she had pretty clothes and her fingernails polished." Meanwhile, Eula's fingers bled from scrubbing the laundry in scalding water. Hired girls performed the intense, physically taxing labor of cleaning and disinfecting houses. The hardest labor was washing the bedding after a woman had given birth or a household member had been ill: first the hired girl stripped the beds and then emptied the feathers from mattresses, boiled the casings, starched the bedding, hung it all to dry, and then refilled the casings with feathers before sewing up the opened end. "It's murder," Eula remembered.[3]

Hired girls also had to learn to navigate relationships with bosses. Eula believed that the people she worked for saw themselves as "better" than the hired girls, who were assumed to be promiscuous. She worked for at least one man who tried to pressure her into dating him, despite being forty-five years old to her fifteen. She recalled thinking, "This is something else. [I'm] washing and scrubbing your old clothes for the money, but I don't have to go out with you."[4]

Eula knew that with an employed husband she could expect greater financial stability and relief from laboring for other people. In 1944, she worked in a boarding house that served gas-line workers. McKinley Hall, the nephew of the woman who ran the boarding house, had just been discharged from the military for medical reasons and often stayed at the house. McKinley was a handsome man, and Eula believed he would make a suitable husband. Eula thought of herself as a promising wife: she had worked hard her whole life and knew how to garden, sew, cook, and keep a home. At seventeen years old, Eula married McKinley, and they moved to neighboring Floyd County.

The young woman who had believed that a husband could relieve her troubles learned the hard truth that a husband and marriage could make a poor woman's life much worse—a living hell even. McKinley was an alcoholic with a temper. "He was one person sober, and another person drunk," Eula explained. He refused to hold a steady job, and he spent his disability check

Figure 6. Portrait of Eula Hall by Kristen Mendenhall. c. 1971. Kristen Mendenhall Collection, Appalshop Archive.

from the Veteran's Administration on whiskey. The promise of marriage soured quickly. But Eula soon became pregnant, and with a child she felt further "trapped" in the marriage.[5]

Like many women prior to the social and legal recognition of domestic violence, Eula found herself in an impossible position. With a husband, she had resources that she felt she could not live without, but to stay in the marriage meant to risk her life. She described herself as "in deeper you've ever been in your life." Varying degrees of irritants set off inebriated McKinley. "If there's no food, he's mad about it and he can't figure out why it's not there. If the child cries it aggravates him, and if you keep a fire you cut the wood yourself." In the three decades she lived with McKinley, he broke her jaw, stabbed her, pulled her hair until she had bald spots, and shot at her. Eula did not have options for employment, so she did what she could to get as much support as possible from McKinley. She dragged him out of bed in the morning, cajoled him to go to work, and she was ready to fight again when he got home.[6]

Eula became expert at navigating social services in her area. She learned that, even when she had him arrested, the police department never kept him more than a night. But she could have McKinley committed to the Veteran's hospital when he was on one of his rampages, and the hospital would keep him for longer periods of time. When she was lucky enough to get the hospital to take him for fifty days or more, she could draw public assistance from Aid to Families with Dependent Children (AFDC).[7] As feminist scholars have argued, because the family unit was legally constructed as a private domain that husbands and fathers headed, there were few legal ramifications for male abusers of women and girls until the late 1980s.[8] Consequently, Eula had little reason to depend on the state to protect her and her children from McKinley. Instead, she navigated the welfare and legal systems and devised her own plans for finding reprieve from McKinley's severe acts of violence.

When federal resources arrived in eastern Kentucky in the mid-1960s, Eula Hall had five children and was doing her best to endure physical abuse and scrounge enough work to keep her children clothed and fed. Along with patching together public assistance, she sold moonshine (from McKinley's operation); she raised gardens to feed the family; and one winter she sewed thirty-five quilts that she sold for income.[9] She was not alone in scraping by. In Floyd County, over a third of families had incomes below the poverty level, and over half of the housing had been deemed substandard.[10] The unemployment rate in Floyd County, indicative of that throughout eastern Kentucky, skyrocketed to 12.9 percent in 1960, seven points higher compared to 1950 and among the highest rates in the United States. Over the course of the 1950s, the Floyd County population decreased by nearly one-fourth, due to the mine closures following the World War II boom in production. At a time when more American women than ever were entering into public work to help support families, in eastern Kentucky there were still few options for women's employment. The bituminous coal and lignite mining industry employed over 60 percent of the civilian labor force in Floyd County in the 1950s and 1960s. With the exception of secretaries and other office workers, all of those workers were men.[11]

The antipoverty programs seemed a promising opportunity to many women living in the coal fields. Hall articulated the eagerness she felt: "When the War on Poverty started I signed up as a worker—anything if there's federal money, I'm going to get my part of it and I'm going to raise hell."[12]

The War on Poverty catapulted Hall into a lifetime of activism, and she would become part of a broad coalition of antipoverty workers and a key leader of the welfare rights movement in Appalachia. Even as the War on Poverty lost funding and faced a backlash among conservatives at the state and national levels, local organizing persisted. Indeed, local activism expanded as local and outsider antipoverty workers embraced "welfare rights" as an organizing platform at the local, state, and national level. Eula Hall's activism was part of a flourishing and diverse welfare rights movement in Appalachia; she joined the Eastern Kentucky Welfare Rights Organization, and from that local group allied with welfare rights activists across the state and the country.

Breadwinner Liberalism and Welfare Rights in Appalachia

As scholars of welfare have shown, in the mid-twentieth century, concerns about welfare dependency began to mount and exploded when black women began to gain access to programs like AFDC.[13] The narrative of welfare as a social ill was not only applied to black women. In the popular histories of Appalachia, a parallel narrative developed, but this one included white, unemployed men and their wives who resided in the economically depressed Mountain South. In the 1960s, policy makers attempted to make sense of their supposedly hopeless condition, drawing upon a range of explanations from economic and psychological dependence to mental defectiveness. The problem, as surmised by authors interested in the history of the "mountaineer," turned on the abuse of land and the exploitation of a once independent and admirable people whose spirit had been broken, first by coal corporations and later by the federal government and its welfare programs.

Harry Caudill pioneered this narrative in his classic book, *Night Comes to the Cumberlands: A Biography of a Depressed Area*. The book was profound in its depiction of how the coal industry controlled regional politics, exploited workers, wrecked the land, and contributed to impoverishment. Picked up by activists, policy makers, and President Kennedy's administration, it influenced policy at the time and the scholarship on Appalachia since. Caudill's book is mostly remembered for its explicit critique of the coal industry and the industrial practice of surface mining. Yet it also laid out a critique of the American welfare state. Caudill framed his argument as an evaluation of *two* pillars of modern America—industrialization and New Deal liberalism—and he saw the two as fundamentally related.[14]

In *Night Comes to the Cumberlands*, Caudill explained that the people of the Appalachian region transitioned from a group defined by independence to a group dependent, first on industry and then on government. Caudill argued that the industrialization of the mountains came with a steep price: mountaineers gave up independence, exemplified by owning land and farming, for wages in the mines and a "modern" life. When the Great Depression sank the economy and busted the coal industry, coalminers and their families turned to the federal government for relief, setting a pattern that would continue into the 1970s. Caudill argued that welfare—including old age insurance, disability, Aid to Dependent Children, and even union pensions—broke the already dampened spirit of the once independent mountaineers. Among those with imperiled characters were the able-bodied men who resorted to "welfare malingerism" and "symptom-hunting" (in order to qualify for disability benefits). In writing about women on welfare, Caudill added to tropes of fertile, immoral women who avoided marriage but birthed children in order to attain welfare. He wrote, "In the deepening destitution of the coal counties astonishing numbers of women resorted to illicit associations, illegitimate children and the certainty of welfare checks in preference to the uncertainty of the holy but penniless state of matrimony."[15]

Caudill's concerns over dependency and his total acceptance of breadwinner ideology put him in the mainstream of liberal thinkers and politicians. During his War on Poverty, President Johnson and his aids promoted employment programs for men, arguing that people (by which they meant men) "needed a hand up, not a hand out."[16] In general, liberal Democrats who believed that the nation must do something to address pockets of poverty in the nation also saw a need to protect or restore traditional family models at the same time, whether that meant discouraging the so-called black matriarchy or preserving white Appalachian families.[17]

The years that Eula Hall began organizing around welfare rights were politically tumultuous. From the mid-1960s through the 1970s, AFDC was linked to and came to symbolize, as historian Marisa Chappell shows, "the failure of the Johnson administration's War on Poverty." With arguments about family, gender, and race at the center of the debates, liberals argued for the expansion of social welfare programs while conservatives charged that "the policies of that discredited liberalism encouraged poor mothers to forgo both marriage and employment to depend instead on government aid."[18] Both ideological camps built their case on the same foundation of a family wage model: conservatives argued that welfare weakened two-parent, heterosexual families, and liberals contended that welfare promised to strengthen them, if implemented in the right way. Blind to alternative models, the liberal coalition ultimately failed to produce a policy that would expand the welfare state in a period in which the family wage model was no longer sustainable. Those alternatives existed, however. Welfare rights activists gave voice to them when they argued for economic self-determination, demanded access to quality jobs and child care, or linked welfare rights to worker rights. In Kentucky, activists and welfare recipients entered into these debates with their own alternative visions of a welfare system that functioned as a "big net."[19]

Welfare rights groups emerged in Kentucky almost simultaneously. On June 30, 1966, black women in Louisville, Kentucky, joined the first nationwide welfare rights protest as welfare recipients marched on state capitals in twenty-five cities and demanded welfare reform. By 1967, the National Welfare Rights Organization (NWRO), made up mostly of black women, had formed. The following year, one of the handful of white male organizers of the national group visited the Marrowbone Folk School after receiving an invitation from Edith Easterling. Before long, welfare rights groups emerged throughout the Appalachian South. Their ranks included enthusiastic outsider activists, locals who saw the welfare system as inaccessible, and young lawyers who had been trained in poverty law. Of the welfare rights groups, some were interracial organizations while others were predominantly white, and almost all were connected to community action agencies organized under the War on Poverty. In 1969, the Eastern Kentucky Welfare Rights Organization, to which Eula Hall belonged, incorporated. By the early 1970s, numerous groups had sprouted in the region, in southwest Virginia, West Virginia, and across Kentucky. Local groups came together in statewide coalitions when laws threatened to weaken public assistance, and they joined regionwide and nationwide campaigns under the direction of the NWRO.[20]

The historiographical implications of the Appalachian movement are threefold. First, from the late 1960s into the mid-1970s, groups like the EKWRO promoted an expansive vision of welfare rights that showed how diverse groups could unify around a concept of welfare that was inclusive and rights-based rather than one that subordinated recipients according to gender, race, and class. When activists from Appalachia spoke of welfare, they did not mean solely AFDC. They almost always included discussions of health care, food stamps, and black lung benefits. But as scholars of the American welfare state have shown, in the 1960s welfare became identified with AFDC on both the political left and right. Conservative politicians, often using race-coded language, vilified single black mothers on the AFDC rolls, and activists on the left celebrated the National Welfare Rights Organization, which focused on the economic positions of black women. While it is true that "welfare" came to be associated with black mothers who disproportionately received public assistance, that process was not immediate or inevitable, especially given the fact that white people made up the majority of welfare recipients.[21]

Second, the history of this movement reveals the importance of grassroots alliances and community organizing in shaping policies and keeping the issue of poverty before elected officials. Emerging out of D.C., policies were worthless if they were not implemented at the local level, a process that involved alliances between local welfare rights activists, antipoverty lawyers, and outsider support, as well as negotiations between grassroots organizations and state and federal officials. While many politicians distanced themselves from the welfare state and focused on employment and infrastructure development, poverty workers and community activists emphatically argued for a broad social safety net as the best antipoverty measure, and they did so in public, at protests and marches. Their vociferous calls for welfare rights indicate how debates about welfare rights were widespread well into the 1970s.

Last, the welfare rights movement in Appalachia was mixed-sex even as welfare was closely associated with poor mothers, and it traversed racial boundaries even as interracial alliances seemed harder and harder to achieve. This regional movement projected an understanding of welfare that would become less popular over the next decade: that to accept public assistance was not a matter of dependency and was not naturally tied to one's race or gender; rather, it was a necessity in an economic system that produced inequality.

From War on Poverty to Welfare Rights

Eula Hall first encountered the War on Poverty through the Highway 979 Community Action Council, an OEO-funded organization named for the highway that cut through the area and composed of community members from each of the twelve hollows along Mud Creek in Floyd County. The Appalachian Volunteer staff had worked closely with the council, applying for grants for a local water system and a community printing press, as well as establishing a community center.[22] In 1965, Hall hosted a VISTA worker, Colleen LeBlanc, a nineteen-year-old college student from Minnesota. Among the first wave of VISTAs, LeBlanc, like many others drawn to the program, answered President Kennedy's call to American young people to serve their country. After training in Michigan for six weeks, she headed to Kentucky, where she was placed in the Mink Branch community of Floyd County. She had moved around to several homes, ending up in an abandoned house with another federal worker. When that person left, she was planning to live alone.

Eula Hall, whom she had met but did not know very well, came to LeBlanc and said, "You can't live by yourself. Come and live with me."[23]

At the time, McKinley was at the VA hospital, and there was room at the Hall household, which sat on a relatively flat piece of land at the mouth of the hollow. Eula and McKinley had four children in 1965, though their oldest was mostly out on his own. LeBlanc worked in recreational programming for kids in the hollow. She helped to clear a baseball field, acquired athletic equipment, led sing-alongs, and organized after-school and summer programs. Yet most of what she offered she probably did not quite realize at the time. She was issued a government vehicle, a big blue Chevrolet sedan. Especially for women, a car was an asset. Colleen gave Eula and other women rides. Eula recalls Colleen taking her to community meetings. Upon request, Colleen also taught one woman, an eighteen-year-old mother of three with whom she briefly lived, how to drive. She helped her study for her driver's license test, too.[24]

Prior to the War on Poverty, Eula had already begun teaching local women how to drive. This may seem like a politically neutral act, yet, as Hall explained, if a woman could drive, she gained a degree of independence. She stated, "Our husbands didn't want us to drive. They can't control you if you can drive and get out and get on a little. You're not going to be home 24 hours a day." If a woman could drive, she could "go to the store, pick out what your kids needed to wear to school, you could go ride to the company store and get groceries. . . . It was just a big benefit to be able to drive a vehicle, especially when there [was] no public transportation, no way of getting anywhere. It was a big benefit to be able to drive."[25] Community action during the War on Poverty expanded on and gave new meaning to such informal networks, as women drew upon them to inform one another of federal resources and to build support for antipoverty campaigns. Hall, whom LeBlanc described as "always moving," recognized opportunity and seized it.

By hosting a VISTA worker, Hall and other hosts helped assure that federal funds would reach communities in Floyd County. Hall likely received payment for room and board from the VISTA program, up to $12.50 per week. As one local priest reported, along with providing human services, VISTA injected the local economy with much-needed funds and made it more likely that community groups in that county would receive federal grants.[26] In turn, the volunteers helped to create opportunities for women who needed income and were eager to change their lives and communities.

VISTA workers also no doubt provided relief from childcare to local mothers by offering tutoring and recreational programs. The oldest daughter of nine siblings, LeBlanc had an especially close relationship with Danny, Hall's youngest child at the time. Danny, who was deaf, was drawn to the new young woman living with his family. He would hang on to her and follow her wherever she went. Danny showed Colleen the woods that stretched up the hills, and Colleen learned how to communicate with the expressive young boy.[27]

The antipoverty volunteers offered Hall a direct line into community organizations. One of the first campaigns Hall worked on was to bring a modern water system into her community, one of the first projects of the 979 Community Action Council. In the summer of 1966, community members began taking surveys about who desired a water system and testing wells for contamination. As a community intern with the Appalachian Volunteers, Hall was one of many community members who helped to gather data. She remembered, "We did a survey and door to door screening, and we found 90 percent had their wells to be contaminated back here. And ours was no exception. Until you got it tested you don't know what you're drinking. You'd just dig a hole and get the water out of it."[28] Community representatives compiled data and began making a case for a water system. In June and July 1966, citizens and local officials made three trips to the state capital before traveling to the nation's capital.[29]

Hall joined the Appalachian Community Meeting in Washington, D.C., where antipoverty workers and local people pushed the OEO to expand programs in their communities. The Floyd County group presented preliminary surveys on well contamination, which they linked to underlying quality of life issues: lack of health care, employment opportunities, and hunger. Eula remembered that they practically begged for a grant. Delegates argued that, with a water system in place, industry could be attracted to the area, a fire department could be established, and their communities would be improved.[30] Although it took several more years before this initiative succeeded, the activists who took the surveys and traveled to Frankfort and then Washington, D.C., burnished grassroots organizing skills.

The efforts of the community action agency primed the community for a welfare rights organization. At local meetings, Eula Hall and others had spoken up about the lack of food and health care in the region, and by 1968, a group of Appalachian Volunteers and VISTAs made an organizing push for a more focused welfare rights organization. They also found allies in a cadre of white, outsider activists who volunteered alongside locals to help make the welfare rights group a powerful force in Floyd County.

Hank Zingg, a graduate of Union College in Barbourville, Kentucky, one of the locations of the first Appalachian Volunteers sites, became the Outpost Director for the Appalachian Volunteers in Floyd County. His wife,

Jo Crockett Zingg, a native of Lee County, Virginia, and alumna of Union College, joined Hank in Floyd County where she found a job in the county welfare office. She recalled meeting women whose husbands had abandoned them or had left them to go North in search of work, often with little luck. She began to see how "badly women were treated in the system," as they attempted to access AFDC. As an AV worker, Hank began to work with local men and women in white communities to organize around welfare rights, an issue identified in community meetings. In 1968, Hank and the AV staff helped more than fifty people secure benefits, and they trained people to understand how the welfare system worked and how to distribute "dependable information so that families do not get their hopes up only to have them dashed."[31]

As welfare recipients were beginning to organize, a new crop of VISTAs arrived in Floyd County, several of whom had a keen interest in welfare rights organizing. Steve Brooks was among the antipoverty workers, and he became a key ally in the struggle for welfare rights. Brooks's path to the VISTA program began when he was in college at Ohio University, where he became part of the student antiwar movement. Brooks's developing political consciousness led him to community organizing in urban neighborhoods in Cleveland. In 1968, he dropped out of college and was accepted into VISTA. At the training in Baltimore, he received a crash course in community organizing, learned about social movement theorist Saul Alinsky, and heard about the growing movement of poor people in eastern Kentucky.[32]

In the fall of 1968, Brooks moved to Mud Creek along with four other volunteers. He and the other VISTAs were told to avoid involvement with the Appalachian Volunteers, who were still reeling from the sedition arrests in Pike County and in the midst of the Kentucky Un-American Activity Committee (KUAC) hearings that helped to undermine the work of the Appalachian Volunteers. The director of the Big Sandy Community Action Program discontinued any support of the organization, and the Floyd County CAP passed a resolution "opposing the activities of the Appalachian Volunteers and further requesting the proper authorities to remove said Appalachian Volunteers from the state of Kentucky and from Floyd County, Kentucky, in particular."[33]

Hall saw through the threats on the antipoverty programs. "A lot of the people would say [outsiders] were communist, you know, and a lot of the political people did not accept them because they could research and find out if the law was being [followed] or it was something illegal that was going on. And they didn't care to let the people know." With that kind of support, local people "could really take action by demonstrating and picketing and doing whatever it took."[34] Local administrators believed that by keeping the Appalachian Volunteers out of the community, they could control the direction of antipoverty programs. But they would soon learn otherwise.

The 979 Community Action Council members soon worked alongside VISTA workers to organize a welfare rights organization. Volunteers and community representatives had already been transporting people to welfare offices and representing them at benefit hearings; now they would form an organization that advocated for better policies.[35] In 1969, as noted earlier, several local men formed Eastern Kentucky Welfare Rights Organization (EKWRO) and signed a document of incorporation.

EKWRO was distinctive within the broader welfare rights movement. Black women led the majority of welfare rights organizations, and they built on the successes of the black freedom struggle. Black welfare rights activists understood their movement as a struggle against racism, especially as experienced by African American women. Made up mostly of white men and women, the eastern Kentucky group drew upon a working-class, masculine rhetoric that emphasized men's labor. Written by the male leaders, the group's bylaws stated that its purpose was to work toward an "adequate income for its members and all Americans." Their guiding principle was that "the fruits of a man's work should be his to enjoy, but wealth created by the resources of this great country should be directed to give an adequate income to all its citizens."[36]

EKWRO also appealed to the sense of many poor people in Appalachia who thought that they were poor because of corporate domination of the land, stating: "We believe people are poor because in this generation or in the generation past, they have been denied equal opportunity. In Floyd County and Eastern Kentucky, this happened when coal companies bought the land and mineral rights for as low as 50 cents an acre eventhough [*sic*] they knew the true value. The results of this exist to the present day."[37] The constitution blended a sense that poverty was unforgivable in a resource-rich nation, with a focus on a history of exploitation by coal companies and how political machines in coal towns controlled who got welfare assistance.

Early on, the eastern Kentucky group's constitution was firmly rooted in a masculine ideal: because men supported their families and protected their countries, they were entitled to a set of benefits, garnered through both the public and private sectors.[38] With references to a universal idea of man and the fruit of his labor, the constitution risked obscuring the bulk of the people who relied upon welfare assistance: women and, more specifically, single mothers. With women as the organizing base, however, EKWRO's leadership would not be able to ignore the special concerns of its women members.[39]

At a time when welfare was associated with women, the EKWRO was a mixed-sex welfare rights organization. Within the National Welfare Rights Organization, middle-class, educated men provided guidance, working as community organizers, lawyers, and lay advocates, and black women provided grassroots leadership. The EKWRO was distinctive in attracting a cadre of *local* men, some of whom received public assistance. And the Appalachian Volunteers employed a local barber as the "welfare rights coordinator."[40] Regional antipoverty organizations like the Council of the Southern Mountains historically emphasized jobs program that focused primarily on the position of male breadwinners. Local men often entered the debate from a similar position, seeking to uplift families by garnering public aid for disabled and unemployed miners and helping them get back to work.[41]

Yet white women recipients were the organizing backbone, and, as was the case for black women, they had the most to gain or lose from welfare policies. Young local women knocked on doors, spread news about current campaigns, and surveyed women about the most pressing issues they faced.[42] Once she began working with antipoverty programs, Eula Hall had access to resources and knowledge that could help her secure welfare for poor people. She drove people to the AFDC, food stamp, and Social Security offices, where she advocated on their behalf. From her own experience of being on and off welfare when her husband was hospitalized for mental illness, to her husband qualifying for disability compensation from the Social Security office, Hall knew that accessing aid often became a political game. The more knowledge you had about the system, the better the chances that you would receive assistance.[43]

To have a broad reach, the welfare rights group depended on informal female organizers, who had better access to local women than men. According to Hall, women would say things to her that they would not discuss with a man; they would not even broach certain subjects if a man was in the room. When she was alone with them they would "open up and talk." Hall knew how to navigate the gender culture of the mountains, where many abided by fundamentalist Christian views of family and society. Moreover, she could relate to women. She "lived their lives," and she understood what it was like to "need food stamps" or "rock sick babies to sleep."[44]

Eula Hall did not need these women to remind her, however, how hard life could be for women living in poverty. McKinley continued to taunt her, and he had a new reason to be angry: now she was active in the community in a way she had not been before. Sometimes if she had been to a meeting, he would lock her out or stand behind the door with a stick ready to hit her. "He couldn't stop me," Eula resolved. Antipoverty work had become her passion.[45]

"Good Resource People": Legal Aid Services

After EKWRO was formed, local activists worked with allies to build a base of knowledge about welfare policy. As Eula Hall remembered, that's what made the group so significant to so many people's lives: it had access to "good resource people."[46] Among the most skillful resource people were allies in the legal aid community. These white, left-leaning, young lawyers and law students (most of them men) put their knowledge and skills to use in the welfare rights movement and fought for important changes to poverty law. In fact, the history of legal aid and the welfare rights movement are intertwined, as the story of one of the first legal aid lawyers in Appalachia reveals.

Recruited by the Appalachian Volunteers to work on legal issues, lawyer Howard Thorkelson provided training to VISTAs as well as community people like Hall so that they could serve as lay advocates at welfare hearings. Thorkelson's commitment to justice developed in part due to the struggles he experienced as a person with disabilities growing up in California. He had contracted polio as a child and was left partially paralyzed in his arms. After graduating from Yale Law School in 1965, Thorkelson took a position at the Center for Social Welfare Policy and Law, affiliated with the Columbia School of Social Work. His work there positioned Thorkelson at the forefront of legal challenges based on welfare rights.[47]

The Center for Social Welfare Policy was founded by labor lawyer Edward V. Sparer, and one of its primary goals was to offer legal aid, not as a charity but as a fundamental right. Howard Thorkelson was among Sparer's first hires. The welfare system was a key area in which Sparer and his associates tested theories that poor people had rights to legal resources and counsel. Under the mentorship of Sparer, Thorkelson's interest in poverty, welfare, and legal rights grew. He began traveling to the South to work on civil rights cases, where he encountered the NAACP Legal Defense Fund and the ACLU's Lawyer Constitutional Defense Committee. He spent a summer working full time on civil rights cases in Selma, Alabama, with a team of civil rights lawyers. That research led to *King v. Smith* (1968), the first welfare case heard by the Supreme Court.

King v. Smith overturned substitute father laws, known as "man-in-the-house" rules, in Alabama. These rules allowed welfare officials the ability to deny benefits to a woman if they found out that the she was in a sexual relationship with a man. The law was almost always applied to black women as a way of denying public assistance to black women and children. The court struck down such laws on the basis that a parent had a legal obligation to care for a child, while a boyfriend did not. Thus the fact of a mother having a boyfriend did not negate a woman's need for welfare to support children.[48]

Working on that case and others in the Deep South laid the foundations for Thorkelson's work in eastern Kentucky.[49] After three years working for Sparer and the Center for Social Welfare Policy and Law, in 1968 Thorkelson moved to Prestonsburg, Kentucky, in Floyd County. There he helped to develop a legal aid program in conjunction with the Appalachian Volunteers.[50]

When Thorkelson arrived in eastern Kentucky, AV leadership was already beginning to recruit young lawyers who were interested in civil rights, mainly from the Law Students Civil Rights Research Council, although VISTA had also begun recruiting lawyers for placement as well. Programs such as these were inundated by requests by young lawyers to be placed in the Deep South, where they could work on some of the most exciting and important civil rights cases of their time. Between 1967 and 1969, the Director of Field Operations of the Appalachian Volunteers began requesting that the Research Council direct students to Appalachia, "an ideal training ground for lawyers," arguing that "their skills are desperately needed if our hopes to affect change in the political and economic system are to be realized." While the Research Council seemed eager to route students to volunteer programs, the future lawyers were not always keen on being placed in Appalachia. In the first summer of the program in 1968, two students did not show up, and others were displeased with the rural area assigned to them and left before their assignments were completed.[51]

Thorkelson helped to remedy the retention problem by hand-selecting law students who had shown an interest in the region. In 1969, he requested fifteen student interns from the Research Council. Their duties included representing defendants in civil and criminal cases and instructing community people on lay advocacy. They also conducted a survey to make sense of the "highly personal" procedures in lower courts, which often ignored formal rules of practice, and sought to address the machine politics of some Appalachian towns.[52] Overall, the main goal of the AV legal team was to raise consciousness about poor people's legal rights, through the courts and through education.

One of the biggest challenges the legal team faced was countering the isolation that "head-of-the-hollow" people, those in the most rural areas of Appalachian counties, experienced in relation to "the law" in the county seats. Thorkelson and his team believed that "many individuals in Appalachia do not know their legal rights. Many think they have greater measures of some rights (such as public assistance) than they actually have. Others know of only a few of their rights." The consequence was that individuals were forced to make "sense out of the rumors and snatches of 'law' that they have heard," usually leading them to conclusions about their legal rights that were vaguely similar to the actual law but ultimately incorrect.[53] The lawyers trained volunteers and local people about the welfare system and how to make appeals. Locals could then serve as lay advocates—people who were not trained lawyers but could offer advice and assistance.

Organizers also helped to distribute information about welfare in Kentucky through the booklet "What Is Welfare?" developed by an Appalachian Volunteer. The handbook provided a comprehensive history of welfare in the United States and an overview of the welfare system in Kentucky. "Who needs welfare?" the authors asked. "The people who need help with their welfare are those who can't provide *the basic necessities of life* for themselves and their families." The community-run Hawkeye Press in Floyd County printed the booklet, and the AV office distributed more than five hundred copies to welfare rights and antipoverty organizations across the state and nation.[54]

"We Had Starving Children"

During the summer and fall of 1969, the EKWRO members mobilized for their first local campaign, a protest to force the school board to follow federal policies on free and reduced lunch, part of the "nutritive welfare state."[55] The campaign reflected the concerns of women members, who, as mothers and caregivers, took on the job of feeding children. As Eula Hall framed the campaign, there was no question that children going hungry "was not right."[56]

The campaign in Floyd County was part of a national current of ideas focused on hunger and welfare rights in the United States. Following the lead of the National Welfare Rights Organization, eastern Kentucky activists exposed the inconsistent implementation of the Elementary and Secondary Education Act (1965) and Child Nutrition Act (1966). They provided (often unwelcome) oversight as local officials did or did not implement recent laws and policies related to public assistance. As Hall explained, "Until you make a noise," they won't make the changes.[57]

In the summer of 1969, the group began petitioning the local school board for a more fair and effective school lunch program. Linda Hamilton of EKWRO wrote a letter to Congressman Carl D. Perkins, explaining why she and a group of local people had begun the campaign. She described a scene in which "poor children [have] to set on the stage and watch the other ones eat their dinner" and how "all left overs was thrown out to the hogs instead of giving it to the poor hung[ry] kids who didn't have anything." She described how local officials refused to talk to the school lunch committee. Hamilton then put the campaign into a broader context, stating that she knew "the government can't feed all kids" but that she and others in Floyd

County were asking for a little help for poor people who "work for what they get" but still did not have enough to eat.[58] Hamilton and other community members and parents called for the Floyd County Board of Education to make public the guidelines for free and reduced school lunches and to treat children from impoverished families with dignity.[59]

School lunches had been in the media spotlight since the beginning of the War on Poverty. For instance, in a 1965 film on President Johnson's "poverty tour," Lady Bird Johnson joined a group of Appalachian school children at their one-room schoolhouse for a hot lunch. "Hot lunches"—as opposed to pails of cold biscuits and gravy or, worse, nothing—became a rallying cry in the early months of the War on Poverty. The issue was easy to get behind. U.S. citizens could surely see the benefit of federal dollars purchasing cafeteria equipment for impoverished schools.[60] Yet, as historian Susan Levine shows, since its inception the school lunch program had "enjoyed widespread support but fed relatively few children."[61] With attention on racial inequality and poverty in the 1960s, civil rights, antipoverty workers, and physicians scrutinized the National School Lunch Program established in the 1940s. Under pressure to feed the nation's poor children, the Department of Agriculture, which oversaw the program, began to push for federal appropriations for free lunches.[62]

In 1966, President Johnson signed the Child Nutrition Act. The legislation expanded and strengthened the National School Lunch Program, providing grants-in-aid to states so that they could fund free lunch programs in low-income areas. It also established pilot breakfast and milk programs for poor children. But there was a problem. The legislation relied on good-faith efforts of state and local officials to establish child nutrition programs, and in 1968, "at least six and a half million poor children, mostly in cities and isolated rural areas, still had no access to free lunches."[63] Local officials needed a push from the people they were supposed to serve.[64]

The NWRO distributed "School Lunch Program Bill of Rights," a pamphlet on how to organize community campaigns to force local school boards to abide by federal law and provide lunches to school children.[65] The bill of rights called for nutritious lunches for all children, even those who could not afford to pay, and declared that they should receive those meals without regard to race, class, or religion. It also laid out the rights of parents, who could request and receive information about school lunch programs in their school district; appeal denials for free or reduced lunch; and form or join a welfare rights organization to enforce school lunch programs. The bill of rights informed parents about how to hold public hearings and demonstrations, bring lawsuits against school boards, and contact state and federal officials when local school boards failed to follow the contract with the U.S. Department of Agriculture.[66]

Drawing from NWRO guidelines, EKWRO members focused their efforts on the John M. Stumbo Elementary School, which served families along the 979 Highway. School administrators there had failed to implement a robust school lunch program despite a large population of children from low-income families. Reporting for the leftist magazine *Impact*, journalist Charles Remsberg (who was known for previous, award-winning articles on hunger in the U.S.) reported that 2000 eligible students in Floyd County did not receive free lunches; children unable to afford lunch or bring food from home sometimes had to sit in the same lunchroom where their classmates ate; and sometimes free school lunches were promised in exchange for votes in school board elections.[67] Eula Hall recalled, "We had one of the finest lunchrooms that you could build in a school," compounding the injustice that some children could not afford to eat. She told stories of children "tantalized" as they sat in the lunchroom and watched other children eat, and children sitting separate from the ones who got to eat. She could not afford for her children to buy lunch. The school lunch cost a quarter for most children, and she had four children in school. "That was a dollar a day. I couldn't come up with a dollar a day better than I could come up with a hundred now," she said. She was able to give her children a hot breakfast in the morning and to send something with them for lunch. "But a lot of children didn't [have that]. A lot of little kids did not have breakfast and they wouldn't have anything to eat until they got home at night."[68]

Community members representing the Eastern Kentucky Welfare Rights Organization provided Floyd County Superintendent of Schools Charles Clark with federal regulations and asked that he force schools to comply. A former high school principal, Clark was a middle-class administrator in his third four-year term who had campaigned on modernizing Floyd County schools. He resented the tone of the campaign, which implied he was not doing his job. He replied that he could not meet the organizations' "demands" (ignoring that the "demands" were in fact USDA guidelines) and stated that the school lunch program did not have sufficient funds to provide for more children. Yet evidence emerged that the school had a surplus of funds but that school officials chose not to use them on free lunches. Instead, the principal explained, funds would be used to purchase new kitchen equipment. He also claimed that, while 50 to 60 percent of the student body lived at or below the poverty line, his program could only afford to offer free lunches to a fraction of those who needed it. Besides, he asserted, many of the students actually had the money to pay but did not want to eat. The principal declared,

"We can't force children to eat. That would be violating their constitutional rights."[69]

Community members told a much different story, in which children of poor women and unemployed miners were denied free lunches and parents were told that their children could work for lunches (a violation of federal regulations).[70] At the same time, rumors flew in the community about mismanagement of school lunch funds. Cooks and janitors at the school were rumored to haul away "enough food to feed every child in that school." The principal of the school was said to have a building for sows to breed and had "beagle hounds that were as slick as a ribbon." The principal's supposed luxuries—plenty of fresh meat and prized hounds—stood in stark contrast to the poverty in the area. "We had starving children in that school," Hall asserts.[71]

In the summer of 1969, the school lunch committee met with Superintendent Clark. The meeting devolved into an argument about whether school lunches were necessary rather than a discussion of policy, as the committee had hoped. Clark explained that he was not ready to provide them a policy and "then went into a long frantic speech, about how the school lunch rooms would go broke if everyone ate free." According to EKWRO members, he lectured them about "how some students had pride and did not want to eat free, telling about his childhood days in an excited voice, of his clothing of which had patches on top of patches and of how he took biscuits and jelly to school, and he would still love to have an occasional bite of those biscuits and jelly." He accused the "outsiders" of stirring up trouble in Floyd County, declaring that the VISTAs were "long-haired foreigners" and that at least one of them was "probably from Russia." The meeting ended with Clark's refusal to speak to the members of the school lunch committee who were outsider volunteers.[72]

As for many middle-class administrators and officials in Appalachia, the idea that local people were willfully working with "outside agitators" disturbed Clark. He saw himself as a public servant who had done his best to provide better schools to the citizens of Floyd County. In a letter published in *The Hawkeye*, he expressed his frustrations that the protests ignored the work he and the school board had done on behalf of low-income school children. He listed in painstaking detail the items and services that they had provided to poor children: 1100 pairs of glasses, 13 hearing aids, dental care, clothing, and 1 million free lunches "although federal support for lunchrooms was hopelessly inadequate." Clark insisted that these services "were provided without demands [and] confrontation. We did these things because we felt that they were needed by children who couldn't help themselves." To him, the outsider activists were the problem: "These people are ignorant of Kentucky people and their laws and customs."[73] While he was likely not incorrect in identifying arrogance of some of the activists and their disregard for the experiences of middle-class administrators, he failed to take seriously the involvement of local people or their desire for rights rather than charity.

In the weeks following their first meeting, Clark continued to refuse information to the school lunch committee. In response, between fifty and seventy parents organized a protest at the offices of the Floyd County Board of Education. A fight started almost immediately between Clark's supporters and some of the EKWRO men. The scuffle led to a few arrests, and the protest crowd dispersed. But the event brought even more attention to the school lunch issue. As Eula Hall remembered, "We had done our homework. We had the news media there, and all we'd say [was], 'We want free and reduced lunches for our children. We want our children to eat along with the rest of the children, and the poor kids should eat if the rich kids do,' and it embarrassed them to death." In the aftermath of the protest, Clark and the Board of Education continued to fight, filing a restraining order that banned all VISTAs, Appalachian Volunteers, and anyone associated with the groups from Floyd County school property.[74]

In a public meeting a few days after the rally, the school lunch committee, concerned parents, and protesters met to discuss the sequence of events and to make follow-up plans. Howard Thorkelson spoke to the group, assuring them that their actions were lawful and that they had a right to petition the Floyd County School Board for information to which they were legally entitled. Thorkelson also pointed out that Clark was trying to divert attention from the rights of poor people by attempting to stir up animosity for outsider volunteers. The group ended the meeting by agreeing unanimously to send one more letter to Clark requesting eligibility standards for the school lunch campaign and calling on him to rescind his injunction against VISTA workers. They also vowed to support all local and nonlocal volunteers, agreeing that the volunteers "had been a help to the community and the community wished to continue to support them."[75]

The school lunch committee's efforts paid off. The protests put pressure on Clark to hammer out the details of a free lunch program with community representatives and an official from the Department of Agriculture. Several weeks after the school lunch controversy, welfare activists accused Clark of not abiding by Title I of the Elementary and Secondary Education Act (1965), another Great Society measure geared to provide resources to schools serving low-income students. The committee reported that many poor children could not afford textbooks and that the school board had not made good-faith efforts to help such students. Clark again resisted, and the activists again pointed to new laws and demanded that they be implemented.[76]

For those in positions of power, it was easier to believe that people had been brainwashed than to accept that people in Floyd County wanted a voice in local politics or that they were savvy political actors. To Clark, charity and services provided at the discretion of local officials should have been enough to satisfy Floyd County residents; for the local and outsider activists, a voice at the table was the ultimate goal.[77] Welfare rights activists in Floyd County and throughout the Mountain South soon joined state and national efforts to shape welfare policy, a battle that would prove much more difficult.

The Welfare Rights Movement Expands

In 1969, with community welfare rights groups in place, VISTA worker Steve Brooks helped to build a bridge between local and state struggles and the National Welfare Rights Organization. After receiving approval from the state VISTA director, Brooks connected welfare recipients, legal aid lawyers, and VISTA workers to form a statewide welfare rights coalition. He also networked with the National Welfare Rights Organization to learn about upcoming national campaigns, with the idea that welfare campaigns would be coordinated between the local, state, and national levels.[78] Based in Washington, D.C. and with its bird's-eye view of hundreds of welfare rights groups across the nation, the NWRO was best positioned to offer guidance on policy.

Even before Brooks's efforts, people from Appalachia had joined statewide campaigns to bolster welfare. In January 1968, representatives from eastern Kentucky joined a coalition of Kentucky welfare rights groups in Frankfort to present a four-point resolution to the state legislature on how to improve the state welfare system. The *Courier Journal & Times* reported on the meeting, with the loaded headline, "Mountain Women Join Negro Mothers to Push for Welfare." The paper reported, "An unlikely coalition of East Kentucky women and Negro mothers from urban Kentucky will petition the state legislature on a common problem this week: not enough welfare." The column exposed the ways many people viewed race and class in the 1960s. "Mountain women" did not need racial or class descriptors; they were presumed to be white, thus the "unlikely coalition" that crossed boundaries of race. The reporter also noted that a handful of men (most likely white) joined thirty-six women; however, they appeared "ill at ease," presumably discomfited by the fact that the coalition was led by white and black women.[79] The reporter's ignorance of the existence of black Appalachians and surprise that white and black, male and female welfare recipients worked in coalition speaks volumes about the racial and gender assumptions of the time.

The welfare rights coalition collaborated on a four-point plan. Activists called for the state to meet 100 percent of the living needs of Kentucky families, based on the national poverty line (as opposed to the 87 percent that they provided at the time); a general emergency assistance program for people who did not meet the requirements for AFDC or aid to the blind, disabled, and aged; an end to the policy stating that child support payments should be deducted from the welfare allowance provided for single mothers; and the creation of a board of independent examiners to hear complaints about mistreatment by caseworkers.[80]

Just as welfare right groups were gaining momentum, so was the antiwelfare movement within the Republican Party. Richard Nixon came to his presidency vowing "law and order" and an end to "government programs" funded as part of the War on Poverty and Great Society legislation. While Nixon's rhetoric was harsher than his actions (many antipoverty programs expanded during his presidency), conservative governors led the backlash by stumping for welfare reform laws and pushing Nixon to the right whenever possible. Governor Louie B. Nunn was among the leaders of the Republican governors, along with Governor Ronald Reagan of California. Winning elections with the support of white middle-class voters, they interpreted their victories as a mandate on Johnson's expansion of the welfare state. Welfare rights activists entered the fray with little power and prestige. While their victories were often fleeting, their history is important for what it reveals about the early 1970s: even as a welfare backlash was gaining steam among white middle-class and blue-collar voters, some poor and working-class whites—including at least some disabled and unemployed white men—continued to argue for welfare as a right of citizenship.

In 1969, activists staged several protest marches, bringing together black and white, male and female participants from the state's major cities and its mountain communities. Civil rights activists, local black ministers, and even social workers who believed the welfare system was "repressive and an affront to human dignity," joined the action. The coalition countered stereotypes; argued for the governor to be more transparent about budgetary decisions; and called for welfare payments that could actually sustain a family.[81]

Calling themselves the Poor People's Coalition, the welfare rights activists made front-page news when they interrupted the Republican Governors' Conference. They hoped to expose the hypocrisy of Governor Nunn presenting the governors with a very fine gift from the Thoroughbred Breeders of Kentucky: a well-bred colt, worth seventy thousand dollars. It represented the blue-ribbon horses—and wealth—that Kentucky was known for (the Kentucky Derby took place just a few days after the conference). Ronald Reagan, governor of California, happily accepted the prize horse on behalf of the Republican governors, each of whom would own a "share" of it.[82]

The Poor People's Coalition had scraped together 65 dollars and purchased a fifteen-year-old mule named "Hope," from Mrs. Rose Cox, a mother of four who lived in a poverty-stricken area with a per capita income of $1100. The coalition presented the "poor people's mule" the same day that the governors received the thoroughbred horse, taking advantage of the national media presence to show the governors the other side of Kentucky. Mrs. Juanita Bain, a white woman who lived in a coal camp read the poor people's statement, describing their desire "to participate in the decisions and activities of government which affects our lives." The coalition urged the governor to force area development boards to appoint more representatives from their communities, returning to the idea of "maximum feasible participation" of the poor. "We give you Hope, governors. It is our deepest desire that all of you may, in another sense, give us hope also," Mrs. Bain concluded.[83]

Nunn—"smiling grimly"—accepted the mule and offered his own beliefs about welfare and projected a new message onto the mule: "I look at the back of this mule and I am mindful of the tremendous burden that is placed upon those of us who share this responsibility, the tremendous burden that is upon the taxpayers of this land who are trying to provide the funds to support the poor." He closed by referencing the "parasites" that resided on the "beast of burden," and, referring to the "rear quarters," said that it would always remind him of some of the protesters. Nunn was weary of protests. In the same week as the poor people's protest, students at the University of Louisville had staged a sit-in to demand a black studies program, and antiwar, SDS, and black student activists from the University of Kentucky also protested the Republican Governors' Conference. Nunn made clear his impatience with activists, telling reporters that he would use "necessary force" if protests got out of hand.[84]

He also continued to promote welfare reform, alongside Governor Reagan, from within the GOP. The conference culminated in the Republican governors criticizing the Nixon administration's welfare policies. They called for Nixon to repeal policies that made public assistance easier to access, close all regional antipoverty offices, and notify and consult governors before making changes to federal welfare policy. Governor Nunn would prove a leader in this movement, signing the Welfare Reform Act of 1970 after its passage in the Kentucky state legislature. The legislation linked work to welfare and was part of the national movement to de-couple AFDC from the idea that welfare would allow women to focus on child rearing.[85] Welfare reform debates ushered in one of the most contentious debates of the period: to what extent should work be tied to welfare, and what were the consequences for women who had the most to lose or gain?

The welfare rights activists' campaigns were not all in vain. In 1972, Elaine Huecker, the first woman and social worker appointed as commissioner of Economic Security in Kentucky, responded to the organization's desire to build bridges between welfare rights organizations and state officials. After a two-day meeting with welfare rights activists from across the state, she agreed to work on new contracts for food stamp issuance offices so that they could be situated in U.S. Post Offices. Currently, they were located only in county courthouses, far from where most rural people lived. At a statewide welfare rights meeting in the fall, Huecker became the first commissioner to address an assembly of welfare recipients. At that meeting, she informed the activists that she would allow the Kentucky Welfare Rights Organization a desk at all public assistance offices so that they could meet with recipients.[86] After years of fighting the governor and commissioners for the chance to simply meet and discuss state welfare policies, Huecker was a welcome change for activists, a sign that perceptions and relationships could indeed change.

The March for Survival

As new battles emerged over federal welfare laws, EKWRO and other Appalachian welfare rights groups allied with the National Welfare Rights Organization to make sure poor people's voices were a part of those debates. Eula Hall and a group of welfare rights and antipoverty activists, including Edith Easterling, planned the Appalachian March for Survival Against Unfulfilled Promises in Washington D.C. over a weekend in November 1971. An interracial group of about three hundred people from Kentucky, West Virginia, and Virginia traveled in seven buses to the capital, where they participated in a welfare rights protest and held a series of meetings with policy officials. They stayed at the Hawthorne School, where three years prior they had commingled, debated, and campaigned with Mexican American, Native American, and African American groups during the Poor People's Campaign. Supported by the Highlander Center, the Council of the Southern Mountains, the Black Lung Association, and the National Welfare Rights Organization, white and black welfare rights activists brought a range of issues to the table that they saw as interconnected: public assistance for poor and single mothers; guaranteed incomes for poor families; benefits for disabled miners and miners' widows; and comprehensive health services for poor people. It was "everything combined: a march for survival," Eula Hall described it. At the heart of the march was the argument that welfare, broadly understood, was a right: the United States government had a duty to ensure that citizens had a "right to live."[87]

The policy focus of the march was Nixon's Family Assistance Plan (FAP). First proposed in 1969, the Family Assistance Plan encapsulated Nixon's conservative version of a guaranteed income plan—liberal Democratic, civil rights, and welfare rights groups had offered their own guaranteed income plans in the preceding months. The plan would have replaced AFDC, focusing on two-parent families—and consequently male breadwinners—rather than single mothers. The Nixon administration argued that the plan would strengthen two-parent families, would tie aid to work, and would likely gain support among low-income whites. In comparison to other proposed guaranteed income plans, Nixon's plan offered low benefit levels, ultimately lower than what single women on welfare already received. Yet the fact that a guaranteed income was on the table at all offered welfare rights activists some optimism.[88]

The March for Survival was part of a wave of protests led and influenced by the National Welfare Rights Organization. In the spring of 1970, NWRO had organized rallies in D.C., lobbied for an improved FAP, and held a sit-in at the office of Robert Finch, secretary of the Department of Health, Education, and Welfare (HEW). In early 1971, the Senate Committee introduced HR1, a revised version of FAP that was even less generous than the original plan. If passed, families would receive less money and potentially lose food stamps, and mothers with preschool-age children would be required to register for work. In response, the NWRO renamed the plan the "Family Annihilation Plan" and lobbied to defeat the bill, not just reform it.[89]

The NWRO requested that groups across the country meet with and write letters to representatives and explain their problems with the legislation. The Appalachian group did exactly that, meeting with representatives of the Appalachian Regional Commission as well as House representatives and HEW officials. But they also had other goals in mind. Along with identifying as welfare recipients, they also identified as Appalachians and organized meetings in D.C. to campaign on issues facing poor people in Appalachia. The title of their march, "The Appalachian March for Survival Against Unfulfilled Promises," suggested that they were weary of politicians, from the local to national level, promising to bring about change in the mountains only to "shortchange Appalachian people" and "do it all with a smile saying how good things are going."[90]

The more than three-hundred-member march forced politicians to see and hear the people who relied on a strong social safety net for basic life needs. The first meeting on the group's agenda was with the Appalachian Regional Commission. Images from the event show a packed room, with officials at a table, surrounded by activists. A group of about one hundred activists started by singing "Amazing Grace." Activists queried the Commission officials about what they were doing for the poor people of Appalachia and what had they done in the six years since the Commission's founding. When one official praised the Commission's plan to build new highways in the mountains, Billie Jean Johnson, an African American mother and welfare rights activist from McDowell, West Virginia, interjected, "Hold the phone a minute." She noted that the roads in her community were in poor condition, adding, "Besides, we can't eat nary a damned highway." Since its inception, the Commission had focused on infrastructure development, with the goal of modernizing the transportation system and attracting industry to the region. But to welfare and black lung activists, the Commission was not doing enough to improve welfare programs, secure benefits for sick miners and their families, or enforce federal oversight of black lung legislation. Plus, highways served wealthier people, not poor people, many of whom did not have cars or did not travel far if they did.[91]

Johnson continued her testimony, schooling the Commission on the realities of poverty. "People are going hungry," she declared. "I'm not telling you what I heard about. I'm telling you what's going on in my neighborhood, going on in my county, what's going on in my community." She also disapproved of Nixon's welfare reform policy, arguing that it would force stay-at-home mothers to go to work. She shared the story of a woman in her neighborhood who had six children and needed welfare to support them, but who would have a difficult time finding employment and—if she did—accessing child care. She also sought to dispel stereotypes of welfare mothers as unwilling or too lazy to work. A conversation about jobs could not be had, she urged, without discussing childcare, as well as the quality of jobs. She asserted, "We want jobs. Us young women, we want something to do."[92]

Following their meeting with the Appalachian Regional Commission, the activists headed to a scheduled meeting with HEW officials. They soon noticed that very few officials were present and that they were "just talking to ourselves." Eula Hall suggested that the activists go to the offices of HEW Secretary Elliot Richardson and demand that he and other officials attend the meeting. She then declared, "Let's stay here until we're heard." She and over seventy activists, black and white, took elevators to Richardson's office and remained until he and several other officials finally agreed to attend a meeting. Upon arrival, Richardson stated, "Tell us what you think we ought to be doing. We're not going to be able to do everything, but we do want to know."[93]

Appalachian activists favored a guaranteed minimum income for single- and two-parent poor families, but like welfare rights activists across the country, they argued that the minimum in the proposed policy was much too low. They also objected to the job requirements, noting that many welfare recipients would be forced to take jobs at hourly rates as low as $1.20 an hour. Moreover, the plan failed to recognize mothers' caregiving labor as a "job," and it did nothing to address the dearth of jobs for women in Appalachia. Finally, they took issue with the elimination of food stamps in HR1, which meant that families on the plan would be receiving even less money than outlined in the original FAP, which had included around $800 annually in food stamps for a family of four. Many activists in Appalachia had fought for more widespread and efficient food stamp programs in the preceding years. They knew the difference the program made in people's lives and they were not going to give it up easily.[94]

In West Virginia, welfare recipients faced a new state policy that would automatically terminate an AFDC recipient's benefits after six months. After a HEW official offered a verbal pledge to assist welfare recipients in West Virginia, Madeline James, an African American activist from West Virginia, explained why poor people had a difficult time swallowing the promises of bureaucrats. "You people have on blue suits, and shoes and clothes . . . what I want to know: Have you ever seen a barefoot child walk up and down and ask, 'Mama, what are [we] going to eat today?'" She demanded a written pledge and action from HEW.[95]

Along with the plight of welfare recipients, the activists put a spotlight on the conditions of miners disabled by black lung disease. At each of the D.C. meetings, representatives from the Black Lung Association spoke about the need for health care provisions and welfare benefits for miners who suffered from the respiratory disease. The Black Lung Association had begun in the late 1960s as progressive doctors, antipoverty workers, and disabled miners began setting up county chapters to address the need for a legislative agenda that would lead to compensation for sick miners. They had successfully lobbied for the Mine Health and Safety Act, which included a section on a temporary black lung benefits program. By the time of the March for Survival, miners were involved in a full-fledged campaign to reform black lung benefits at the federal level. They wanted claims processed more quickly, and they fought for "claimants' rights" to impartial examinations and explanations when they were denied claims.[96]

Led by retired African American coalminer Fred Carter, the Black Lung Association issued thirteen demands, from an expansion of medical services and benefits for people who suffered from black lung, to greater oversight of mining companies and assurances that widows and dependents of miners would also be eligible for black lung benefits. Most powerfully, miners who suffered from the disease spoke directly to the formerly "faceless bureaucrats." At the HEW meeting with Secretary Richardson, James Hamilton, a white, seventy-seven-year-old, disabled miner testified that he had been a coalminer for forty-seven years until he had to retire because of black lung disease. When he retired he "went through all kinds of hell before getting help from the government."[97]

Among the small victories, mothers from West Virginia successfully campaigned for oversight of state welfare policy after Madeline James's complaint to HEW officials about welfare termination. Federal policy stated that assistance should be provided to eligible individuals until they were found to be ineligible. West Virginia officials were putting the onus on recipients to prove their eligibility every six months, which struck many as punitive and unnecessary. Soon after the march, HEW officials contacted West Virginia officials and requested that the policy be revised so that it was consistent with federal policy.[98]

Overall, however, the march had a limited impact. In October 1972, Senate conservatives voted down the Family Assistance Plan, and a more generous welfare package did not replace it. The NWRO had hoped to help write a new piece of legislation, but by 1972 the political tides had turned and they were not able to build momentum for the effort. Appalachian welfare activists, like their counterparts across the nation, continued to look for other ways to strengthen social welfare programs in their own states and communities.[99]

A week after the March for Survival, a small group of people who had gone on the trip came together to reflect on the meaning of the march, what they had learned, and what they saw as next steps. A white welfare rights activist from West Virginia, Shelva Thompson commented that she was proud of her compatriots, who showed politicians that they weren't "talking to a bunch of old, stupid, poor people." Eula Hall noted that it was obvious that many of the politicians did not understand welfare policies or how they affected recipients. Edith Easterling, who was unable to attend the march but who kept up with it every step of the way, argued that Appalachians needed to organize and make demands as a group. She also noted that the march "opened people's eyes to how politics work; you get more educated when you can get outside the community and learn new things." Before the meeting ended, Eula Hall declared, "I think we ought to send a woman to be president." Someone else chimed in, "What about a hillbilly?" Laughing, they all agreed that Washington politics could use a good shake-up.[100]

The optimism of the activists exhibits how open political debates over welfare appeared to them, even in the face of a mounting backlash. Little did they know that within the next year guaranteed income plans would become politically untenable, as debates about poverty began to narrow in the 1970s. As other historians have shown, the left's arguments against AFDC would eventually feed into antiwelfare debates, cutting off alternatives to the two-parent or family breadwinner model. The Appalachian welfare rights movement, with its unifying message, was limited in its ability to transform the systemic racism and sexism of the welfare system, and welfare rights coalitions lacked the power necessary to survive a powerful backlash. Moreover, their inclusive vision of welfare rights simply did not resonate for a majority of working- and middle-class white voters, who grew to loathe the idea that their tax dollars should support families headed by single mothers. Many would ditch the Democratic Party by the end of the decade. The broad coalition in Appalachia, of white and black, men and women, would soon be forgotten as a story of resentful white southerners fleeing the Democratic Party came to dominate the narrative of 1970s politics.

Yet that narrative obscures a lesser-known story. Some low-income whites shunned the dog-whistle, antiwelfare politics of the 1970s and carried the war on poverty forward, often in mixed-sex and interracial alliances. Their involvement in welfare rights points to the contingency of 1970s political history, that the backlash of working-class whites was not fated, but was in part an inability of liberal politicians to reframe the debate about poverty. When Eula Hall and others returned to their communities, they continued to mobilize antipoverty programs and to fight for better services for poor people.

In Floyd County, Eula Hall emerged as the leader in the next battle of the EKWRO, which by the early 1970s included 150 dues-paying members. The group spearheaded a campaign for a community health clinic that addressed the interrelated health, work, and environmental issues facing poor people, as well as the overall lack of services in rural Appalachia. "We was hollering [for] health care. We were pleading for health care," she remembered, and she had ideas about what to do next.[101]

5 "The Best Care in History"

Interdependence and the Community Health Movement

When reflecting on her life in the Mountain South, Eula Hall summarized: "The worst thing about it was no health care." She continued, "The saddest thing in the world was when children was getting sick, no doctors, no nurses, and people tried home remedies—some worked, some didn't. Some was a disadvantage." Hall's mother, whom she referred to as a "good Samaritan," would "go in and cook, help take care of the other children while the mother took care of the sick one." Because she was the oldest daughter, Hall would often join her mother. She recalled people getting sick from untreated wounds, mothers dying in pregnancy, and children suffering from dysentery. Preventable deaths were common. After a neighbor woman suffered a wound from a rusty nail and died of lockjaw, she worried that if her own mother died nobody would take care of her. Her own family had experienced numerous tragedies. Her mother's parents had died young and her grandfather perished in a sawmill accident. Her father's second wife and three of their children had died of tuberculosis, and he told stories about the 1918 flu epidemic, when neighbors would hang buckets of food on the doors of sick families in order to avoid exposure. She saw "all the suffering from [illness], the emotional strain put on the family. . . . You was the doctor, the nurse, the undertaker and everything. It was scary to get sick." As a child, she often "wondered what makes the graveyard get filled."[1]

By the time she was an adult, health care had expanded, especially for those employed in unionized mines, but gaps in care persisted. Some working-class and poor people who lived in rural areas, including Hall, had never seen a doctor; for those that had, it was only intermittent. Beginning at age seventeen, Hall had six pregnancies. The first four babies, Randy, Colleen,

Nanetta, and Troy, were born at home. Her second child, Colleen, died on a winter night when she was three weeks old. The child had never seen a doctor: "You worry about what really happened," Hall reflected. Troy was born premature and was deaf. Only Dean, her youngest, was born in a hospital. As a lay advocate with her welfare rights organization, Hall began to connect the deep-rooted health care problems in Appalachia to a systemic failure to serve certain populations. She saw people who were sick but had no transportation to hospitals and so she drove them when she could. She met others who were turned away from hospitals because they could not afford to pay for medical services. As early as 1965, Hall talked about her dream of opening a community health clinic.[2]

In describing her life as a health activist, Hall often points to one event that displays her understanding of systemic failures in the medical system. One night Hall was called upon to take a pregnant woman to the hospital. Two hospitals refused to admit the woman because she could not pay for services. By the time they got to the third, the woman was in advanced labor and the hospital still refused to take her. At her wit's end, Hall wheeled the woman inside and dared the hospital attendants to leave the woman in the waiting room in front of the other patients. The attendants finally gave in and provided the woman with a room, although they turned her out soon after she gave birth.[3] Hall told this and other stories of health injustice as she became a leader of the community health movement, which grew out of the welfare rights movement and expanded in the early 1970s. A decade after Hall articulated her dream of opening up a community clinic, she and the Eastern Kentucky Welfare Rights Organization (EKWRO) founded the Mud Creek Health Clinic in Floyd County, Kentucky.

The Mud Creek Health Clinic was part of a regionwide and nationwide community health movement. The first community health centers in the country opened in Mound Bayou, Mississippi, and at a housing project in Boston, Massachusetts, in 1965. By 1974, more than eight hundred community health centers, serving more than four million people, had opened, most of them funded by the Office of Economic Opportunity.[4] By the early 1970s, about a dozen clinics had opened up in the mountains, many of them a part of a confederation of councils that organized under the Council of the Southern Mountains Health Commission. A generation of medical students, professionals, and legal aid volunteers—inspired by the civil rights movement and influenced by the energy and ideas of health equality organizations—labored in the community health movement. They sought to provide medical services to poor communities and assist locals with setting up clinics and health education programs throughout the South.[5]

The delivery of health care to the poor was a central concern in the Great Society legislation, most notably in the creation of programs to finance care for the elderly (through Medicare) and the poor (through Medicaid). These programs reimbursed physicians and providers and gave poor and elderly people unprecedented access to health care. They did not, however, address fundamental problems in the health care system: many people lacked access to care because they lived far from hospitals. Others faced discrimination or avoided hospitals because of racial and class barriers. Civil rights activists pioneered the community health movement in 1964, when doctors served in Mississippi Freedom Summer, the campaign to organize for voting and civil rights in the state most hostile to the movement's goals. They provided medical care to white and black activists who were refused services locally. They went on to form the Medical Committee for Human Rights (MCHR) and to open up community health centers in underserved towns and neighborhoods. Advocates of "community health" sought to provide new models of care by opening neighborhood clinics, where primary care and preventive services would be the focus, along with building relationships with community members in order to address environmental and social concerns related to health.[6] According to historian Jennifer Nelson, the Medical Committee was guided by three principles: medicine as "a tool for community transformation," medicine as a human right, and medicine as a way to promote personal empowerment.[7] These health activists envisioned health care as more than tending to individual bodies. It was the ability to see those bodies as part of a web of life, work, community, environment, and history.

Mud Creek Health Clinic and the many others that were part of the community health movement had a common goal of using health as a platform to address a host of interrelated issues that shaped poor communities. Leading community health activist Dr. H. Jack Geiger argued that, along with making health care more accessible, neighborhood clinics used "social and political change to affect those powerful determinants of health status that lie in the economic and social order."[8] Activists in this movement insisted that health concerns could not be divorced from economic and social factors in the community. Between 1970 and 1973, community health emerged as a central concern in the coalfields, and activists adopted a series of strategies to expose systemic health injustices. They spotlighted occupational disease and disability, expanded access to health care, joined movements to expose environmental hazards, and made visible the health impacts of gendered poverty. As they traversed campaigns and made a case for health rights, they sought to build on a sense of "community," which was sometimes key to their success but other times a stumbling block in a difficult political and economic system, too often hostile to their claims of fairness and justice.

Occupational Disease and Disability

When David Allen was thirty years old, his breath began to catch. It happened when he was working in the mines as a hand-loader, shoveling coal into hoppers that carried the coal above ground. He would find himself doubled over, holding onto the shovel for support, a sharp pain in his chest. He noticed that he felt weak and tired more often than not, and he had developed a cough that clung to his lungs. When he went to a doctor, chest x-rays revealed that rock dust filled his lungs. The doctor told Allen that he could no longer work in the mines and should seek a job less demanding on his worn-out body.

David Allen had worked in the mines since he was a boy of fourteen. The work was hard, punishing even, but it was the best work around for supporting a growing family. With a third-grade education and a broken body, Allen had few good options. He enrolled in a jobs training program and was soon placed as a bus driver and tender of coal-burning stoves at a school. His salary of $250 was insufficient to support his family—a wife and three children—and medical expenses, so he applied for public assistance from Aid to the Permanently and Totally Disabled (APTD), a parallel program to AFDC that was administered by the state. When he applied for disability, he must have hoped that his sixteen years in the mines and his crippled body were a steep enough price to have paid to be able to receive public assistance. The Kentucky Department of Economic Security, which handled APTD, agreed that his medical condition was poor: he had a perforated eardrum, calcium deposits in his lungs, and symptoms, like spitting up blood, related to the lung disease that was bound to develop into a severe impairment. Yet the report concluded, "At this point, the medical evidence and testimony indicates that the claimant's disease has not progressed to the point of incapacity," making him and his family ineligible for aid. The department administrators seemed to prove the belief among many miners suffering from occupational disease and disability that "you have to be practically dead" for a claimant to be found eligible. Allen and hundreds of others soon became the focus of legal aid lawyers, who linked disability, health care, poverty, and welfare rights.[9]

In 1969 and 1970, legal aid lawyer Howard Thorkelson, who had been hired by the Appalachian Volunteers and directed the Mountain Legal Rights Association, started a disability study in Appalachia. David Allen participated in it, seeking one more opportunity to secure assistance. Driving the study was the concern that "in the United States sickness attends poverty, and the inability to work compounds sickness." The 1954 amendments to the Social Security Act included aid for the permanently and totally disabled, but significant hurdles remained, especially for nonelderly adults (only people age fifty and older qualified). In Thorkelson's view, the program expressed the fear of middle-class professionals that poor people looked for ways to escape work. Welfare officials, he argued, hold an "essential concern that poor people would not see sickness as an alternative to working," and they failed to consider the "serious impairment of earning capacity because of sickness."[10]

Poor and working-class people often faced insurmountable hurdles when applying for disability benefits. Unable to afford an examination from an independent doctor, they had to rely on exams performed by doctors employed by the welfare department, who, in Thorkelson's estimation, had a vested interest in "reducing the dole." Consequently, poor people did not receive fair exams, and they faced high rates of rejection for public assistance. Born out of his interactions with miners and their families, Thorkelson's hypothesis—that poor people in Appalachia did not receive fair hearings—was verified in the study.[11]

Merging health care and economic welfare, Thorkelson's study showed how poverty compounded sickness and vice versa. He worked with Harvard professor and antipoverty advocate Robert Coles to assemble a team of doctors from the Boston area, where ideas about doctors' role in community health first took root.[12] Thorkelson hypothesized, "If a group of claimants were provided professional, competent medical examinations by doctors who were solely responsible to the conditions of the claimants" (and not the welfare department), previously denied claimants would qualify.[13] He recruited to the study 114 people from eastern Kentucky and West Virginia who claimed to be significantly disabled and unable to work or to find jobs that fit their physical needs. The majority were disabled men—mostly miners—but a handful of women and people from other occupations were included as well. After receiving medical exams, the individuals decided whether or not to resubmit claims. Of the eighty-nine people who reapplied for aid, all of whom had been rejected previously, 59 percent qualified. The study revealed a need for reforms within the system and more qualified doctors to evaluate patients. More broadly, the study concluded that disability benefits had to be considered within the context of the economy. For instance, what comparable jobs were available to a miner who suffered from severe pulmonary disease? And to whom could working people in Appalachia turn for fair treatment when they were at their most vulnerable?[14]

In 1970, Thorkelson connected with activists in the community health movement in New York City. He contacted the Health Policy Advisory Center (Health/PAC) to request assistance in advising miners with disabilities, including black lung disease. Founded by civil rights and New Left activist Rob Burlage, Health/PAC promoted community-centered approaches to health care in New York's crumbling medical system, and it critiqued the two-class system of health care in the "medical industrial complex."[15] Health/PAC organizers created a map of the New York City medical system, charting systems of profit and exposing undemocratic planning. They imagined a countermovement to the system of health care that dominated American society, and they offered technical services for planning community health campaigns.[16]

The first Health/PAC staff person hired by Burlage, Maxine Kenny volunteered to go to eastern Kentucky when Thorkelson called. Kenny had spent three years with Health/PAC as an assistant, writing for the organization's bulletin, leading workshops for community groups and medical professionals, and contributing to two books on the ideas underpinning the community health movement, *American Health Empire* and *Race and Politics in New York City*. In Kentucky she held workshops on community health organizing and recruited a medical student to spend a summer in the mountains to assess the feasibility of community-controlled health services there.[17]

Before long, Kenny decided to relocate to eastern Kentucky, where she believed it was important "to build links between the progressive medical forces around the country and the people in the mountains." Kenny also had personal motivations for the move. Her parents relocated her and her siblings from their farm in northern Ontario to Flint, Michigan, in the early 1940s, drawn by the opportunities created by the auto manufacturing industry. She understood a life of "sporadic work, commodity foods, and getting by." After attending the University of Michigan, she spent her early adult life working for social change, first as the deputy director of OEO in Vermont, as a peace activist, and then as an organizer and journalist at Health/PAC. The burgeoning community health movement in Appalachia seemed a natural next step.[18]

The issues surrounding occupational disease and disability were the initial focus of community health efforts in eastern Kentucky. Two mine disasters served as rapid reminders of the risks that miners took daily and the extent to which the coal industry ignored safety standards. In November 1968, Consol Mine No. 9 exploded in Farmington, West Virginia, leaving seventy-eight dead and more wounded. About two years later, the Hurricane Creek Mine erupted in Hyden, Kentucky, killing thirty-eight miners. In both, company neglect and a lack of inspections had led to tragedy.[19]

In the same years, new studies showed that black lung disease—acknowledged by the medical community beginning only in the 1950s—plagued miners at an alarming rate. New technologies that allowed for faster drilling increased the concentration of coal dust, and doctors believed it would yield even higher rates of illness. Coal operators ignored or downplayed black lung disease. The same companies that looked the other way when safety violations were reported had long denied the disease's existence, and they fought new regulations at every turn. What's more, after the passage of the 1969 Mine Health and Safety Act, miners faced a bureaucratic maze when attempting to seek compensation administered through Social Security. Required medical tests were difficult to obtain and often misleading, and the burden of proof of disability fell squarely on individual miners or their widows.[20]

Miners led a movement to address the intertwined concerns of health, safety, and economic issues. Fundamental to it was the Miners for Democracy, a democratic movement within the UMWA to unseat corrupt leadership that had mismanaged the UMWA Health and Retirement Fund and had failed to address miners' central concerns. Made up of a coalition of disabled miners, widows, and health advocates, the Black Lung Movement shone a light on the failures of the coal industry and the federal government to acknowledge and treat the lung disease. The Health/PAC reported on these movements and saw their greater significance in the battle for occupational and environmental safety and health. One Health/PAC reporter stated in a monthly newsletter, "The workplace makes up one-third to one-half of every worker's health environment, and if the health movement is to address the causes of poor health rather than simply its treatment, it cannot ignore occupational health and safety conditions. In attacking the causes of black lung, mine explosions and roof-falls, miners are truly conducting a struggle for environmental and preventive health." The miners were the canaries, their health needs at the whim of capital interests.[21] And they were one segment of the growing community health movement, closely related to another led by the welfare rights movement.[22]

A Community Health Movement

When Maxine Kenny arrived in Kentucky, community activists were embroiled in a controversy over the Floyd County Comprehensive Health Services Program. Funded by the OEO beginning in 1967 and implemented by the Floyd County Health Department and Big Sandy Community Action Program, the program was supposed to follow federal guidelines to "assure services" with the input and participation of residents of an area. The OEO outlined the need for "truly responsive" health programs that valued and implemented the perspectives of those being served. Director of OEO Sargent Shriver warned that programs could all too easily morph "into a form of the dole—paternalistic, unilateral, and degrading." To many residents of Mud Creek, that was exactly the problem they encountered.[23]

Welfare and community activists had two major problems with the Floyd County Health Services Program. First, it did not provide direct care but was a "referral and coordinating mechanism." Patients could go to an outpost where they would be seen by a nurse and then possibly referred to a physician in town—creating a "two-class system" in the parlance of Health/PAC.[24] Instead of providing comprehensive health services within the community, the program provided transportation from the rural outpost to the doctors' offices in town. Welfare rights activists argued that poor people needed direct care services, not a "taxi service."[25] Second, community activists argued that the program was politics as usual, with no local input, and it served "to strengthen the control that a few people in Floyd County have over the majority of county residents."[26]

OEO officials' review corroborated local critiques of the program. In 1968, a site evaluation team found that the program made no "basic changes in the existing medical care system" and that the medical services provided were very poor quality.[27] Two years later, the Office of Health Affairs, which soon replaced the OEO in oversight and funding of health centers, sent another evaluation team, which also reported that the program was fundamentally flawed: it was dominated by middle-class people and failed to include input from representatives of the population served, and the health educators it employed spent little time with patients. The health programs simply came nowhere close to being comprehensive. Some medical outposts were inaccessible, and even when a person was referred to a physician in town, the offices were so packed that doctors had little time to provide adequate care. Other elements of the program were so fraught as to be unhelpful to the majority of the population. The family planning portion of the program, for instance, required women's husbands to agree to their participation in the program, creating a barrier to women's health services. And there appeared to be a conflict of interest: the doctors who helped to design the program (and to assess the fees) were the same physicians treating the patients.[28]

As chair of the EKWRO's health committee, Eula Hall led the charge to reform the OEO-funded program and force the middle-class residents who headed the program to relinquish control. She had been a consistent volunteer since the mid-1960s, but now she was a woman in the spotlight, leading the health committee and testifying at public hearings. To the people threatened by the welfare rights group, Hall was a well-intentioned woman who was being manipulated. One board member stated that welfare rights activists "pushed" Hall "out front," and continued, "every time something popped up she had a written statement." Questioning Hall's capabilities, the board member stated, "Now, she isn't qualified to make those statements.

Every time I saw [EKWRO activists] they had three or four attorneys with them and somebody was putting words in their mouth. I don't know who it was, but I know damn well it wasn't Eula Hall."[29] It was unimaginable to this particular board member that Hall had knowledge of the problems in her community or that she was capable of analyzing the strengths and weaknesses of the health program.

Following evaluations, in 1970 the OEO discontinued funding of the Floyd County health program and called for reorganization. In 1971, the Office of Health Affairs accepted a new proposal by the Floyd County Health Department that promised accessibility and teams of public health nurses and community health aides. Yet again, a battle between local elites on the board of health and the EKWRO heated up. According to federal officials and welfare rights activists, the local administrators of the program, made up of middle-class professionals, failed once again to provide a truly comprehensive health care system. The committee fired Dr. Arnold Schecter, a former instructor at Harvard assigned by the Office of Health Affairs to direct the program, who had objected to the machine politics in Floyd County. He soon filed an extensive complaint with the OEO. While federal officials pressed the committee to work toward fully functioning clinics, EKWRO focused on what they perceived to be the root of the problem: the program illustrated "what easily happens when programs to provide valuable medical service to poor people are not controlled by the poor people themselves."[30]

In early 1971, as they continued to face resistance among local elites in charge of the comprehensive health care program, welfare rights activists began a publicity campaign with the hopes of pushing the Office of Health Affairs for real reform. They picketed the health program's central offices, the Floyd County Courthouse, and the Prestonsburg General Hospital. Using her connections to journalists, Maxine Kenny helped to generate interest in the story. Picking up the news, the national press sympathized with the activists' position that the countywide health program failed to meet its standard of providing comprehensive health care to poor people. Kenny also helped EKWRO organize a public hearing, during which a group of medical professionals, activists, and local people came together and testified. Eula Hall and a legal aid lawyer chaired the meeting, and speakers included a doctor representing Health/PAC, Dr. Schecter, and patients who testified about the inadequate treatment they had received at regional hospitals.[31]

Welfare rights activists made their clearest statement about their vision for health care in their "Bill of Health Rights." In the tradition of President Roosevelt's economic bill of rights and on the heels of the NWRO's welfare bill of rights, the "Bill of Health Rights" declared: "Health care is a *right*, not a privilege for those who happen to have money." Activists called for an end to the exploitation of poor people by medical professionals; for the University of Kentucky Medical School to commit funds to training the sons and daughters of coalminers; and for the involvement and leadership of poor people in the design and implementation of a comprehensive health program. The bill closed with the statement: "The Eastern Kentucky Welfare Rights Organization pledged to fight for decent health care for all people in Eastern Kentucky. We believe all patients should be treated with respect and dignity and should receive quality services in well-equipped hospitals and clinics near their home."[32]

Ultimately, the Office of Health Affairs decided to defund the Floyd County comprehensive health program, but the EKWRO health committee was not willing to give up their fight for medical services. Over the next several years, EKWRO led campaigns that addressed the immediate health needs of residents, sought structural reforms in the existing system, and connected health care to occupational and environmental hazards in the region.

The welfare rights group launched a legal challenge in 1971, focusing on hospitals that, despite having nonprofit status, refused to serve more than a handful of people who could not afford services. *Eastern Kentucky Welfare Rights Organization v. Simon*, a class-action lawsuit against the Internal Revenue Service, became part of the Hill-Burton cases, a series of class action suits that claimed that "hospitals receiving construction funds under the Hill-Burton Act had incurred an obligation to provide free care and community service to the medically indigent and poor." Leading up to the legal challenges, a pair of lawyers from the National Health Law Program of the Legal Services Corporation had published two articles explaining that the Hill-Burton Act contained provisions that hospitals constructed or expanded under the legislation were required to provide care to persons unable to pay for services. Marilyn G. Rose, one of the lawyers leading the research, had been involved previously in cases against Hill-Burton hospitals that discriminated on the basis of race. In the late 1960s, Rose sought test cases around the country in which clients had been denied hospital services because they could not pay. Although the EKWRO case did not have standing in the courts, it informed a series of cases that ultimately led to amendments to the Hill-Burton Act requiring that private, nonprofit hospitals with tax-exempt status must post their obligations to treat people for free or below cost if they could not afford services. All in all, the Hill-Burton cases helped to rectify the assumption that Medicaid and Medicare solved the problem of poor people's medical care and prevented hospitals from refusing treatment to poor people.[33]

But the legal challenges did not remedy one of the primary problems facing poor people in rural areas—that they could not easily access medical facilities. In the 1940s and early 1950s, health care had expanded with the success of the UMWA Welfare and Retirement Fund, but by the 1960s the fund had decreased assistance in order to maintain solvency, revoking health cards and forcing the closure of Appalachian hospitals. Unemployed miners and widows began the roving picket campaigns in 1962 to make a case for labor rights, especially the "cradle to grave" health care that they believed was their due.[34] The community health movement of the 1970s was a part of this longer story of progress followed by setbacks. Activists considered how to bring comprehensive health services to rural and working people in Appalachia for good, by designing programs in which local people had greater control.

Health fairs were crucial to the expansion of the movement. They offered an opportunity for poor people, many of whom had never received a full medical exam, to access needed care; only after those needs were provided for could activists tackle large-scale problems. In the summer of 1971, Maxine Kenny recruited Vanderbilt University's Student Health Coalition to partner with the EKWRO health committee for a weeklong health fair. Initiated in 1968 by Vanderbilt University and Meharry Medical College students, the Student Health Coalition worked with rural communities throughout Appalachia and the rural South to provide some semblance of health care for people who otherwise rarely received it. Medical students would often see up to four hundred people in a week. The students usually stayed in the homes of community members, symbolic of the way that they sought to break down barriers between professionals and clients. They also trained local people to provide lay services, including taking blood pressure and analyzing urine samples.[35]

At the same time that health fairs addressed the needs of a community, they were effective organizing tools. One doctor who worked with the Student Health Coalition explained, "Health was used as an entree because of its common interest to all, health in its broadest sense meaning physical and spiritual well-being and proper economic and social environment." The health fairs were free to the public and had a festive quality, unlike what so many poor people experienced in hospitals. As Eula Hall explained to reporters, many poor people avoided going to the doctor because they feared being turned away: "They dread the harassment, the charges that come when they can't afford it because they don't have some kind of medical card."[36]

Health fairs also provided an opportunity to bring up issues of workplace safety and environmental hazards.[37] In Floyd County, medical students and professionals associated with the Student Health Coalition offered physical exams and diagnostic tests, seeing five hundred residents over the course of one week. For two days during the fair they focused on lung exams for miners who were at risk for black lung disease. With a diagnosis, miners could take steps to apply to the Social Security Administration for black lung compensation. Public assistance for miners was still threadbare, but a diagnosis could put them on track to secure more.[38] Along with providing health screenings, medical volunteers worked with communities to identify areas of research and set up local clinics. They identified common themes in the communities where they worked: "generally characterized by the lack of control over factors affecting health care, lack of adequate financial resources for delivery of health care, [and] lack of effective influence on authorities over health-related aspects of their environment."[39]

The EKWRO health committee also began plans to build a permanent, physical clinic. A clinic required devoted medical professionals who understood the importance of community-controlled health care. The welfare rights group found allies in Drs. Elinor Graham and Jim Squire, whom Maxine Kenny met through her New York contacts.

Elinor Graham was not new to Appalachia. She had worked in Myers Fork, Kentucky, as a VISTA worker in 1965, leaving Appalachia after a year to pursue a degree in medicine. Her plan was to gain a skill and then move back to the mountains. While in medical school at the University of Rochester, Graham joined the Health/PAC and helped to set up inner-city health projects. After she graduated, she was part of the Lincoln Collective, an effort by activist medical residents, community members, and hospital staff to reform the Lincoln Hospital, a former charity hospital in the Bronx that served low-income, Puerto Rican communities. Community members referred to the hospital as "the butcher shop" because of the abysmal quality of services.[40] By the time of her residency at Lincoln, Graham had married Jim Squire, who had lived most of his life in Brooklyn, New York. After two years of pediatric residency, Graham looked for a place to start practicing in the mountains, and she convinced Squire, who was also a pediatrician, that they should locate to Appalachia.[41]

In 1971, Graham met Eula Hall and learned about the EKWRO health committee at a meeting of the Medical Committee for Human Rights in Lexington, Kentucky. Maxine Kenny had helped to convince the committee to hold its annual conference in Kentucky to expose the medical profession to health care issues in Appalachia. The conference included sessions on the EKWRO health committee, strip mining as a health concern, and information about black lung disease and organizing efforts by the Black Lung

Association. Within a year of the conference, Graham and Squire joined the community health movement in eastern Kentucky.[42]

In the summer of 1972, Drs. Graham and Squire helped to set up a two-month summer health project in Floyd County with a goal of building interest for a permanent health program. The project employed eleven teenage health workers who were trained by six medical volunteers. By employing young, local people, the doctors hoped to encourage community involvement and introduce young people to health careers. The teenage workers, ranging in age from fifteen to eighteen, participated in spring training sessions where they learned the basics of taking health histories and doing lab work. At first, some of them were uncomfortable entering the homes of family members or acquaintances, but they soon were "self-assured," as "they quickly learned their way through a maze of record forms, new medical terms and names, and a lab full of equipment like microscopes, incubators, centrifuges and pipettes."[43]

The medical team visited over 700 people and 184 homes in Floyd County, selected by the health committee based on need. Over a third of the people visited had no medical insurance, while the rest had partial benefits either through the UMWA or public assistance. The health team performed comprehensive health tests: evaluating hearing and vision; taking urine, stool, and blood tests; and examining for TB, diabetes, and high blood pressure. Once they had the results, the medical workers provided patients with a copy of their health record and offered them medical advice or referred them to health department services.[44]

The results of the project were sobering. Ten percent of patients had untreated tuberculosis. Over 40 percent of patients had mild to severe anemia. Chronic ear infections and hearing loss were common problems in children, and nearly a third of the adults tested had poor vision but could not afford eyeglasses or treatment for cataracts.[45]

The most pervasive problem turned out to be parasite infections. About half of the patients were tested for a variety of parasites and, of those tested, 50 percent had some form of parasite due to water contamination. Medical workers set up a "micro-biology lab," and as Graham recalled, it was not long before the teenage health workers learned to recognize parasite eggs in stool samples. They also began to understand the association between well water, outdoor privies, and contaminants. Of the families visited, 80 percent used outdoor toilets. Graham remembers, "As soon as they learned what was going on with the sanitation and how it impacted families in terms of the contamination of the wells, they were real crusaders." The youth medical workers educated the community about water contaminants and spread information about moving outhouses away from gardens and water sources. They also helped to distribute medications to families who tested positive for parasites, and they provided information on how to clean wells and purify water. More than most health issues, the epidemic of parasites could be solved largely with community education. Once they were treated for parasites, other health problems, such as anemia, would also begin to improve. Offered resources and medical support, community members could take action to improve their own quality of life.[46]

Following the success of the health fair, EKWRO activists wrote a proposal to establish a permanent health clinic in Mud Creek through the National Health Services Corps, but the application was not approved. Activists refused to settle and began a fund-raising campaign.[47] The Appalachian Volunteers, which was closing its doors, donated the last of the funds in its account to the project.[48] Once established, the clinic worked with the UMWA Health and Retirement Fund, which paid a monthly stipend to the clinic for each of its members who enrolled there. Amounting to about $5000 a month, the funds were enough to support the clinic for the time.[49] A local man offered to rent a house he owned so that it could be converted into a clinic, and within a year Eula Hall donated her own home to the clinic. Drs. Graham and Squire worked for an annual salary of one dollar each. They were able to do so because they worked part-time at a hospital in a neighboring county.[50]

The Mud Creek Health Project officially opened on February 11, 1973, with a community celebration befitting its origins: more than six hundred people attended the opening of the clinic. A headline captured the mood: "This Clinic Is a Dream Come True." As staff person and public face of the clinic, Eula Hall declared that the clinic belonged to the people of Mud Creek. "They can go and feel assured to see a doctor and they don't have to worry about being turned away."[51] Hall also placed the clinic within a history of antipoverty activism: "We're having the best care in history. This is the first clinic ever on Mud Creek." She noted that people on public assistance could afford exams at a low cost, which meant "more money for the poor."[52]

The structure of the clinic reflected EKWRO's desire to involve poor people in planning and implementation and to connect individual and community health. The community board included retired or active miners, low-income, community representatives, and staff people. Once the clinic had a solid budget, all of the staff received equal salaries. The bylaws laid out plans for the clinic, but they also outlined more expansive goals, including working "for the improvement of the health and welfare of poor people in the region," educating people about the health care needs of rural people, and assisting members "in all ways possible to obtain good quality health care."[53]

The clinic was an immediate success. For the first time, poor people in the community could count on receiving comprehensive care from a physician. Patients were charged a four-dollar office fee, but if they had no money, they were not turned away. If a patient could not afford medication, the clinic provided it at no cost. At first the clinic was open only two days a week. Although the staff stopped registering patients at five o'clock, they often continued to see them until eight o'clock in the evening.[54]

The EKWRO maintained an ongoing relationship with the clinic. The group received funding for a community van, which it used to shuttle people who did not own cars or who could not drive (typically the elderly, sick, or disabled, but also young mothers) to the clinic as well as to other social service offices. In the summer of 1975, Naomi Little, a housewife and EKWRO cochairman, was hired as a driver three days a week. She kept records of her travels, which give a sense of the needs of the community at the time. She took "loads of people" to the food stamp and legal aid office, shuttled patients from the clinic to the hospital, and carried mothers to offices where they could pick up vouchers for baby formula. When she was not needed as a driver, she provided assistance to the clinic staff. The van services, which the EKWRO referred to as the "transportation co-op," epitomized the group's community work. In a newspaper article, one of the members, disabled miner Woodrow Rogers, stated about the group, "Any problem, we'll work on it!"[55]

Reflecting its relationship with the UMWA and deep ties to the labor movement, the clinic provided special services for miners. The board hired respiratory therapists to treat miners who suffered from black lung disease. It also hired Eula Hall as a social worker. In that position, she advocated for people who had been diagnosed with or potentially suffered from black lung disease. She visited homes to educate people about the clinic and coalminers' pneumoconiosis. Once someone was diagnosed, she helped them sign up for benefits.[56]

Hall's advocacy on behalf of disabled miners was part of a longer movement. Before the clinic opened, the EKWRO had built important alliances with the Black Lung Movement. During the March for Survival in Washington, D.C., a coalition of welfare rights and black lung activists circulated petitions to improve black lung legislation. In 1971, black lung activists founded a statewide organization, the Kentucky Black Lung Association, so that they could better lobby for effective and fair policies for disabled miners. William "Bill" Worthington, a disabled miner and African American leader in the UMWA, was elected the first president of the organization, and Eula Hall followed as president a few years later.[57] The Kentucky association built on a legacy of interracial organizing in the UMWA and reflected the importance of women activists in the union. Along with providing much-needed medical services and screening for miners with black lung disease, the clinic offered space to black lung activists when they needed to organize a petition or lobbying effort.

As the social worker at the clinic, Eula Hall bore witness to the difficulties facing miners who sought black lung benefits, even after the 1972 amendment expanded provisions. She described her impression that once a miner retired from the industry, he did not go "to green pasture" but "home to suffer." She remembered those years when black lung was common: "You can go up and down this road in the summer any hour of the night, you'll hear somebody talk, it'll be dark, it'll be a light on, you hear somebody coughing and there'll be a man sitting on the porch trying to breathe." She continued, "I've stopped [and asked,] 'What're you doing up, what're you doing out?' 'I'm trying to get my breath. I just couldn't sleep.' You don't hear them complaining. They may not even come into the doctor the next day. They come in when they think they're going to smother to death."[58]

In her own community, Hall acted as a lay advocate for miners who could not afford attorneys. She remembered the impact black lung benefits had on

Figure 7. Eula Hall on the front porch of Mud Creek Clinic, explaining black lung treatments to a couple, 1976. Courtesy of www.earldotter.com ©.

miners and their families, how it lifted hundreds of people out of poverty. She recalled, “Every time [miners with black lung disease] got any kind of money over what they had to live on, they repaired their house. They would put [in] indoor plumbing, and they'd add a room on, or they'd remodel and make their house a lot more comfortable. They'd get a better vehicle, and they could buy better clothes for their children, educate their kids better.”[59]

The idea that a health movement would be holistic in addressing a community's problems was borne out at the Mud Creek Clinic. It was part of a web of activism locally and regionally, operating as much as a community center in the early years as it did a medical facility. Its staff and the members of the EKWRO soon joined the struggles of other working people and their organizations. Through word and deed they argued for a broad vision of community health rights.

To Save the Land and People

In 1971, Bessie Smith, a mother of nine who lived at the head of Lotts Creek in Knott County, Kentucky, went to the courthouse to get a warrant. She hoped that officials would arrest coal operators who continued to illegally strip the mountains near her home. She got the warrant, but the state police refused to serve it at first. When they finally did, a judge dismissed it. Coal operators, police officers, and the courts proved they cared little for the damage wreaked on the landscape. Smith was irate. Her children had not been able to attend school for seven days because of a mudslide related to the stripping that made the road impassable, and nobody seemed to care. She and several other local women took matters into their own hands. They decided, “if the law wouldn't enforce the ban on strip mining, that we would go out and stop overweight coal trucks ourselves.” Raising her arms in the air, Smith stood inches from the grill of one truck. She successfully stopped three coal trucks, their beds overflowing with coal.[60]

Smith was a member of the Knott County chapter of the Appalachian Group to Save the Land and People (AGSLP). The Knott County group had been involved for years in protracted battles to stop strip mining in their communities. They saw how surface mining exposed the earth; the loads of spoil from the sites dumped to the side, creating mudslides and clogging creeks. They documented the sickness related to a polluted watershed. Children had developed ulcers from drinking acidic water, and some contracted hepatitis after exposure to toxins. Strip mining and the run-off that it created ruined the hillsides that people had long farmed. People lost crops, orchards, and the fields where they kept cows, hogs, and goats as the coal industry skimmed the earth for more minerals. As one woman put it, "one swipe of that blade" destroyed life. She continued, "I'd set for hours, and there wouldn't be a bird ever fly by that place."[61] She did not have to be a scientist to know that when birds—an indicator species—stopped showing up, there was a bigger problem.

Strip mining had devastating psychological effects, too. At one of the hearings to expose the hazards of the practice, a woman testified that a coal company stripped the land where her deceased child was buried and did not inform her until after rocks and dirt were piled on top of the graves. She expressed grief over the fact that she would never again be able to visit the gravesite.[62] Strip mining put stress on the community, pitting men in need of work against their neighbors who pressured the local and state governments to close down work sites. But it also revealed the interdependence of people and land, and how a lack of economic power strained and stretched that relationship.

By the 1970s, the Council of the Southern Mountains passed a resolution that condemned strip mining and called for federal, state, and local officials to take immediate action in banning the practice.[63] The CSM regional magazine *Mountain Life & Work*, which enjoyed record-high subscriptions, covered surface mining, along with welfare and health rights, as one of its key issues. The Council also hosted public hearings on the practice and distributed information on the movement and on legislative efforts. Sally Ward Maggard, staff of the Council, learned that Bessie Smith and Eula Hall were planning a direct action at a strip mine site in late 1971. The Appalachian Group to Save the Land and People had been active for several years, and a band of men had formed a covert group that sabotaged equipment at strip mine sites. But the women were ready to try something different. They wanted to occupy a strip mine site and force a shutdown. They hoped to be arrested, at which point they would draw wider attention to the practice and support for a strip mining ban.

Maggard took the idea of the direct action protest to the CSM board. Jim Somerville, a Presbyterian minister and president of the board, was passionately opposed to strip mining after witnessing its impacts. Antipoverty activist Edith Easterling was the vice president of the Council. She had long been outspoken about strip mining, going back to the Appalachian Volunteers' support of Jink Ray's protest to protect his land from strip mining in 1967. Eula Hall was on the board of the CSM, thus her word also carried weight. The board voted to endorse the sit-in movement, giving credibility to the campaign and gesturing to the fact that the direct action protest was part of a multipronged working people's movement in Appalachia.[64]

On a cold, rainy day in January 1972, women who worked at the Mud Creek Clinic and were members of the EKWRO joined the protest with Bessie Smith, Sally Ward Maggard of CSM, members of the AGSLP, members of Mountain People's Rights legal aid, and others opposed to the industrial practice. Led by Smith, the group of twenty-one women coordinated a civil disobedience action at the Elijah Fork surface mine operation in Knott County, Kentucky, owned by Sigmon Brothers. Their hope was to get arrested, create media attention (two journalists accompanied them), put pressure on Governor Wendell Ford to enforce regulations, and inspire opposition to the practice of surface mining.[65]

The women chose a site that was owned by a coal operator, distinguishing them from past protesters who had been landowners. Those activists often drew some sympathy from politicians who respected property rights. Historian Chad Montrie argues that activists in the movement against strip mining "maintained a reverence for the institution of private property, albeit property on a different scale."[66] Yet the women's actions spoke to values that went beyond property rights, as they spoke about their inability to provide for families if coal companies ruined the land. Choosing an industry-owned site, they would bring attention to the fact that coal operators who owned a site could rip up the land however they wanted, regardless of the destruction it caused or how it affected the people living nearby. The leaders also decided to limit protesters to women, for they believed that the guards and workers at the site would be less likely to incite violence against them. Whether it was conscious or not, the move was also symbolic. Bessie Smith and other women had not been silent about how strip mining made their work as caregivers difficult, if not impossible.[67]

The morning of January 21, the women walked the muddy road to the "bench," the carved-out part of a mountain where miners worked and kept their equipment. Their arrival heralded a work stoppage. The women carried with them a tarp, coffee, and sandwiches, and they settled in and built a fire to keep away the chill. Some sat in the bucket of a bulldozer, taking shelter from the rain. They began with high spirits, but as it got later and the sheriff refused to arrest them, they realized their plan was falling apart. To make matters worse, they learned that some of their male compatriots at the bottom of the mountain had been assaulted and younger women faced harassment and threats of rape on the road to the mine site. After fifteen hours, the women abandoned the site.[68]

As many activists perceived at the time, the protest revealed the importance of a multi-issue, broad-based movement that could bring together a community. Sally Ward Maggard recalled, "It wasn't just a lone bunch of women who said we're going to go do this, who had different strands of interest." They saw themselves as part of something larger, a movement of working people who realized how domains of power—in this case, the coal industry and the politicians in the industry's pocket—operated in their lives on multiple levels.[69]

Their action made the national and regional news, and it was one of many protests that helped to attract attention to the practice of surface mining. Later the same year, EKWRO joined another effort to shut down a stripping operation along the Floyd-Knott County border that had destroyed bridges, roads, and homes and had led to the death of one person. The group garnered a thousand signatures on a petition to close the operation, and two months later they organized a direct-action protest during which two hundred people forced a strip mine operation to shut down.[70]

Ultimately, however, the campaign failed in the sense that the action, and the movement it was part of, did not lead to the abolition of surface mining. While the Mud Creek Clinic demonstrated how community health could unite people and lead to positive change (with relatively little pushback), the movement against strip mining revealed complex fractures within the community. Although the state was the focus of activists, the struggles nonetheless pitted anti–strip mining activists against strip miners, who often lived in the same place and worked at the sites. Strip mining was catastrophic for many people, and certainly for the ecosystem, but it was also one of the only jobs in a depressed region. While strip mining harmed some people when it destroyed their land and water, to ban it meant that some men would have no work in the short term. Even then, some of the workers at the Knott County site, sympathetic to the women's protest, admitted that they preferred not to destroy the landscape, but surface mining was the only job available to them. Like many people who had to choose between jobs and protecting the environment, many chose jobs. Reflecting back years later, one of the protesters summarized: "You can't successfully . . . fight such an issue without trying to change the whole system. The need to protect the environment is deeply intertwined with people's need for good jobs and means of protecting themselves and their family economically. Save the Land cannot be separated from Save the People."[71]

The limitations of the campaign revealed the difficulties in building a movement that truly connected issues—welfare rights, health care, and an end to surface mining. In 1970, welfare rights activists had joined with disabled miners to argue for a guaranteed income. Had that movement succeeded, one can imagine that some miners—who saw no other choice than to surface mine—might have had more options. When politicians hampered the welfare rights movement at its peak, other movements that did not have a solution for the economic crisis in the region would continue to hobble.

To many looking back on the period, the protest bookended the grassroots movement against strip mining in Kentucky. Direct action protests and legal challenges did not lead to a ban, as most activists had hoped, but to watered-down regulatory measures. The coal industry easily maneuvered around them and soon developed even more drastic and damaging techniques to extract coal, with the development of mountaintop removal. To see the protests only as a failure, however, is shortsighted. As historian Chad Montrie argues, activists witnessed a breakdown in the democratic process as few state politicians listened to the people who organized to expose the hazards of the mining practice. Nor did representatives fully consider or care about the long-term health and environmental effects of surface mining on a region that was already economically depressed.[72] Last, when considered within the context of the community health movement, the protests against strip mining emerge as the unfinished work of activists who saw the profound connections between environmental, economic, and health justice.

Gendered Poverty and Women's Health

Community health activists' anti–strip mining protests and their work on black lung proved that they saw it necessary to take on structural issues in the mountains and buttress campaigns that were already underway. Although those campaigns always included a gendered element—in that female spouses of miners benefited from black lung benefits and environmental destruction made women's caregiving work more difficult—women activists rarely used language of "women's issues" to describe those campaigns. But with large numbers of women involved and its commitment to self-help and a patient-centered approach, the community health movement offered a gateway to publicly discussing gender inequality in women's lives.

Not long after opening, the Mud Creek Health Clinic became a space to discuss women's health issues. While the anti–strip mining and black lung movements have been remembered as some of the most powerful movements in Appalachia in their day, women's health activism has received relatively little attention. Yet, the regional women's health organizing—though difficult to measure by policy—carried great significance to women who had been mistreated by physicians because they were poor and rural, had been denied information, or lacked basic care for most of their lives.

In previous health care battles in Appalachia, the focus had been on miners' health, union benefits, and access, with an emphasis on class inequality in health care systems. Those previous debates, although important, did not capture the intimate, personal, and specific health care concerns of women. In the community health movement, women joined in public conversations about women's health to discuss their own bodies, from experiences of childbirth and reproductive control, to the sense of the mysterious that their bodies inspired. As women, as poor people, and as Appalachians, their willingness to speak about sexuality and private experience was a radical act that ran counter to the images of poor and mountain women that circulated broadly.[73]

Popular lore portrayed mountain women either as wholesome, strong, and asexual, or barefoot, pregnant drudges, suspicious of modern medicine, and implicitly hypersexual, with a houseful of kids. The reality was much more complex. Some women had more children than they could handle, not because they were hypersexual but because they lacked access to information about birth control. Others were aware of the traditional herbal medicines that their mothers and grandmothers had used but were eager to receive comprehensive, modern medical services.

Working-class and poor women in Appalachia faced numerous barriers to receiving medical care. By the early 1970s, women testified in public forums that they often had a difficult time getting to clinics or hospitals because they could not drive or feared being turned away. When they made it to a doctor's appointment, they often encountered sexist and classist barriers to quality health care, including doctors who disrespected them or withheld information. They often lacked reproductive health care and access to information about family planning. Through meetings and publications, women's health activists in Appalachia began to carve out spaces where they could speak openly and address these needs.

The Mud Creek Clinic facilitated some of these early discussions. The staff held a monthly family planning clinic where women could learn about birth control methods. The clinic also boasted a female doctor. Elinor Graham recalls that, though she was a pediatrician, she often cared for female patients. "As a woman I had to do a lot of women's health care work," she remembers. The clinic also had steadfast leadership in two female community workers. Eula Hall and Alice Wicker, mothers of five and seven, respectively, spoke openly about their personal health experiences and the struggles of female kin and neighbors.[74]

Alice Wicker was particularly vocal about the poor health care she received as a young mother. A longtime member of the EKWRO and the treasurer of the Mud Creek Health Project in its early years, Wicker shared her history of childbirth in public forums. Wicker had her first three children at home, with her aunt serving as her midwife. Discussing the mixed blessings of midwifery, she noted that midwives were more affordable than doctors and that she received care from "a bunch of neighbor women" who arrived to help her through the labor. But some midwives, including Wicker's aunt, were not well-trained and gave women castor oil and turpentine, which were considered cure-alls. The home remedies did little to ease her birth pangs and instead added to her discomfort. Wicker recalled that the neighbor women "held me in bed until I had the baby, held my hands, knees, and feet. I was screaming of course." Wicker had her last four children in the hospital, and the situation there was not much improved. The male doctor gave women drugs that would prevent or stimulate births in order to arrange the births around his schedule. When Wicker told the doctor that she had suffered for two days and no longer wanted to delay delivery "he just walked out."[75]

In the fall of 1972, Wicker joined nearly a hundred women from West Virginia, Virginia, and Kentucky in Pipestem, West Virginia, for a "Women's Weekend," where she told her story. Those in attendance ranged in age from ten to sixty. Some ascribed to socialist feminism and were full-fledged participants in the women's liberation movement; others were new to the women's movement and came along to see what it was all about. Represented in the audience were outsiders and locals, lesbians and straight women, mothers from Appalachia, and radical activists. While the weekend organizers explored a variety of themes, from labor to welfare rights, and provided film showings and entertainment by female-led bands, women's health was a primary concern.[76]

Dr. Elinor Graham of the Mud Creek Clinic was among the health experts at the conference, and she later recalled the spirit of discovery and camaraderie there. Four months pregnant at the time, Graham led a workshop on women's self-care, showing women how to do breast and pelvic self-exams. Graham demonstrated on herself, which worked well since she had "this nice little lump" of pregnancy and her uterus was well defined. After she inserted the speculum, she invited the attendees to look at her cervix. Graham recalls that one "regular Appalachian" woman in her sixties looked at her cervix before declaring, "Well! I've had eight kids, and I never knew where they came from!" "The light bulbs were going on everywhere," Graham remembers. "It was wonderful."[77]

The Women's Weekend was a family affair for some. Linda Elkington, who had been an Appalachian Volunteer, attended the conference with her mother, Bessie Cooper, and her three younger sisters, ranging in ages from sixteen to ten. Linda, her mother, and her sixteen-year-old sister Joyce attended the workshop where Graham demonstrated self-exams. Linda wrote that they "learned about caring for our own bodies so we won't have to be totally dependent on those chauvinist gynecologists." The women received free speculums "to remind [them] that no longer does it have to be only the doctor who sees our inner goings on."[78]

Self-care clinics had become staples of the women's movement in the early 1970s and were related to the underground abortion services in many of the nation's cities. Self-help clinics could arise anywhere: at gatherings in women's homes, off-hours at a formal clinic, or at a conference. In feminist lore, the self-help movement was born when a feminist in Los Angeles demonstrated a pelvic self-exam in a feminist bookstore. Typical of women's movement narratives, this creation myth places the women's movement in a coastal city; yet these feminist acts emerged across the country within a year and in a variety of locations that shaped their meaning. As historian Finn Enke argues, self-help clinics operated as "a stake claiming women's sexual autonomy in the public landscape."[79]

In Appalachia, acts of women's health autonomy, in the context of class battles, allowed working-class and poor women to assert control over their health care. Having fought for access to medical care and against class and gender discrimination in many hospitals, some Appalachian women saw self-care clinics as one more way to reject the abuses that they had experienced in traditional medical facilities. By becoming more informed about their own bodies, moreover, they could make better decisions as consumers when they did visit a hospital or medical clinic.

The women who organized these early meetings sought to spread information about the women's movement and the women's issues that came up at retreats and in meetings. The CSM magazine, *Mountain Life & Work*, published news about women's organizations and provided information about a variety of women's concerns. Since the Council "takeover" in 1969, women had more prominent voices in both the magazine and at the annual conference. The magazine covered women's issues, including the women's health conference, and in 1974 it published a special "Women's Issue," after seventy women at the CSM annual meeting decided that there was a "need to relate across class and county lines about life as women living in Appalachia." They decided that an issue devoted to women "would be a good tool to emphasize the commonness of women's struggles," and the editors signed the introduction "sisters in mountain struggle."[80]

While the editors, who were white, chose to use the language of sisterhood here and in other articles, they were careful not to ignore differences between women. In fact, the very idea of sisters in a *mountain struggle* engaged the diverse challenges that shaped the lives of women in Appalachia. But the editors also believed it was important to unify women around common goals, so they chose the theme "women's health" for their first special issue. Why health? The editors explained that women visited doctors more frequently than men, but almost always as the primary caregivers of children. "So we need to share our experiences in the health care system" and learn how to "maintain our health and regain our dignity," the editors concluded.[81]

The writers distributed a wide range of medical information. They discussed the purpose of gynecological exams, the legality of abortion in the U.S., how abortions were performed, and a list of clinics that offered abortion services. They also included a section titled "Facts for Women" that discussed breast self-exams, various types of birth control, and how to prevent venereal disease. Recognizing links between high poverty rates and poor medical care in Appalachia, the editors offered information about welfare benefits, from Social Security to food stamps, public assistance, and black lung assistance. In a section on job protections, they reminded their readers: "don't forget that federal law prohibits discrimination on the basis of sex, race and age."[82]

These conferences, meetings, and publications offered women the space to have frank discussions about the meaning of womanhood in the mountains and to create a gender-conscious community of women. Women discussed the culture of gender in the mountains and explored the ways that women's bodies had been defined, treated, and abused. A moment of grassroots feminism, it was also among the seeds of a regional women's movement that grew in subsequent years.

• • •

The community health movement exemplified organizing efforts that continued into the 1970s. As the War on Poverty's visibility receded, antipoverty activists continued to seek ways to trigger broad social change at the same time they addressed the immediate needs of poor and working-class communities. As Dr. H. Jack Geiger described them, community health activists were part of "the most extensive concerted public effort in the history of the United States to expand ambulatory care resources in poverty communities on a nationwide basis." At the same time, the community health movement implemented a new version of modern health care in which clinics responded to the needs of the community by offering an array of programming. They tackled policy issues related to disability benefits and worked toward providing basic medical services, as well as helping people navigate social provisions that would improve their health. They allied with other groups fighting for basic life necessities, like clean water and livable environments, and they exposed the effects of gendered poverty on women's health.[83]

It is not surprising that women led these efforts. As the caregivers of families, tenders of gardens, providers of food and water, and nurses to the sick and disabled, they saw more immediately how community health was tied to many elements of life. But they also faced an economic and political system that was not equipped to address interrelated problems with multifaceted solutions. While efforts to provide health care to hundreds of people and to expand assistance to disabled miners or to address women's health needs met with broad community support, large protests to stop strip mining—which had negative impacts on health over the long term but also signified a lack of economic power—were more difficult to ignite. Nonetheless, to the people fighting those battles, the relationship was clear. They understood that it was not possible to change one single issue and improve people's lives substantially; a multi-issue, broad understanding of power was imperative, even if the barriers to building that movement often seemed insurmountable.

In 1973, women activists would once again make a case for the complexity of social justice struggles in Appalachia. Eula Hall and other clinic staff and members of the EKWRO joined the labor struggles that had begun to rock eastern Kentucky, bridging the militant labor movement to the antipoverty efforts of the last decade.[84] When a miners' strike began in Harlan County in 1973, Hall, clinic staff, and EKWRO members joined their sisters and brothers on the picket lines. The labor struggle captured the nation's attention to an extent not seen in years. It signaled a moment when the issues that had animated women activists since the mid-1960s—the burden of social reproduction in the coalfields—became even more pronounced.

6 “I’m Fighting for My Own Children That I’m Raising Up”

Women, Labor, and Protest in Harlan County

During a miners’ strike in 1973, Earl Dotter photographed Minnie Lunsford, the oldest among a group of women who stood on the picket lines in support of striking miners. She carried a sign that stated, “Duke Power Company Owns the Brookside Mine, But They Don’t Own Us.” Her statement boldly addressed a history of exploited workers. The coal industry thrived in part by stealing lungs and bodies. Men labored for years only to be tossed aside when they were sick or disabled, or worse, killed in the mines. Part of the power of the statement is where it appears. In the hands of a woman who had never been employed in the mines, the declaration exposed the company’s control over the above-ground world of mining communities, where women lived, worked, and cared for families.

Lunsford’s fellow picketer Sudie Crusenberry cut out a magazine print of the photograph and pasted it on the cover of one of her scrapbooks, where she documented the strike, past and present battles in the coalfields, and the activities of the Brookside Women’s Club, an organization founded by female kin of striking miners. Along with the picture of Lunsford, Crusenberry included an image of Mother Jones and her famous battle cry, “Pray for the dead and fight like hell for the living.” On another page, she inserted the lyrics of a song by Aunt Molly Jackson, the wife of a miner who affiliated with leftist organizers in the 1930s. Her song “Dreadful Memories” captured the gendered class divide in the coalfields where “the coal operators and their wives and their children / Were all dressed in jewels and silk” while the miners’ wives cannot afford to feed their children and are haunted by the “dreadful memories” of seeing children “sick and hungry, weak and cold” who “starve to death and die.” Crusenberry positioned these lyrics alongside

Figure 8. Minnie Lunsford holds picket sign after striking miners' arrest, Brookside, Kentucky, 1973. Courtesy of www.earldotter.com ©.

a portrait of herself, taken at an organizing meeting. Last, she tucked into the pages of the book an International Women's Day button, from a local women's rights meeting where she had been a speaker after the strike had ended. The photograph of Lunsford along with Crusenberry's bricolage—and the stories that led to these material artifacts of a 1970s miners' strike—offer windows into these women's worlds, where the class struggle between miners and coal operators also exposed a gender struggle, as women revealed the ways in which the beneficiaries of coalfield capitalism thrived on the toil of caregivers even as they weakened the social supports necessary for that labor.[1]

Lunsford and Crusenberry joined miners as they fought for union recognition. In September 1973, miners at the Eastover Mining Company, a subsidiary of Duke Power Company, in Brookside, Kentucky, walked off their jobs after the company refused to recognize their vote to form a local of the United Mine Workers of America (UMWA). Following an injunction that limited pickets to three miners per entrance, wives, daughters, and mothers of miners stood in for male picketers and soon founded the Brookside Women's Club. Over the course of the next year, they continued to recruit women to the picket lines and to organize in support of the striking workers. During the yearlong strike, the club's ranks grew to nearly one hundred active members, including relatives of miners and women leaders from various community organizations in eastern Kentucky, and it had dozens of supporters from across the country.

The women of Brookside were working-class caregivers; some worked for wages part time and others were full time homemakers, but, during the strike, most of them positioned themselves as sustaining and caring for life. Their gendered class status and union politics converged to create a grassroots feminism that exposed how unrestrained capitalism held little promise for caregiving, female dependents in the coalfields. They argued that coal companies owed them something: along with better benefits that would come with a union (and would aid the family), they yearned to lessen the burdens of care work by better protecting men on the job.

The antipoverty campaigns of the previous decade informed the women's activism and also offered continuity to the key struggles of the grassroots war on poverty. Seen in this light, the militant labor strike was the culmination of many of the arguments promulgated by antipoverty activists, who exposed corporate control as the primary driver of poverty in the coalfields. The Brookside women, like welfare rights activists, acted from their positions as caregivers in the coalfields. Yet in popular memory they are remembered for their plucky commitment to a labor strike that was fomented and led by their male kin. Their support of men on strike has symbolized a hopeful moment of working-class solidarity. The women's own activism and their explanations about their motivations, however, reveal a more complex story about the inner workings of gender, class, and white womanhood, as well as the ways in which the labor movement propelled some of the women into feminist struggles of the 1970s, in which they served as heroines. They were never simply devoted, working-class wives or women's liberationists, as they teetered between movements that did not fully integrate their lives.[2]

The women of Brookside exposed the gender and class fault lines in the capitalist coal industry. Women's unpaid reproductive labor had for decades lent stability to the coal industry, as they took on the arduous work of caring for and reproducing a labor force. Their work was "an indispensable background condition for the possibility of capitalist production."[3] As the class struggle between miners and coal operators exploded, mothers, daughters, and wives of coalminers argued that the coal economy drained their communities of lifeblood and strained their ability to do the work of caring. For them, the politics of care could not be divorced from the politics of class. Their involvement in the strike dramatized the "contradictions of capitalism"—that industry relied on the reproductive labor of women, yet created a hostile environment in which that work took place.[4]

Collective Memory and Working-Class Struggle in the Coalfields

Pro-union miners in the Appalachian South worked tirelessly to build support for the labor movement and faced many setbacks between the 1930s and 1970s. Setbacks were not always the result of company antiunion tactics: strikebreaking and disagreements among workers about what constituted rights are as much a part of working-class history as the union movement. Women supporters in Brookside, however, employed collective memory of working-class solidarity to make sense of their own responsibility to stand up to the union busting of the Eastover Mining Company. And in stories they told at the time and in years after the strike, they cast themselves as women kin and neighbors who sought vengeance against the industry that had caused destruction in their lives.

By the early 1970s, Brookside was one of the region's last remaining coal camps, as most companies had shifted away from providing housing to workers. The women who led the Brookside Women's Club had lived either there or in other coal camps as children. Founded by the relatively small Harlan Collieries Company in 1924 and purchased in 1970 by Eastover Mining Company, Brookside was a modest community. Its four-room homes did not have insulation or indoor plumbing, and the community lacked the amenities of urban planning, such as the modern water systems of larger coal towns.[5] Nonetheless, there was a strong sense of community. Men worked together in the mines, and families gathered in schools, churches, and community centers.[6]

Community ties were also staked on the individual and collective memories of miners' labor struggles. In the 1920s, the United Mine Workers of America began campaigns and, in the early 1930s, the communist-led National Miners

Union organized miners and faced off against company-hired guards, leading to the famous "Bloody Harlan" battle between miners and the local sheriff.[7] During the 1970s strike, three generations of women were represented on the picket lines, and their activism reflected a living memory of the 1930s labor movement. Some were children during the 1930s labor battles. At least one woman was a young mother in the 1930s, and others were granddaughters of men who had been pro-union miners.[8]

Lois Scott, who became an outspoken leader in Brookside, was born on November 3, 1929, just days after the stock market crash.[9] Scott, her parents, and twelve siblings lived in the Benham coal camp in Harlan County. In the 1930s, Lois's father, Dave Jones, could find work only two days a week. Scott's country-dwelling relatives kept the large family from starving by sending food.

Coal operators reacted to the Depression and an overall decline in coal demand by cutting wages by 10 percent and reducing hours of operation. Miners and their families faced severe poverty, and they found that the Red Cross, controlled by local elites, used the organization as one more way to control workers. The UMWA saw the opportunity to act and initiated what would become a nine-year unionization campaign in eastern Kentucky and Tennessee.[10]

Dave Jones began organizing for the UMWA and soon met punishment from the coal operators. The Harlan County Coal Operators' Association, established in 1916 by local firms to facilitate political control of the county government, including the sheriff's department, kept close watch over union activity.[11] Moreover, the mine bosses employed guards, spies, and "gun thugs" in their attempts to quell labor protests. When miners tried to organize a union, they risked their jobs, their housing, and sometimes their lives. People who were children during the 1920s and 1930s in eastern Kentucky towns grew up with the chilling stories of gun violence, protracted standoffs, and murders stemming from labor struggles.

"This is important to me, and this scared me," Lois Scott remembered. One night company guards invaded her home and made the children get out of bed so that they could search underneath the mattresses for union literature. "They'd kick the door open and shine the flash light in our eyes," she recalled.[12] She knew that her father was pro-union, and she feared for his life. Another night, the guards came into the house and told Bessie Jones that her husband had been shot. Later that night, the family learned that Dave Jones was alive, uninjured, and hiding. The guards had lied in an attempt to frighten his wife into providing them information about the union organizers' whereabouts. Later, Scott declared that the Brookside strike "gave me the opportunity to show the feelings, I guess you'd call it the hatred, I feel for the coal operator—for what he done to my father and to my brother and the family."[13]

Seventy-year-old Minnie Lunsford, who had been a young woman in the 1930s, often used stories of the 1930s labor battles to rally supporters. She recalled the times during the Great Depression when mining companies cut wages and fought the union. When violence broke out between union workers and anti-union security guards, the National Guard was called in to quell the labor protests. Lunsford remembered that she stayed inside with her children, and she kept a close watch on the machine guns that sat atop hills surrounding the coal company town. "I would put my children to sleep and I would walk the floor and worry about my children's safety," she said. During the Brookside strike, she feared that the situation could become a repeat of the repression she witnessed earlier in her life. "We're living in a critical time," Lunsford stated as she compared the 1930s to the 1970s strikes. One of the biggest changes in Lunsford's eyes was that more women could publicly support the men. In the past, she had stayed indoors with the children; now she joined the men on the picket line and helped make decisions about how to support the union.[14]

For younger women, stories of the past helped them to make sense of contemporary problems. For instance, Lois Scott's twenty-five-year-old daughter, Bessie Lou Cornett,[15] explained her own participation in the strike as an attempt to reverse the decades of injustice her family had known. Cornett's early life was marked by the rocky relationship of her parents (her father was abusive), and for a time she lived with her grandparents. Bessie set out on her own at an early age. By the time she was fourteen, she had quit school and moved to Chicago to work in a factory. At the age of sixteen she married a coalminer and moved with him back to Harlan County. He got a job at Brookside, and they moved into the community where they raised their only child. Cornett pieced together restaurant work with other service jobs to help support her family and eventually returned to school for her GED and trained as a dental assistant.[16]

When the strike began, she returned to the stories that her grandfather Dave Jones had told her of life in the coalfields. As a child she sat at the dinner table and absorbed his tales of UMWA organizing in the 1930s. "That's mostly what we talked about," Cornett stated. Her sense of injustice grew as she watched her grandfather die of black lung disease after forty-two years of working in coal dust. When the Brookside strike began, Cornett was eager to participate. "When I watched [my grandfather] die and suffer like he did with that black lung disease," she reflected, "I knew that something could be done about it. And I told myself, if I ever get the opportunity to get those coal operators I will. Because I thought, you know, [the company] was the enemy. So when this strike came up, I saw the opportunity, and I jumped right in there."[17]

These stories of pro-union workers clashing with powerful capitalists offered a framework for making sense of coalfield politics. They were also gendered narratives: a mother worrying or a daughter seeking revenge for the harms inflicted upon fathers and brothers. As the strike became more heated, women would continue to draw on a collective past—specifically from the perspective of coalfield women—as they exposed the worst abuses of the coal companies.

Women's Mobilization and Gendered Narratives of the Strike

In the boom-and-bust cycle of the coal industry, the early 1970s were considered relatively stable, but the workers knew how quickly the tide could turn. At the Eastover Mine in Brookside, workers made relatively good wages—$45 per day. Decent pay, however, did not make up for the fact that the company union installed and controlled by management failed to secure medical benefits and pensions, and it made no effort to address dangerous working conditions. Because the union's leadership had been handpicked by the company, workers did not believe that they could report their problems in good faith. In 1972, the Mine Enforcement Safety Administration found that the rate of disabling injury at Brookside was twice the national average. It documented an array of mechanical and structural problems in the mines, such as "loose, broken, or missing roof bolts" and dangerous flooding. Each day that miners went below ground, they risked serious injury and even death. Over the long term, they were prone to developing black lung disease from inhaling coal dust day in and day out.[18]

As Brookside miners grew wary of the constant threats to their safety, UMWA miners nationwide erupted over their union's corrupt leadership under Tony Boyle, who had overseen the murders of rival Joseph "Jock" Yablonski and his family, and who had done little to address the dangerous working conditions that miners faced in his years as president. An internal movement called Miners for Democracy pushed for democratic reform in the UMWA beginning in 1970, leading to the election of Arnold Miller, a retired and disabled coalminer from West Virginia who had led the Black Lung Movement.[19] Reform leaders of the UMWA held a rally in Harlan County in 1972, promised an organizing drive, and declared Harlan County a "cornerstone" to a successful organizing drive in the region.[20] Inspired and supported by the movement for democratic reform, Brookside miners voted 113 to 55 for the UMWA to be their representative in June 1973. In July, the company refused to recognize the UMWA as the workers' union or to accept a contract, and all 180 miners employed at Eastover walked out.[21] Eastover promptly hired nonunion workers and, by September, obtained a court injunction to limit the number of striking miners who could picket.[22]

Wives, mothers, and daughters stepped onto the picket lines in late September 1973. The women noted that while it was illegal for more than three miners to picket, the injunctions said nothing about women. As Bessie Lou Cornett recalled, "We wanted to be able to help the men stop the scabs and get a contract without all that violence. And so what we did was we talked to each other. We had a march and said, 'Why don't we just [go] down to the picket line ourselves. We can stop the scabs. The court don't have an injunction against us.' We saw that as a tactic for getting around the injunction. So, that's what we did."[23]

Almost as soon as they joined the picket line, women from Brookside and their allies formed the Brookside Women's Club. The club was open to all wives of Brookside miners on strike and any women who supported the union. After electing officers, the members met at each other's homes and at the community center to make decisions about when and where to meet for protests, how to raise money in support of the strike, and how to distribute funds. They recruited new members to the club, including pensioners and their wives, who understood the stakes of a strike for better benefits. The group helped to pay for prescription medications for miners who were out on strike, and it supplied families with clothing and women with the gas money they needed to be able to drive to the picket lines. Women stood on roadside corners with gallon milk jugs and signs stating, "Striking Families Need $ Please Donate." The women always saw the strike as a community effort; whole families were on strike with the miner, and the women expected the working-class community to come together and support the families.[24]

The club advertised itself as a supporter of pro-union families, but the women also had practical reasons for joining the strike: they believed that their presence would prevent extreme forms of violence between antiunion and union men. Minnie Lunsford recalled that, early on, some male strikers did not want women to protest because they wanted to "battle it out" with the strikebreakers.[25] But the women continued to recruit picketers. Although their presence may have prevented gun violence, they soon found themselves targets of gendered violence. According to several women, in the early days of their participation strikebreakers shouted obscenities at them as they drove their cars through the throng of protesters. Some of the women collected "switches"—the sturdy sticks used in tobacco fields—and they responded to drivers who threatened them by sticking their switches into open car windows and hitting the strikebreakers.[26] The local paper, sympathetic to the coal industry, reported, "What began as a peaceful demonstration . . . ended in an alleged brawl."[27]

The women publicized acts of aggression in the hopes of attracting more members. In one of the early recruiting fliers, the club listed the attacks on women picketers and union miners, naming some of the strikebreakers who threatened them. They reported that one strikebreaker hit a woman picketer with his car, another threatened to shoot protesters, and one antiunion man shot into the truck of a union supporter.[28] After two days of confrontation between picketing women and strikebreakers, the group of supporters grew to include women from across eastern Kentucky. Female bodies on the line may have prevented potentially explosive violence, as many of them believed, but their presence also helped to expose pervasive duress. As the strike wore on, the women dramatized the ubiquitous forms of violence that informed coalfield politics, from preventable workplace accidents that maimed bodies to state-backed repression of the strike and the company's exploitation of working people and their families.

A month after the strike began, filmmaker Barbara Kopple traveled to Harlan County with a colleague to document the strike, soon to be joined by a film crew. Kopple had grown up on a vegetable farm in New York and had briefly attended college in Charleston, West Virginia, where she became familiar with coalmining and the labor movement. After graduating from Northeastern University in Boston, she moved to New York City and became a film editor and worked on political documentaries, including the anti–Vietnam War film *Winter Soldier*. As she made her way to eastern Kentucky, Kopple also learned about Miners for Democracy and hoped to work with the UMWA to boost its efforts. However, as Kopple shot film in Harlan County and worked closely with the miners and their families, living with them throughout her time there, the Executive Committee of the UMWA—still made up of Tony Boyle supporters—began to question her motives and accused her of having communist affiliations. The committee eventually refused to support the making of the film despite an initially positive response. Free of union oversight, however, Kopple was able to focus more emphatically on the local miners, their families, and the Brookside Women's Club members, who would become central to the film.[29]

Not long after arriving in Harlan County, Kopple and her film crew caught one of the most dramatic moments of protest on film. At daybreak on October

23, 1973, dozens of women prepared to hold the picket line. Dense fog silhouetted the gathering crowd. State police stood on one side of the road, forming human fences to keep protesters out of the street. "Very tough looking women" stood on the other side. Events from the past couple of days portended conflict. Ninety strikebreakers had arrived, and the state police were prepared to escort them and mine bosses onto company property. Meanwhile, hundreds of union supporters from Kentucky and Virginia mines joined locals on the picket line. Tensions broke when one carload of strikebreakers made it past the picketers. Before the second car could pass through, Lois Scott called out to her comrades in the Brookside Women's Club, "Come on, girls! Lay down! Lay Down!" Scott, Betty Eldridge, and Melba Strong stretched across the road to block a car from entering the company gates. If the men wanted to break the picket line, they would first have to run over the protesters. Despite jeers from the crowd, the state police quickly intervened.[30] The police dragged the women into police cars and arrested them for blocking the road.[31] Betty Eldridge reported that the police officer slammed her knee in a police car, crushing it "to a pulp." She interpreted the aggressive act as evidence that the law at Brookside was "all one sided."[32]

While the arrests angered the women, they also gave them the opportunity to expose the political machines of Harlan County and the unjust operations of the local court. F. Byrd Hogg, the Circuit Court Judge who presided over the trials of those who disregarded the strike injunctions, became so notorious for siding with the company and against strikers that he was widely rumored to secretly be a coal operator. Those rumors were eventually verified when the *Courier-Journal* reported that he had been a major stockholder and sole incorporator of A&G Coal Company and principal operator of a Knott County mine.[33] According to Eldridge, Hogg did not like the idea of women participating in the protests or the legal process. When she questioned a police officer's testimony, Hogg told her she was a "big-mouth, interfering woman" who was "sticking her nose" where she had no business, and he indicted her for contempt of court. She saw the indictment as an attempt to intimidate her and to pressure her to reveal the UMWA's tactics. The judge asked her if the union was paying her to picket. Eldridge responded that she picketed on "principle." To her, supporting a union comes "from the inside of you. It's not money." The courts and the company people couldn't seem to understand that people would stand up for their beliefs "without [someone] loading their pockets with money."[34]

Women referenced their sex frequently, from their declarations that they would use their female bodies to prevent violence to accounts of sexism as they entered into spaces where they contested power. In these moments, they often drew upon their wifely and motherly roles to defend their stance. For instance, when Judge Hogg sentenced Nannie Rainey along with six women and eight men to six months in jail or $500 for violating the injunction, Rainey took her seven young children to jail with her (five other children also went to jail with their parents). Rainey told a reporter that her only crime was "trying to protect my husband's job." She added that she was following in the tradition of her own father, "who went through this same kind of battle years ago."[35] News of the arrests spread and photographs of the women and children behind bars circulated through the media, showing up in union literature, regional newspapers, and leftist publications. Following the arrests, Brookside strikers upped their protests in response, leading the judge to suspend the jail sentences after two days (though he kept the $500 fines in place).[36]

Throughout the strike, women employed language to position themselves as wives, mothers, and daughters who were mobilizing in defense of the men in their lives and for their families. In this way, they signaled that their activism was not meant to threaten gender hierarchy. But as the strike wore on, women more frequently pushed the boundaries of their activism's meaning, especially as they engaged more direct action protest. Moreover, the rhetoric of "protecting" a man's job elides the bold actions of women; even as they spoke in deference to gender hierarchy, they paradoxically challenged gender and class boundaries by showing up in male-dominated spaces, such as the picket line, the jail, and the courthouse. This point was not lost on their adversaries. At a press conference, president of Eastover Mining Company, Norman Yarborough, said, "I wouldn't like to think that my wife would do that."[37] Another woman reported that antiunion men would yell things like, "If you was my wife, you'd be home where you belong."[38]

Social Reproduction in the Coalfields

On the face of it, a class struggle was at the heart of the Brookside Strike: miners mobilized against the corporate greed of Eastover and Duke Power Company, and their female kin embraced their fight. There is evidence that some in the UMWA leadership were wary of strike activity and that the Executive Committee did not approve of women's coordinating activities. But among striking miners and union organizers, the women were invaluable supporters.[39] Observers described the women as "allies" to the men and as "the strong reserve troops of the workers."[40]

More than supporting workers, however, the involvement of women in the strike importantly dramatized the "contradictions between the economic system and its background conditions," in this case their reproductive labor.[41] During and after the strike, women gestured to the fact that social reproduction and capitalist production did not exist apart from one another but always operated as a pair. In building their arguments for supporting the strike, they interwove stories about childrearing, doing housework, supporting disabled husbands, and caring for loved ones who were dying of black lung disease, all the stuff of maintaining family and social bonds.

Take, for example, Minnie Lunsford, who often linked the strike to the union benefits that eased the burdens of care. She explained her activism years later: "At Brookside, we weren't striking so much over wages as over benefits and safety." When the strike began, her husband "was just skin and bones from where that rock dust had collapsed his lungs." The two of them relied upon the UMWA Health and Retirement Fund for medical care. "I know what a union card is worth," she explained. "It paid for my hipbone, it paid for my eye, and it would have paid for my husband if he'd had to go stay in the hospital. When we got his pension money, we took it and fixed this little old shabby house so it would be warm for me and him." Referring to her life after the strike and following the death of her husband, she said, "Being a widow woman, I don't draw too much from the union. I draw about half of what my husband did, but without the union, I wouldn't draw nothing." This despite the fact that she had raised eight children, and it was her caregiving labor that had buttressed her husband's working life, a life that she described as one full of worry for the fate of her husband and her children.[42]

Lunsford described how during the strike she tried her hardest to explain to strikebreakers why the union was important, beyond higher wages. She posed questions to strikebreakers when they drove past the picket lines: "Do you have a daddy or a granddaddy that's drawing black lung? Is he sick and unable to work? What do you think is gonna happen if you live that long and work at a non-union mine?" She continued, "If you're crippled up in the mines and sitting in a wheel chair, do you think that company is gonna take care of you?" The subtext, of course, was that a female family member would most likely support them if they were unlucky enough to be injured in the mines or to wind up with black lung disease.[43] And she would be better able to with union benefits.

Other women explained similar motivations at the time of the strike. Mary Widner, wife of a coalminer, told a reporter, "I don't want to go back to jail, but if it means helping Kentucky and helping my kids, I'll do it."[44] Sudie Crusenberry explained on camera that she was fighting not only for the miners but "in support of my own children, too, that *I'm raising up*."[45] Male leaders of the strike also made these connections. For instance, Darrell Deaton, the vice president of the Brookside UMWA local, testified before an audience of five hundred: "All our lives we've seen companies like Duke Power, which run mines for profits and don't care about how many of us go home battered and broken, companies which buy up a coal camp community like Brookside and think they've bought the lives of the people who live there."[46]

In a fitting gesture, one of the Brookside Women's Club's protests involved stopping trucks that carried deliveries to the commissary, or company-owned store, shutting it down temporarily. Women were barred from employment in company mines until the late 1970s (their presence was considered bad luck), but they were the primary consumers at the commissaries, where they bought food, clothing, and household supplies. These company-controlled stores served as physical reminders of the extent to which social reproduction and corporate profit were intertwined. Commissaries were notorious for gouging working families, who had few other options for purchasing goods. Some stores in Harlan County reportedly hiked prices between 18 and 21 percent and generated up to 170 percent profits. Up until the 1940s, coal companies paid miners in "scrip," company-minted money that could be used only in the commissary. As activist Hazel King stated of the coal companies: "They liked to keep a captive audience with their miners."[47] While scrip had been phased out by the 1970s, the legacy of exploitation persisted in the commissary, where workers' wages went back into the company owner's pocket.

The politics of caregiving in the coalfields were on full display when, nine months into the strike, members of the Brookside Women's Club spoke on a public stage about their experiences as women and mothers in the coalfields. In March 1974, women joined the Citizens Public Inquiry, a forum to discuss the abuses of the coal company. Funded by the Field Foundation, the Citizens Public Inquiry was modeled after a 1931 citizen's inquiry to investigate coal company intimidation and was headed by the radical novelists Theodore Dreiser and John Dos Passos.[48] UMWA President Arnold Miller proposed the 1974 meeting and Daniel Pollitt, a University of North Carolina law professor who was committed to civil rights and labor justice, moderated the meetings at a community center near Brookside. He and local religious leaders, a former U.S. Secretary of Labor, faculty from Duke University, activists from various regional councils, and members of the Brookside Women's Club joined miners to testify in support of the UMWA contract.[49]

Women documented the litany of problems they faced in raising families in the coalfields. Many rented homes in the coal camp owned by Eastover, homes that lacked running water and indoor toilets. They relied on well water, but it was of poor quality because the privies polluted the creek, and the company dumped mine waste into the water. Bessie Lou Cornett reported that she had urged the Health Department to test the drinking water a year earlier because she feared that the outdoor spigots were not safe. The Health Department found that the water was highly contaminated with fecal bacteria. Another woman stated that at times the water was so black from coal dust that she had to strain it with a cloth. The women then pointed out that, because the company owned the wells and the water in the camp, the Health Department refused to do anything to remedy the problem. They also testified that they did without recreational areas or "niceties of any kind."[50] Along with the poor conditions of the residences, workers believed that the company threatened to tear down housing or evict residents as a way of maintaining control over them.[51] U.S. Secretary of Labor Willard Wirtz noted that the strike raised not only "a collective bargaining contract issue" but also a social issue. Wirtz recognized that the women's involvement brought attention to the strike as a community issue that went far beyond a dispute between business and labor.[52]

The women participated in the meetings as a gender-identified group ("The Brookside Women") invested in the general well-being of their community and others like it. During public hearings in the 1930s, officials had questioned miners' wives on the witness stand and focused on the treatment of their pro-union husbands. In the 1974 hearing, women were much more involved in shaping the meeting as they testified as a group. They all sat together at one table, some of them with children, and they were a formidable presence as they charged the coal company of crimes and the local government of circumventing the law. The issues that the women discussed—housing and the ability to care for families—hearkened back to other miners' wives protests, yet their presence as a group points to a pronounced gender-consciousness that was not a part of the earlier protests.[53]

Sudie Crusenberry's testimony emerged from the Citizens' Inquiry as the most damning indictment of Eastover's treatment of workers and their families. For Crusenberry, past and present tragedies were the markers of her life trajectory and underpinned her activism. Perhaps more than any other woman involved in the strike, Crusenberry's life experiences pointed to the constant threat of tragic accidents that disrupted women's lives, revealed the forms that everyday violence took, and showed how a lifetime of unfair treatment could motivate and shape women's activism.

Like Lois Scott and Minnie Lunsford, Crusenberry belonged to a generation that had witnessed instability and violence in the coalfields. She had lived all her life in Brookside, where she was born in 1933.[54] Sudie's father was a coalminer who had begun work as a child. As an adult, he worked at a mine that was walking distance from the home he shared with his wife and children. When a man was hurt or if an accident occurred, such as a collapsed roof, the company sounded an alarm. Young Sudie would run to the mine to make sure her father was not the injured man. On numerous occasions, she had seen men carried out of the mine with injuries or, sometimes, dead.[55]

Before the Brookside strike, Crusenberry was like many women in her community: her husband worked in the coalmines; she went to church on Sundays; she tended a large hillside garden and canned all the produce; she sometimes cleaned houses for money to help support her family; and she kept a close watch over her three daughters and two sons, whom she was determined would get the high school diploma she did not have the privilege to obtain. Her worst fear came true a few years before the strike when her husband William, whom she had begged not to work in the mines, got caught underground during a cave-in. His back and pelvis were broken, and his doctors doubted he would be able to walk again. After two months he was healed enough to come home from the hospital. Sudie worked with him daily, massaging his legs and helping him regain strength in his muscles. Sudie, her ailing husband, and her young children lived on worker's compensation, which paid significantly less than the regular paycheck, and the company continued to take out rent for their house. Fortunately, the family had a large store of canned goods that Sudie kept under the beds and along the walls. When hard times fell on her family, she was prepared.[56]

But Sudie could only withstand so much. Once her husband was declared unable to work in the mines, the company evicted her and her family out of the coal camp house. This last injustice—the company forcing her family out of their home when they were at their most vulnerable—lit a fire in Sudie. She believed that if William had been in a condition to work the family could have kept the house, but as soon as company officials learned the extent of his injuries, they told Sudie that they were going to tear down her home. Sudie's father, who suffered from black lung disease and also lived in the camp, was also forced to move.

Sudie told her story at the Citizens Inquiry, and the *UMW Journal* printed her narrative in April 1974, at the peak of the strike. She testified that the destruction of the houses and the displacement of miners and their families was cruel. The wood-frame houses may not have appeared special to an outsider, "just shelters from the storm," but, for Crusenberry, the landscape of the coal camp held a lifetime of memories.[57] Her husband had been crushed in the mines, and she had known deep poverty much of her life. Yet she had made a home in the coal camp, and now the company was taking that away, too. Sudie recalled going back to the camp and standing in the spot where her house had been. Two of her children, one who died at birth and

Figure 9. Sudie Crusenberry with her husband and family, Brookside, Kentucky, 1973. Courtesy of www.earldotter.com ©.

another who died at ten months old from pneumonia, were buried in the camp cemetery. After the company tore down the houses, they built a road that made it difficult to get to the gravesite.[58]

The protectors of coalfield capitalism—coal associations, managers, state and local officials—often claimed to care about the working-class families in their communities. But their words often betrayed them. Pressed by a reporter about the poor quality of housing that the company rented to its workers, mine owner Norman Yarborough responded that the company was attempting to "move our people into trailers." He claimed he would "upgrade our people into better housing." The image of unkempt houses was arguably a public relations nightmare more than it was a moral issue for Yarborough. Perhaps he hoped to show a sense of unity by claiming miners as "our" people, but the language, in the midst of a labor struggle, suggested that he expected loyalty to the company without question. His reference to "upgrades," moreover, cast the workers as commodities, not people.

For Crusenberry, the company's unwillingness to honor a UMWA contract and their treatment of families who had lived in coal camps for two and three generations were of a piece. Coal companies had too much power, and they wielded that power over the workers and everyone in the community. Crusenberry often pointed out that the company had forced her and her family out of their home before they had a new place to live. If anyone questioned the relationship between housing and union organizing, Crusenberry put doubt to rest when she covered the walls of one of the rooms of the house with UMWA bumper stickers before it was demolished.[59]

By the time of the strike, Sudie had two young sons, along with her three older daughters. She was especially concerned about the future of her male children growing up in a place where there were few jobs for men outside of coalmining. This point became especially clear in one club meeting when two club members got into an argument. One woman accused another of committing adultery. Sudie interrupted the argument and emphatically reminded the women what was most important: "I don't care who takes whose man, who lives with whose man, what they do, they can take mine, take him on, they can have him! I'll shed no tears. I'm not after a man; I'm after a contract! I'm raising two boys!" Sudie then began discussing her own experience as the wife of a disabled miner, the daughter of a sick miner, a girl who grew up poor in the coal camps, and a woman who had lost her home to the company. She punctuated memories of a coal camp life with the poverty, hardship, and physical violence that existed in the coalfields. As she shared these memories, the pain became so great that she began to sob.[60]

As the once-bashful Crusenberry was swept into a gender-conscious movement in the coalfields, she expressed her and her group's moral visions: that children in the coalfields deserved better options, that miners and their families needed social supports that a union provided, and that until they were freed from the everyday violence of the coalfields, mothers would continue to speak out.[61] Some of them would continue their activism under the banner of the women's movement, where they grappled with a movement that too often downplayed or ignored the caregiving labors of working-class women.

"Wearing the Pants": Feminist Politics and the Brookside Strike

Throughout the yearlong strike, Brookside women connected with a regional network that raised issues of power, class, and gender injustice in the mountains and sparked broader discussions about the meaning of women's rights for working-class women. Their radical and gender-conscious activism both garnered attention from self-proclaimed feminists who traveled to Brookside to meet club members, and led some Brookside women to count themselves among the movers of the women's movement, molding feminism to fit their visions of gender equality.

Female leaders of social justice causes across Appalachia joined the picket lines and helped to publicize the events. For example, welfare rights and community health activist Eula Hall heard about the Brookside women at a health fair she had organized. Hall soon joined the club, arrived early in the mornings to picket, and helped plan rallies. Florence Reece, who wrote "Which Side Are You On?" during the 1930s labor struggles in Harlan County and who had become a heroine to 1960s activists, traveled from Tennessee to show her support for the Brookside picketers. She led sing-alongs and posed for pictures with strikers.[62] A network of younger, militant women and men who had been instrumental in youth and poor people's movements in Appalachia joined in, too, as well as young people who traveled to the region specifically for the strike, like the *Harlan County, USA* filmmakers. Along with making films, young people picketed, photographed the strikers, and wrote many of the articles that appeared in progressive and left-leaning publications.

The strike at Brookside came to symbolize the power imbalance in the mountains for many and garnered support from a host of regional social justice organizations. Among supporting organizations were the Black Lung Association and the Eastern Kentucky Welfare Rights Organization. The Brookside Women also joined picket lines and found supporters in the mostly female strikers at the Pikeville Hospital, who went out on strike on June 10, 1972, after the Pikeville Methodist Hospital in Pike County, Kentucky, refused to recognize the employees' union representation. Some Brookside women were again arrested for violating strike injunctions, but this time at the hospital strike. Supportive networks developed outside of Kentucky as well. For instance, the Appalachian Women's Organization of Cincinnati held a rally attended by two hundred people in a migrant community there. Numerous unions backed the strike, as well as four major Christian church denominations. And in the summer of 1974, up to 4500 people from across the country traveled to Harlan to attend a UMWA rally.[63]

The Brookside women's activism made national news when *New York Times* reporter Judy Klemesrud wrote a story on them. A leader in changing the newspapers' masculine culture, Klemesrud covered the women's movement in the 1960s and 1970s, publishing the paper's first articles on the movement. Even though she was sympathetic to the movement, she adopted a mocking tone in her article about the Brookside Women's Club, revealing class dynamics within, and potential barriers to, feminism. Klemesrud headlined her article "Coal Miners Started the Strike—Then Their Women Took Over," playing on stereotypes of downtrodden, emasculated men. She described the women as "bored housewives who find picketing more exciting than scrubbing floors," doubtless alluding to Betty Friedan's *The Feminine Mystique*.[64] Club member Betty Eldridge countered later, "If somebody's looking for excitement, I wouldn't recommend going to a picket line. There's no excitement. It's just a whole lot of trouble!"[65] Eldridge had little patience for the "New York woman" who demeaned the circumstances of the protests and failed to recognize the weight of the situation: women risked their homes, physical safety, and financial stability by participating in the strike; their husbands hazarded being blacklisted; and the women faced criminal charges for their activities.

In spite of her errors, the *Times* reporter captured some of the women's thoughts about feminism. Thirty-four-year-old Nannie Rainey, who when arrested took her seven children to jail, asserted that women were willing to protest and spend time behind bars because they saw "all those women libbers picketing on television, and we didn't see why we couldn't, too." Barbara Callahan, a twenty-three-year-old woman from Harlan, responded to a reporter's query about whether the women were supporters of women's liberation by saying, "Right on!" She then qualified her statement, adding that she was "all for families and motherhood," too.[66] At least some of the women saw their protests in relation to the women's movement, which reveals the ways that women negotiated the meanings of the women's movement and gender equality to make a space for themselves. As sociologist Sally Ward Maggard reported in her study of the Brookside women, the strike led many of them to reconsider their domestic roles in light of their labor protests. For instance, some reported that they slacked off household duties so that they could spend more time picketing. Betty Eldridge asserted, "[Y]ou've got to have priorities. . . . Something had to go."[67]

Klemesrud was not the only self-identified feminist the Brookside women encountered. Throughout the strike, they met and had discussions with socialist feminists and other young women, like Kopple and her film crew, who may not have belonged to feminist organizations but were nonetheless influenced by women's liberation. By focusing heavily on the Brookside Women's Club in her film, Kopple helped to bring attention to working-class women's struggles for justice. She was also invested in the women's group during the months that she filmed, living with local women and supporting their efforts. As she learned from and was inspired by the women, she helped them to make connections between their own activism and other working-class women's movements. For instance, Kopple arranged for the 1954 film, *Salt of the Earth*—based on the 1951 zinc mine strikes in New Mexico—along with other labor films to be sent to Harlan County.[68] By the 1960s, *Salt of the Earth* had gained a following as student leftists, unionists, and socialist feminists adopted it and began showing it in union halls, community centers, and university forums.[69] The Brookside women's activism on the picket lines paralleled that of the women in *Salt of the Earth*, as it addressed not only class inequality and an abusive mining company, but also gender relations in the home and community. The club showed *Salt of the Earth* at several meetings.[70] While we do not have direct accounts of how the women responded to the film, it is likely that some of them related to the protagonist of *Salt of the Earth*, Esperanza Quintero, a passive housewife who develops into a leader, argues for women's equal participation in the male-led strike, and freely expresses the needs of working-class women.[71]

The Brookside Women's Club was also visited by some of the leading voices in the women's liberation movement, especially those who theorized a socialist feminist approach and sought to build coalitions with working-class communities. Barbara Winslow and Sheila Rowbotham visited Brookside for four days in 1973. They met with members of the club, interviewed some of the women, and gave them copies of Rowbotham's recently published book, *Women, Resistance and Revolution*, which documented women's involvement in modern revolutionary movements in Russia, China, and Latin America. As Winslow later recalled, the Brookside Women's Club inspired her and others to push the newly formed Coalition of Labor Union Women (CLUW) to open membership to working-class women who were not officially members of unions. Though these efforts were unsuccessful, they show how the campaigns of the Brookside women, and others like them, shaped debates within national feminist organizations. They also reveal the forgotten alternatives within the women's movement, when a critical mass of women fought for a women's movement that integrated a class analysis and a labor movement that adopted feminist politics.[72]

It is little surprise that the Brookside women's activism sparked interest among women calling for women's liberation. Even if they had not declared theirs as a feminist struggle, the symbolism of much of their activism was part of the zeitgeist. They organized a "women's club" to call attention to injustice; they practiced civil disobedience; and they challenged gender norms. Like women across the country, they demanded to be heard, and they entered into spaces often closed to them and acted in ways that some men found unbecoming. They did it all with a flourish.

Even in stories told years later, feminist tropes stand out. For instance, Minnie Lunsford was recruited to the strike when a girlfriend called and invited her to protest. Her initial response was, "Well, what must I wear?" Her friend said, "Wear your britches!" Lunsford then disclosed, "That's how come I got started wearing the pants, you know." She continued, "So the phones went to ringing and everybody got their pants on and went out there together."[73] Lunsford's pairing of the women's decision to join the strike to "wearing the pants" (older women in particular still wore housedresses as their standard garb) represents the ways that women, in a moment of class upheaval, saw fit to challenge a host of gender norms.

Gender and Race Politics in Brookside

In the summer of 1974, nearly a year into the strike, strikers and their female supporters insisted that they would not back down, even as the company tried new tactics. In the spring, two men from the company-supported union attempted to bribe UMWA organizers with up to $5000 each to give up the strike and urge men back to work. The miners, working with UMWA lawyers, documented the bribe and reported it to the National Labor Relations Board.[74] Although Governor Wendell Ford had, after a meeting with union representatives, dismissed state troopers from the picket lines and halted activity to assist strikebreakers into the workplace, company-supported men increased intimidation of union miners and families. In July and August, a company-hired security guard shot twice at a sixty-six-year-old pensioner who stood on the picket lines at the Highsplint mine (he survived); "gun thugs" went on a rampage one night and shot 150 rounds into union homes; somebody smashed the windows of a strike leader's truck and poured sugar in the gas tank; and early one morning, the ring leader of the company-hired security, Basil Collins, shot at the documentary filmmakers and called for his men to attack one of the only black people on the picket line, the activist Bill Worthington. In late August, a strikebreaker fatally shot striking miner Lawrence Jones after a skirmish. On August 29, 1974, hours after Jones's death, Eastover Mining Company finally signed the UMWA national wage agreement and recognized the collective bargaining rights of the Brookside miners.[75]

The local male leaders of the UMWA appreciated the women's support and realized the important roles they played in helping the men win a contract, often making statements like, "If it hadn't been for the women, we'd have lost this strike."[76] The union victory was bittersweet; Lawrence Jones left behind a young wife and baby. Many of the women had hoped to prevent such violence. Nonetheless, the Brookside women and supporters of the strike considered Jones a martyr, as his death spurred Eastover into a contract with the UMWA.[77]

After the strike was won and the camera crews left the scene, the Brookside Women's Club continued to meet and women began to participate in new causes, including those that were explicitly organized in support of gender equality. Bessie Cornett described the continued activism: "The lessons that were learned at Brookside weren't lost."[78] These "lessons" went beyond the labor struggle itself and encompassed the options available to women in the coalfields, their relationships to men, and their contribution to the burgeoning women's movement. In the months after the strike, some of them attended women's rights meetings where they spoke about economic injustice in women's lives. Others began to consider working in the mines and breaking down gender barriers in the coalfields. Some women negotiated new relationships with their husbands as they decided to go back to school or start jobs outside the household when the strike was over. At least five women returned to school, and two women started their own businesses. Others joined community and labor organizations, including the Black Lung Association, and the women who figured most prominently in Barbara Kopple's documentary film *Harlan County, USA*, which won an Oscar in 1976, went on speaking tours.[79]

Even as they entered new arenas, they could not avoid a hard truth: their activism, which called into question coalfield capitalism and exposed the patriarchal underpinnings of it, put them at grave risk and hinted at the fragility of working-class solidarity that did not integrate women's and racial equality. Bessie Lou Cornett, among others, faced the direst consequences of speaking out. Emboldened by her year of hard-nosed activism, she disclosed the intimate violence that she suffered in the wake of her participation in the strike and other social justice causes in Harlan County.

Cornett's problems began with her husband, who physically attacked her when she became involved in the strike. Gender violence was not new to Cornett. Her own mother, Lois Scott, had left her father because of his violent outburst and threats to kill her. Cornett's activism during the strike seemed to be the kindling that sparked her husband's rage. Cornett described her relationship: "My husband said, 'you can't go' [participate in the strike]. He even beat me or locked the doors. He said a woman's role was in the home, cooking and cleaning and so on. And there was a lot of jealousy. If you were exposed to a lot of other social activities, you might begin to broaden your interests a little outside of the home, and see that you had more potential."[80] Her husband's fear—that women would question other injustices in their lives if they joined the strike—rang true. Once she was involved, indeed, Bessie realized her potential as a social justice activist and carried her fight into new struggles.

During the strike, Cornett had helped to develop the left-leaning newspaper *Harlan Labor News*, "a weapon for the coalminers for defending and uniting the various efforts of the whole community around issues which affect all of us."[81] Divorced and fully committed to activism in the months after the strike, she continued to organize in eastern Kentucky as part of the Brookside Women's Club and to write for and distribute *Harlan Labor News*. That work carried her into interracial organizing against the "urban renewal" of Georgetown, a black neighborhood in Harlan that was being zoned out of existence.[82] Bessie used her platform at *Harlan Labor News* to garner attention to the crisis in Georgetown. She also helped to expose the reorganization of the Ku Klux Klan, which recruited members with ads in the Harlan County newspaper. After an African American student told her that the school home economics class was required to make outfits that looked like Klan regalia, Cornett published the outrageous news. She connected the Klan to antiunion activity and argued that it divided workers, making life worse for everyone.[83]

As Bessie's activism continued, her ex-husband sought new ways to punish her. He filed for full custody of their eight-year-old son, Stephen, citing Bessie as an unfit mother. He used Bessie's strike activities and other progressive organizing—including working in alliance with black people in Harlan, and writing for the *Harlan Labor News*—to make his case. The presiding judge corroborated his view and awarded him full custody of Stephen.[84] As the ruling of the judge indicates, gender violence was not contained to intimate partnerships, and it could not be separated from racism. In the eyes of her ex-husband and in the opinion of the law, Cornett's union activism in conjunction with her crossing the color line made her especially unfit to care for a child. In the months after the strike, Cornett was not alone in drawing the ire of men who opposed women's activism, and who drew upon time-tested taboos that forbade contact between black men and white women.[85]

The UMWA had long promoted an interracial union, and during the Brookside Strike, white women joined picket lines and attended union meetings that often included black miners.[86] The Ku Klux Klan also had a long history in the county, and African American communities carried collective memories of racial terror and lynching in the early twentieth century.[87] During the strike, racial epithets had been one of the weapons of the antiunion ranks. For antiunion men—widely believed to be working within the boundaries of the KKK—the union and its supporters threatened white male supremacy. During the upsurge of Klan activity in the 1970s, white, working-class women who straddled movements for labor rights, racial equality, and women's liberation posed a great threat to intertwined racial and gender hierarchies.

On July 14, 1975, police officers arrested Cornett and charged her with kidnapping a woman and her children. The woman had accepted Cornett's help in escaping her husband's abuse, but when her husband threatened her with further violence, she agreed to testify that she had been kidnapped. Bessie and her mother, Lois, identified the man as a Klan member and connected him to the resurgence of white supremacy in Harlan County.[88]

Three days after her arrest, the Louisiana Klan leader David Duke held a rally in Harlan County, one of a string of meetings in Kentucky as part of Duke's plan to reinvigorate the white supremacist group. He spoke at an event in Louisville to oppose school busing as a way to achieve integration, followed by rallies in eastern Kentucky and West Virginia, where he argued that "reverse racism" was one of the consequences of the civil rights movement. The Harlan County event drew about four hundred and fifty people, although the Klan had predicted three thousand attendees. Reports noted that the Klan met on the property of an antiunion coal operator. In his speech, Duke knit together the black freedom movement, the so-called communism of the labor movement, and women's activism, all of which led to immorality, he argued. Several white UMWA members went to David Duke's rally to observe and reported that most of those in attendance were known "scabs," painting the Klan as an organization that weakened the labor movement.[89]

A few days after the event, someone shot into and then set fire to the home of two sisters. The women, who were divorced, said they were accused of hosting "wild parties," and they believed that the Klan was responsible for the attack.[90] The Klan also targeted labor activist Sudie Crusenberry. Members burned a cross near her home and sent her hate mail, threatening to harm her family.[91]

In response to Bessie Cornett's arrest and the surge of Klan activity, UMWA members began petitioning the Kentucky governor to release her. After Lois Scott called the FBI, officials investigated the case and ruled that Cornett had been falsely charged, forcing her release. In the *Harlan Labor News* and during her speaking engagements after the release of *Harlan County, USA*,

Cornett continued to publicize the Klan's activities in Harlan County. She summarized the larger concerns in her community: "What the people at Brookside was fighting for was just a better way of life, a better way of living." Drawing parallels to the ongoing black freedom struggle, she continued, "But it still didn't mean there was full equality, and we still have to carry it forward. If you let down your guard and you don't keep up the fight or keep struggling, they can take away all the gains you got. And that's why it needs to be pointed out that the Ku Klux Klan is around to take away the things we won during the strike."[92]

Bessie Cornett ultimately could not tolerate the harassment, rumors, and gossip that she encountered in her community. The threats against her and others became too much to handle, so she left Harlan County, leaving her son, family, and the Brookside Women's Club behind to start a new life, first in West Virginia and then in California.[93] While many of Appalachia's women activists in this period were lauded as heroes by their sympathizers and fellow activists, Cornett's story was a stark reminder of the stakes of challenging the status quo and the losses incurred during hard-fought battles.

Cornett's story also captures the tenuous solidarity in white working-class communities, families, and households, especially as some women mobilized for greater autonomy or voiced militant political views. As some joined militant movements and subverted racial and gender norms, the possibility of paying a high price was ever present. Despite these stakes (perhaps because of them), by the mid-1970s, some white, working-class women came together to form an explicitly feminist group, the Appalachian Women's Rights Organization, and others voiced their own vision for the feminist revolution. Building on years of activism, they articulated a feminism that encompassed the issues at the heart of working-class communities, which included labor rights, environmental justice, support for caregivers, and a clear-eyed reckoning with an economy that benefitted some to the detriment of many.

7 "Nothing Worse than Being Poor and a Woman"

Feminism in the Mountain South

On March 9, 1975, the Appalachian Women's Rights Organization held a meeting to celebrate International Women's Day, as women around the globe marched for women's rights. Over seventy women and men gathered at a community center in Wheelwright, Kentucky, a once booming industrial town that had been fading since the 1950s. Some of the busiest and best-known female leaders in Appalachia shared their untrammeled vision of a feminist revolution.

Eula Hall, Sudie Crusenberry, and Bessie Smith Gayheart sat before the gathering, three middle-aged mothers who had participated in some of the most dramatic struggles in Appalachia since the 1930s. Leader of welfare rights and community health campaigns, Eula Hall opened the discussion by asserting the goals of the newly formed Appalachian Women's Rights Organization: "to protect women and to encourage them to get involved in their equal rights." She then emphasized what she saw as the most significant problems facing mountain women: managing a family on welfare, job discrimination, and domestic violence. These problems compounded to keep women poor and powerless. "I don't think that in Appalachia there's anything worse than being poor and being a woman," declared Hall. She closed her speech by calling for women "to fight back" against discrimination and to do so in solidarity: "It's much easier to combat a problem if you've got support."[1]

Representing the Brookside Women's Club, Sudie Crusenberry shared how women had rallied behind the UMWA organizing drive in Harlan County, Kentucky. "When we first started we had three members. Then we gathered a few more. We seen it rough, and we was treated rough, but we won victory. I believe in standing up for our rights together," she stated. Although the women's labor activism was often characterized as auxiliary to the men's strike, to show up on picket lines with men also meant going on strike in their own way—against the gender roles enforced by coalfield capitalism. Bessie Smith Gayheart summed up her experience as an activist who led a group of women, including Hall, during a sit-in at a strip-mining site. "I was born and raised in east Kentucky and I am going to stay; but to stay here you're going to have to fight like hell," she declared. She told the women in the crowd that they were as capable as men and that women could do anything "if we put our minds to it." Her phrase echoed the statements one might hear from middle-class women climbing the professional ladder or newly arrived in universities. Coming from Gayheart, however, the phrase took on new meaning: if they fought hard enough, women could bring a strip-mine operation to a halt and effectively protect communities and homes. Gayheart implied more than women's individual achievement; these were women fighting for their homes and livelihood.[2]

On the stage with local women, veteran activist Lyn Wells had traveled from Detroit, Michigan, to discuss the meaning of International Women's Day and to dispel myths about the women's liberation movement. Wells began participating in civil rights demonstrations in Washington, D.C., at age fourteen, and she had been a member of civil rights and student organizations as they unfolded in the 1960s—first SNCC and then Students for a Democratic Society (SDS) and Southern Student Organizing Committee (SSOC). By the time of the Wheelwright meeting, she was a member of the October League, a Marxist-Leninist faction that had broken away from SDS and sought to organize the U.S. working class. The League stated in its constitution, "Women's liberation is a component part of proletarian revolution, and the October League firmly upholds the revolutionary struggle for the full equality and the emancipation of women." It declared that for the "revolutionary struggle" to succeed, "the broad masses of toiling women" must be part of the "working class army."[3] Wells emphasized that women's rights included more than "the right to be mayor"; they included the right to decent jobs and child care as well. She argued that the women's movement was not about giving up "children and family in order to be free," but about giving women basic economic rights so that they could make better decisions for themselves and their families. Wells passed out International Women's Day/October League buttons, one of which Sudie Crusenberry placed in her scrapbook.[4]

The International Women's Day celebration in Wheelwright capitalized on the coalitional work that defined women's organizing in Appalachia, bringing together welfare rights, labor, women's liberation, and anti–strip-mining activists.[5] Speakers focused on social transformation that would improve life for poor and working-class families in the coalfields. At the same time, they sought to bring visibility to Appalachian women and to integrate their own ideas and experiences into the women's movement platform, which was not settled but in process.

Claiming their place within national and global women's movements, they defined for themselves the meaning of women's rights based on their years of activism. When the United Nations renewed the celebration of International Women's Day and declared 1975 to be International Women's Year, women across the country and world took the opportunity to proclaim their feminist desires and goals. In eastern Kentucky, the occasion offered a banner under which women activists could celebrate female leadership in community organizations, recognize the injustice women continued to face, rally for change, and continue the discussion of what fairness and equality looked like in their communities. As Jocelyn Olcott has written of the International Women's Year conference in Mexico City, its "proliferating diversity of women's concerns . . . under the umbrella of 'women's issues'" undermined "essentialist ideas about a universal female subject."[6] As Appalachian feminists proclaimed themselves a part of the women's movement, they also created and re-created the notion of "women's issues."

At the Wheelright meeting, women countered an exclusionary understanding of second-wave feminism—that it was about an ideology that started with the desires of professional, middle-class, or college-educated white women. As multiple historians have shown, that tidy and delimited narrative of the women's movement soon became the orthodox history of the movement, despite the hundreds, if not thousands, of moments like the Wheelwright meeting that displayed a grassroots feminism that grew from local antipoverty campaigns and responded to national feminist currents.[7] Feminists in Appalachia proclaimed the centrality of women activists in the previous decade of militant activism and asserted their own vision of a class-conscious feminism on the contested terrain of the 1970s women's movement.[8]

This chapter considers the emergence of an explicitly feminist, regional women's movement in the Mountain South and how it evolved, encountered, and responded to feminist policy making in the 1970s to the early 1980s. Not long after the celebration in Wheelwright, the Appalachian Women's Rights Organization presented a statement at a public meeting of the Kentucky Commission on Women, which represented white, middle-class feminism. Initially hostile to antipoverty efforts, the commission soon promoted the advancement of women through equality measures, focusing primarily on workplaces. The commission represented the movement's gradual shift toward accepting the terms of capitalism and breaking down barriers in workplaces, albeit in ways that rarely transformed them into spaces conducive to the complexities of women's lives. The encounter between the AWRO and the Kentucky Commission on Women would put on full display ideological tensions captured in Lyn Wells's statement about moving beyond the "right to be mayor," in other words, basic economic rights versus the narrower fight for access to traditionally male jobs. Working-class women in Appalachia found themselves in a tenuous position, to which they reacted with a combination of accommodation and resistance. Although many embraced new employment opportunities that opened up in the wake of feminist policy making, they continued to press the issues—rights to economic self-determination and caregiving—that had long defined their activist positions.[9]

Feminism, the War on Poverty, and the Kentucky Commission on Women

The Kentucky Commission on Women was among a host of state commissions established in the mid-1960s in response to the President's Commission on the Status of Women (PCSW) under the Kennedy administration in 1961, the culmination of the work of social justice feminists. A twenty-two-month undertaking, the PCSW's final report, *American Women*, sold thousands of copies and exposed barriers to women's full equality in the United States. It called for bold changes in workplace and governmental policy, as well as a revaluing of women's reproductive labor. As historian Dorothy Sue Cobble notes, the report was deemed conservative and outdated by the 1970s, but in fact its argument that "women's family and marketplace identities were equally valid" was a "bold and progressive formulation in 1963" when the report was published.[10]

The Women's Bureau of the Department of Labor sought to build on the federal commission and encouraged governors to establish state-level commissions that could implement social and political changes outlined in *American Women*.[11] But by the time the state commissions formed, feminist politics had begun to shift after the passage of the Civil Rights Act and the inclusion of "sex" as a protected category. Commission agendas differed by state, where governors appointed the commissions, but, by and large, the focus tended toward job programs, implementation of Title VII of the Civil Rights Act, and the passage of the Equal Rights Amendment (ERA), a constitutional amendment guaranteeing equality between the sexes. By 1966, most states had commissions on women, including Kentucky, although its activity ebbed and flowed for the first decade. Governor Louie B. Nunn resurrected the commission by executive order in 1968, and in 1970 the state legislature narrowly passed a bill making the commission an official state agency.[12]

The first appointees of the Kentucky Commission on Women centered the needs of white, middle-class women, departing from the PCSW's focus on working women. Affiliated with women's clubs and representing a who's who of prominent Kentucky families, the members offered a narrow feminist agenda at the first meeting. Their list of demands featured programs that promoted political and economic advancement of white middle-class and elite women and would support philanthropic programs to assist women they saw as less fortunate than themselves, primarily poor white women. Underpinning their vision was a sense that a culture of poverty was to blame for the high rates of poverty among women and, given the opportunity, their commission would help break that cycle through counseling and steering poor women to employment. Blind to the fact that women in Appalachian Kentucky had been organizing for years, the commissioners saw themselves as trailblazers for women's equality in the state.[13]

The first chairperson of the Kentucky Commission, Marie Caldwell Humphries, worked closely with Governor Nunn to establish it. Humphries grew up in Aberdeen, Mississippi, where she was the only female in her high school class of eleven. Although she was the valedictorian of her class, like many precocious young women of her generation who faced a world of limited options, she became a secretary, soon working in the War Department during World War II. After the war, she married a salesman, left the workforce, and moved around the South for her husband's work. She devoted her time to her husband and children but also managed to maintain an active role as a volunteer in the communities where she lived. By 1968, she and her family resided in Frankfort, Kentucky, the capital. Humphries would begin a new phase in her career, working for Governor Louie B. Nunn and leading statewide efforts to promote the advancement of some women.[14]

In the same year as her appointment to the commission, Nunn sent Humphries to the White House's "Women in the War on Poverty" conference. On the face of it, this was an odd choice given Humphries lack of involvement in antipoverty programs, but it was also in keeping with Nunn's relationship to the War on Poverty—he had promised to dismantle the major antipoverty programs in his state. At the conference, Humphries encountered feminists of the same generation and class as herself whose ideas about women's equality were forged in the labor and civil rights movements. Humphries, however, would interpret the conference as a confrontation with radicals.

The 1968 conference was the second held by the Women's Advisory Council on Poverty. The speakers responded to the events unfolding around them: the

Poor People's Campaign and the release of the Kerner Commission's report on civil disorders. The speakers included representatives from government offices like the OEO and the Department of Justice, Dorothy Height from the National Council of Negro Women, and Esther Peterson from the Department of Labor, among others. These civic leaders encouraged the women in attendance, all of whom were delegates from women's organizations or State Commissions on the Status of Women, to recognize the significance of new challenges and to take action.[15]

Sensing that some of their middle-class audience had mixed feelings about growing militancy and chafed at civil disorder, various speakers pleaded with delegates to find it within themselves to understand many black and poor Americans' frustrations with inequity and slow progress. On the topic of urban riots that had exploded in 1967, Esther Peterson declared, "The Kerner Committee and the report . . . should be like a branding iron on the conscience of every one of us." Another speaker representing the Civil Service Commission narrated the civil rights movement of the preceding ten years. She then turned to the present, urging the delegates to connect current demonstrations to the ongoing movement. She stated that the Poor People's Campaign was "an extension of the civil rights movement across the economic frontier." Dorothy Height led several sessions at the conference, including one on the meaning of the Kerner Report and another workshop called "proposals for action." The conference brought together the issues of the day: poverty, the state of the civil rights movement, urban unrest, women's advancement, and the implementation of antidiscrimination laws. And speakers called for delegates to build bridges, create spaces for dialogue, and develop action plans to cure the ills of society and build on the progress of the last decade.[16]

Marie Humphries perceived the event in a completely different light. Her evaluation of the conference revealed the racial anxieties that beset many Republicans in this period and that would also come to inform the Kentucky Commission's early platform. In her opinion, African American women and their radical white allies were forging a path of destruction. The conference, she argued, was more "about White Racism than Poverty itself." Racism had nothing to do with poverty, in her estimation. Using the politically charged terms of the period—"Black militant," "dirty, long-haired" hippies, and "sympathizers"—she described the participants of the conference and concluded that "negroes" had overtaken the War on Poverty. Humphries also played on old gender tropes. Embodying a fragile, southern white womanhood, she explained that she dared not speak up at the conference because she feared "bodily harm." She signaled an idea strongly held throughout the South that whites, in particular white women, were at risk in a world in which black people had access to power.[17]

Her conspiratorial report suggested that she attended the conference as an act of surveillance, likely heightened in the aftermath of the Louisville riots in the spring of 1968 (she submitted her report two months after tensions exploded in the city). The Kentucky Un-American Activities Committee was in the process of organizing, in part a response to the riots. She chided speakers for blaming "everything—riots, shooting, looting, what-have-you" on "White Racism."[18]

In direct defiance of the conference leaders' calls to build cross-class and interracial coalitions, Humphries reported on an African American woman, also a Kentucky native, in attendance. The woman had shared a story about being grateful for a federally funded health center in her community. Humphries convinced herself that the woman's primary concern in life was avoiding white people. Perceiving the woman's testimony as a threat of some kind, she asked for her name and address, which the woman gave her. Humphries included it in her report to Nunn. She assured the governor, "I gave her no information about myself."[19]

Humphries's evaluation concluded that the conference was a "stage set for threats, a feeling of national guilt." She was astonished that the federal government funded it. To her, the conference offered cover for radical activism, and Democrats were in cahoots. The conference was one more piece of evidence that "the Republicans MUST win this fall."[20] She positioned herself as part of Nixon's "silent majority," silenced by the rabble-rousers of the 1960s (even as her account ignored the overwhelmingly middle-class, professional makeup of the conference).

When Humphries returned to Kentucky, she took her seat as chairperson at the first meeting of the Kentucky Commission on Women. There, she made clear that she had in mind a different kind of women's organization than the feminist leaders of the PCSW and the leaders of the conference on Women in the War on Poverty. Her version of a women's rights organization reflected a commitment to preserving racial and class hierarchy.

Humphries's background as a "chief volunteer"[21] as well as her views on the War on Poverty—that it had been infiltrated by dangerous groups and was a threat to national security—informed her thinking about how the commission should operate, whom it should serve, and in what ways. In the only other documented meeting that year, the commission outlined its purpose: to "promote advancement of young women, the uneducated women" and, in a telling turn of phrase, to support "the unqualified women."[22] Once elite women—"qualified women"—rose in the political ranks, they could offer services to the "poor" and "uneducated." Their statement made clear their ideological leanings, characterizing poor people as a potential drain on taxpayers in the state and dismissing welfare programs that largely served women, seeing instead private enterprise and employment as the best options for women's advancement.[23]

Even under the leadership of a Republican woman, the commission faced a backlash. Governor Nunn, who initially supported the commission, backed away from it when Republican state legislators chafed at the idea of a state agency that promoted the advancement of women, however narrowly defined. Two of the only women officials in state politics, both Democrats, rallied for legislation to create a permanent commission on women, and while they succeeded, the agency acquired very little funding and thus did not establish programs until a few years later. Meanwhile, in the early 1970s, as previous chapters have illustrated, women activists in Appalachia continued to fight for robust rights of poor and working-class women in the region. For some, that activism led them to proclaim themselves a part of the women's rights movement.

Appalachian Feminism

"One woman alone can't do anything," Eula Hall declared at the inaugural meeting of the Appalachian Women's Rights Organization. The group had met for the first time at the Mud Creek Clinic in Floyd County, in February 1975. The regional magazine and media outlet for social movement news, *Mountain Life & Work*, documented thirty people in attendance, mostly women, including Eula Hall and Dr. Elinor Graham of the clinic, as well as several women who had traveled from surrounding areas. A few "interested men" attended as well, including Woodrow Rogers, the chairman of the Eastern Kentucky Welfare Rights Organization. Following a three-hour discussion, the group decided they needed a formal organization to promote women's rights in the region.[24]

To several of the supporters in attendance, a women's movement made complete sense given the history of women's activism in Appalachia. They reminded each other that women in the Mountain South had often been the strongest, most dependable fighters in times of crisis, and the women's rights meeting marked a moment to consider what women as a group needed to thrive. Woodrow Rogers reflected that women were "the most powerful" at "rallies, picketing, and everything else." During her eight years of community work, declared Sue Fields, a community organizer in southwest Virginia, "It was the women that got things done." For the past decade, Appalachian women had led numerous social justice efforts, from welfare rights campaigns and women's self-care meetings to civil disobedience actions to draw attention to poor conditions in the coalfields. The new organization would build on that energy but bring a new gender-consciousness to their analysis of power in the coalfields.[25]

The AWRO members identified two areas that they believed most important to organizing for women's rights: gender violence and economic hardship. Too many women simply did not have access to decent, well-paying jobs, and the employment most often available to them—so-called "unskilled" labor—paid too little to support a family. With the tightening of social welfare programs, many women in Appalachia saw few routes to economic stability. Those economic concerns entangled with gender violence in the home. As explained by Dr. Graham, the intersection between poverty, a failing economy, and domestic violence could lead to tragic outcomes. "The job situation in Appalachia is bad. Men get disabled young. Tension builds up at home. Beating begins on the wife and often children . . . the whole thing comes down on the women."[26]

The AWRO's steering committee set up four working groups: workplace organizing, day care, driver's education, and shelter. All of the areas of interest pointed to the ways that women often felt isolated and without options when they lived in unstable or violent households. Without access to day care or good-paying jobs, they had few resources when facing life with an abusive, sick, or absent partner. That many women could not drive aggravated feelings of helplessness.

Eula Hall's imprint was hard to miss here. Her pitch for a women's organization reflected her own experience of domestic violence, personally and in her work with female patients. "Day after day we [the clinic staff] see the need for a women's group to counter the things we live with: physical abuse from men; husbands objecting when women try to do anything like take a job or work in a local organization. When a woman tried to do anything, she must fight her husband to do it. If we have a group women won't be so scared to try."[27] By 1975, Hall had survived physical and emotional abuse by her husband McKinley for over thirty years. His violent attacks had begun soon after they married and had escalated over the years as she became a more assertive and committed activist. Only when she had enough money to pay rent and feed her kids did she finally leave him in 1976. He continued to harass her when he saw her, so she bought herself a gun and "never went back for no more." In 1977, she was finally able to divorce McKinley.[28]

Class-conscious, antipoverty feminism buttressed numerous women's organizations in the 1970s: from community organizations in Atlanta, New

York, and Las Vegas, to new lobbying organizations in Washington, D.C., like the National Council on Women, Work, and Welfare.[29] The Appalachian Women's Rights Organization was a part of a surge of welfare rights activists and their allies who sought to influence emerging feminist policies, especially as related to welfare, work programs, and economic security. Armed with their own stories of resistance and a history of activism that linked women's liberation to economic security, AWRO members imagined what feminist revolution would look like in their lives. A few days after the AWRO International Women's Day celebration, members presented demands to the Kentucky Commission on Women, where they hoped to convince commission members, who saw themselves as the vanguard of the women's movement, to expand their understanding of women's rights.

By 1975, the Kentucky Commission on Women had reorganized, and its Democratic leadership showed more interest in interacting with women across the state, including poor and working-class women. Democratic Governor Wendell Ford appointed Marie Abrams, his former administrative assistant, to chairperson of the commission in 1973. She oversaw twelve public meetings when commission members traveled the state in order to compile information about sex discrimination in a series of categories. Although the commission was no longer outright hostile to the concerns of poor women, it continued to reflect a middle-class ideology, focusing on credit, employment, salaries, real estate, day care, and the campaign to pass the ERA. The commission invited women to speak briefly on these topics, and the hearings would be included in an annual report, with recommendations to the governor's office.[30]

On a wintry evening in March 1975, commission members traveled to Hazard, Kentucky, on a charter plane. Local women activists from across eastern Kentucky navigated difficult road conditions in the dark, as they made their way to the courthouse in Hazard. There they met the commissioners, and they pressed them on the meaning of equality for poor and working-class women.

Dr. Elinor Graham read a statement prepared by the AWRO. Although she was not from Appalachia, nor was she working-class, she had aligned with antipoverty feminism. The statement pushed the commissioners to "take up the genuine problems of the vast majority of the women in this area and to bring these problems to the attention of the public and government officials." It continued, "These are problems of finding jobs, getting decent pay and work conditions, trying to feed families with constant inflation of food prices, increasing unemployment for them and their husbands, having to fight for state and federal social service benefits and food programs that should be easily available and now may be cut back, and trying to hold their families together economically and morally in a time of general economic crisis." The AWRO representatives pressed the commission to use its platform to work toward solutions to the economic crises they faced and to expand services that benefited women and families, including strong welfare and jobs programs. The appeal made one of the commissioners "choke up" and declare that it was "an absolutely stunning statement." However, at least some women left the meeting skeptical that the Commission on Women had the ability to bring about significant change in the mountains.[31]

Even as they found some of the testimonies emotionally appealing, commission members failed to take seriously the policy implications of the group's statement. For instance, even as Appalachian feminists urged the commission *not* to create a false binary between work and welfare, Chairperson Abrams responded by asking about Manpower programs. Created under the Nunn administration before becoming federal policy, these policy initiatives required that welfare recipients enroll in work programs, with the goal of permanent employment and a decrease in the welfare rolls. A discussion followed, during which Appalachian women explained the problem with welfare-to-work programs in a time of economic crisis. One woman stated, "we can't demand jobs for women and not jobs for everyone."[32]

The commission's vision of women's advancement by individual uplift made little sense in the single-industry coalfields and in a period of mechanization and deindustrialization. Local women also discussed the conundrum of caring for disabled men but also needing to become the family provider when men could no longer work. Their feminism was bound to structural issues that the commission failed to perceive in their narrow definition of women's advancement.

The commission's plan of action simply did not reflect the concerns of eastern Kentucky women who filed into the courthouse that evening. Credit and equal salaries were the "concerns of professional women," the AWRO noted.[33] Few women in Appalachia could even find opportunities for well-paid employment. Not only were they not considered for industry jobs, the highest paying jobs in the region, they knew the risks that one encountered when employed in the mines. Still, they were open to traditionally male work if it was available, but even that option disrupted gender norms of some middle-class women who could not imagine doing hard labor. Sally Maggard of the Council of the Southern Mountains reported, "When women brought up problems in getting jobs in heavy industry, the Commission members were surprised. . . . [They] had not expected women want these jobs." The AWRO summed up the meeting: the Commission could not "offer many concrete suggestions to the problems presented to them, the problems of the majority of the women in the area who are in the working class or trying to support their families on a fixed income."[34]

The Kentucky Commission on Women of the 1970s proved more invested in women's equality than the Commission of the late 1960s, yet its set of policy concerns defined equality in ways that too often gave short shrift to the problems facing working-class and poor women, a pattern in liberal feminist organizations. For instance, some of the debates about the relationship between work and welfare, and more generally what it meant for a woman to live a fulfilling life, had arisen in organizations such as the National Organization for Women (NOW), which had built coalitions with welfare rights activists and poor mothers. Yet tensions often came to define the relationship, most notably after the defeat of the Family Assistance Plan by the GOP. In the aftermath, liberal feminists argued against a male breadwinner model that circumscribed women's economic independence, something that class-conscious feminists supported, but the liberal coalition practiced "benign neglect" when it came to supporting generous public assistance for poor mothers, as AFDC became increasingly stigmatized.[35] As historian Marisa Chappell shows, by the late 1970s "the diffusion of liberal feminist ideology, liberal demands for full employment, and a political climate increasingly hostile to welfare—along with the continuing flood of mothers into the labor market—prompted a shift in emphasis. Now, employment took center stage."[36] Like liberal feminist organizations more generally, the commission promoted equal employment as the surest way to help lift women out of poverty, even as many women continued to point out the gaps in that formula.

The AWRO's encounter with the commission is important for what it reveals about the lost promises of the feminist movement, but also how feminist ideas from previous decades persisted into the 1970s, as well as how women sought to negotiate competing feminist ideologies. Appalachian feminists took a holistic view, arguing for structural changes that would manifest in support of working-class communities. No single approach could solve their problems. They wanted access to well-paying, union jobs, but they also called for robust state support for those who cared for children and other dependent family members.

In this way, they looked more like the "social justice feminists" who were active between the 1930s and 1960s than they did second-wave feminists. As stated by Mary Anderson, appointed the first director of the Women's Bureau in the 1920s, a feminism that focused on "doctrinaire equality" without "social justice" would fail to improve the majority of working women's lives. Anderson and others like her were opposed to "equal rights feminism," which focused on equality between women and men but failed to address the ways that race and class also structured women's lives.[37] Their conceptions of feminism promoted an expansive social safety net, a robust labor movement, and the valuing of women's labor in the market *and* the home. Moreover, like the social justice feminists before them, feminists in Appalachia built on the ideological frameworks of antipoverty, labor, and civil rights movements.

The commission offered Appalachian feminists a narrow agenda focused primarily on employment. It aimed to remove barriers standing in the way of individual women's advancement, whereas the AWRO called for structural change and demanded that feminists grapple with the intersections of gender and class. As legal challenges wended their way through the courts and feminist policy organizations solidified their platforms, the former won out. In the following years, the commission continued to feature prominently in its newsletters information about how women could apply for credit, claim property rights, access higher education, and utilize affirmative action. By the late 1970s, it put its resources toward lobbying for domestic violence legislation and providing support networks for victims of rape and domestic violence. While women in Appalachia certainly took advantage of many of these policy changes, their broader vision of a justice that dealt with the distribution of economic power did not gain a hearing. Without a broad agenda, the Commission on Women and the liberal feminism it represented held limited possibilities for working-class women.[38]

The AWRO and feminists in Appalachia ultimately turned their attention to the one area of feminist policy where they might make economic gains: access to higher paying jobs in male-dominated industry. They began mobilizing for an end to employment discrimination, especially in the coalmines. Over the next several years, they realized success in legal challenges and in breaking down barriers in workplaces. In making this shift they muted their previous indictments of the mining industry, as well as their commitments to a guaranteed income and rights for caregivers. A woman donning coalminer's garb became the new, iconic image of the Appalachian feminist.

From Welfare Rights to Workplace Rights

Two cross-cutting developments in the mid-1970s shaped the future of feminism in the Mountain South. On one hand, the antipoverty efforts that had expanded social welfare programs and energized a welfare rights movement gained little to no support from the women who led policy efforts at the state level and faced a political backlash nationally. On the other hand, feminist organizations such as NOW forged new paths for women as they fought legal battles to open traditionally male workplaces and to end sex discrimination. Following the passage of Title VII of the Civil Rights Act (1964) and other antidiscrimination laws, feminist organizations arose to fight court battles on behalf of women who wanted access to jobs in the nontraditional employment sectors. Riding that wave, new organizations emerged in Appalachia to fight for women's employment in well-paying jobs, and for some time they were successful. This strengthening strand of feminist mobilization—jobs as a way to lift women out of poverty—became dominant, and campaigns that put caregivers at center faded.[39]

Like many professional women, Appalachian feminists began to use affirmative action to bring gender equality to the workplace and to institute gender-neutral practices in hiring. The women who applied for masculine work were a part of a widespread movement of women across the country that used Title VII to challenge sex discrimination in the workplace. Women in pink-collar jobs, especially clerical work (one of the most sex-segregated types of work), demanded equal pay for work of equal value. Others questioned the logic that some jobs were naturally masculine while others were feminine. Propelled by the momentum of the women's movement, they applied for jobs as steel workers, firefighters, construction workers, and miners. These were not quiet gestures. Many of the women who applied for these jobs—and who often were quickly rejected by the companies—took their stories to the media, built coalitions with women supporters, sought lawyers to represent their cases, and eventually made progress.[40]

On the heels of the Brookside Strike in Harlan County, where women were among the most militant protesters, a handful of women applied for jobs at unionized mines, among the first to do so in the region. Several factors contributed to the small but highly significant wave of women who applied for jobs in the mines in Kentucky in the mid-1970s: concerted efforts on the national stage, most notably by the National Organization for Women, to interpret new sex equality laws; the commitment of the Women's Bureau's of the Department of Labor to help women transition into traditionally male workplaces; and, most important for mining women, the formation of region- and state-level organizations that applied new civil rights and antidiscrimination laws in local and regional contexts. But perhaps most significant, women at the grassroots were poised to take advantage of new laws.

Regionally, the Kentucky Human Rights Commission (KHRC) was instrumental in aiding women's employment activism. Conceived by a black newspaper publisher from Louisville, Frank Stanley Sr., the commission was sanctioned by Governor Bert Combs in 1960 to desegregate public accommodations and promote fair housing, setting Kentucky apart from other southern states that led assaults on desegregation efforts. By the early 1970s, the biracial commission worked toward implementation of Title VII under the leadership of the white civil rights lawyer Galen Martin.[41] The Human Rights Commission emerged as a response to racial discrimination but came to benefit white women as well.

The Kentucky Human Rights Commission led the charge to eliminate sex discrimination in Kentucky workplaces. In 1974, the commission oversaw the addition of a clause to the Kentucky Civil Rights Act (1966) that prohibited sex discrimination in credit, insurance, and public accommodations. A year later the Kentucky Commission on Women effectively lobbied to replace gendered phrases in Kentucky statutes with gender-neutral language.[42] The Human Rights Commission began accepting sex discrimination cases, investigating companies charged with it, and negotiating with companies on behalf of women. Several of the women who challenged sex discrimination in hiring at coalmines contacted the commission to file complaints, leading to negotiations and public hearings.[43]

By the mid-1970s, Kentucky women spread word of antidiscrimination suits through informal and organizational networks, prompting many to test employers in their own communities. The Appalachian Women's Rights Organization stood at the intersection of these early efforts and helped to promote the idea of women coalminers in public hearings and meetings where they called for increased job opportunities for women. In their newsletter, they recruited women, stating "we would like to encourage and support any woman interested in applying for a job in the mines," and pointed especially to newly built mine complexes that had refused to take applications from women.[44] They were witnessing a boom in the coalfields, as the oil crisis of 1974 fueled a rise in production and hiring in coalmines, and women wanted equal access to new jobs.

In September 1975, the Kentucky Human Rights Commission held a series of public hearings on sex discrimination in the mines. Mountain feminists were on hand with other progressive groups to pass out leaflets and inform attendees about workplace discrimination against women and minorities. Earlier in the year, four women who had been backed by the Appalachian Women's Rights Organization had filed complaints with the Kentucky Human Rights Commission. Three white women—Melba Strong (one of the Brookside Strike picketers as well as daughter of Lois Scott and sister of Bessie Lou Cornett), Cindy Williams, and Deborah Hall—and one black woman, Joetta Ann Gist, applied for positions at Harlan County mines.[45]

Challenging the gender division of labor proved a powerful demonstration of feminism. With the exception of wartime work and some family-owned operations, industrial mining had historically been closed to women in the United States. Coal companies routinely turned women away from underground production jobs, and women also had a difficult time securing positions as secretaries and clerks.[46] Moreover, the industry adhered strictly to the sexual division of labor: while men performed public work for wages, women were in charge of the reproductive labor of caring for children, the elderly, and people with disabilities. As women sought jobs in the mines, they encountered and challenged "age old superstitions about women in the mines bringing 'bad luck'" and coal companies' insistence that "women did not want to work in the mines."[47]

About a year after the group of Harlan County women challenged hiring practices in coalmines, the Kentucky Human Rights Commission put in place a template for making broader changes in the mining industry. The commission reported that settlements with two coal companies in 1976 were "expected to have far-reaching effects on opening of mining jobs to women in the state's coal industry." One company agreed to hire one woman for every three men until the number of females reached 20 percent of the nonclerical workforce. Another, International Harvester's Wisconsin Steel Coal Mine in Benham, Kentucky, paid back wages to Cindy Williams, who had been a guest speaker at an AWRO meeting a year earlier.[48] She and another woman had applied at three different mines, saying that they wanted "to find decent-paying jobs with benefits." They had both been waitresses, working six to seven days a week for ninety cents an hour.[49] Williams's two-year struggle led to a conciliation that included the granting of seniority based on the date that she applied for a job and an invitation for twenty-seven women who had applied for positions at the mine to renew their applications with the company.

The Human Rights Commission also made headway in the case against U.S. Steel, which resulted from complaints by Melba Strong and Joetta Ann Gist. Gist's case also brought to light the overlapping forms of discrimination black women faced when they applied for traditionally male employment in which the majority of underground workers were male and the clerical workers were white men and women. Gist charged that the U.S. Steel Company in Harlan County denied her a clerical position due to her race and rejected her application for underground work because of her sex. The commission ordered the company to pay Gist back wages from the date she had applied to work as a teletype operator (January 1975) until she was eventually hired in September. They also issued an order requiring the company "to implement an affirmative action plan for increased employment of women in mining jobs."[50] U.S. Steel appealed the implementation plan that called for one woman to be hired for every four men in production positions, and for one African

American to be hired for every two white people hired for clerical positions, but the Harlan Circuit Court upheld the decision in 1981. The series of cases in the mid-1970s set the stage for the first class action lawsuit filed by women against a mining company in Kentucky.[51]

The handful of women who applied for mining jobs in 1975 were among the first in the mountains to use Title VII. Their early efforts were a part of an upsurge of such challenges. Between 1975 and 1985, the Kentucky Human Rights Commission facilitated conciliation efforts for complaints brought by thirty-four women against eleven different companies. Six major coal companies in Kentucky agreed to affirmative action plans and, by 1984, Kentucky companies had hired 791 women miners, compared to zero in 1973.[52]

By the mid-1970s, several regional, women-centered organizations took up the question of women's employment in blue-collar, traditionally male work. The leaders of these organizations rejected the family wage model—that men were breadwinners and women dependents. Among them was Lesley Lilly, a former VISTA worker, who became a leader in the movement for women's transition into male-dominated industrial work. She argued that, despite massive efforts to defeat poverty, women in Appalachia remained "among the poorest, most underemployed women in the country." The problem, as Lilly saw it, was that development policies in Appalachia had continued to focus on men as the breadwinners and "failed miserably to address the needs of women in Appalachia, that like women nationwide, have become an integral part of bringing home the bacon." Despite their important role in providing household income, working-class women were confined to segregated, female-dominated jobs that paid low wages. Lilly argued for policies that addressed "job equity and economic opportunity" for working-class and rural women.[53] Lilly became the director of the Southeast Women's Employment Coalition (SWEC), which sought to raise women's economic status and to expand employment opportunities for women by training them in nontraditional work. Other local and regional organizations picked up similar mantles of nontraditional job advocacy, including the Coal Employment Project (CEP), an organization that promoted women's employment in the coal industry.

The Coal Employment Project (CEP) formed in 1977 after staff members at a Tennessee legal aid organization realized that females were not allowed to enter mines for tours, much less work in them, and they soon contacted Betty Jean Hall. A lawyer from eastern Kentucky who worked for the Appalachian Regional Commission in the 1960s as well as public interest firms tied to the War on Poverty, Hall sought to find out if women wanted jobs in the mines and discovered more interest than she had expected. Under her leadership and with the networking of coalmining women, the CEP boldly tackled sexism in the coal industry, in which nearly 100 percent of the workers were men.

Hall initially worked with the Kentucky Commission on Human Rights to identify women who had been turned away from the Peabody Coal Company, which had federal contracts, in hopes of gaining momentum at the federal level. Fifteen women had filed complaints against Peabody with the commission, prompting Hall and the CEP to file suit with the U.S. Labor Department of Federal Contract Compliance. An office created by the Carter Administration, its purpose was to force companies with federal contracts to follow new antidiscrimination regulations. The company refused to admit to discrimination, but it agreed to pay $500,000 in settlements and implemented new hiring practices: one woman for every three inexperienced men. Officials also agreed to recruit women from a list of five hundred who had applied for jobs but had been passed over for male workers.[54]

The CEP began as a legal project to help women gain access to the coal industry. It recruited women with an effective media campaign and, after a year of its founding, had filed, according to Betty Jean Hall, "a major lawsuit against 153 companies" and did so "with great fanfare in the national press." Gaining access to employment was only the first hurdle, however. Once in the mines, women faced a new set of challenges, from questions about safety and equipment to sexual harassment. The CEP fostered what it called "Support Teams" where women miners could share information, offer advice, and develop a group identity. It also published a monthly newsletter, with articles by staff and coalmining women, in which they distributed information, offered advice, and celebrated success stories. Finally, it began an annual conference that brought together women miners. While the CEP's earliest campaigns took place in Appalachia, it soon expanded nationally, supporting women in all mining industries.[55]

The women who went into the mines fit more squarely in popular conceptions of the women's movement than the activists who had led antipoverty movements. Women miners often described themselves as outliers and rebels. Not surprisingly, they became icons for their courage to break down gender barriers. As Brenda Brock described, "It takes a certain breed of women to go underground. I think we're women who aren't satisfied with the role we've been put in all our lives. We're bored with it."[56] The feminist publication *Ms. Magazine* wrote cover stories on mining women and published images of women donning hardhats and coveralls. The CEP coordinated with NOW and the Women's Bureau, and it supported the ERA and sent a delegation to the 1978 March for the Equal Rights Amendment in Washington, D.C.[57]

Yet women miners rarely described their employment activism as explicitly a feminist drive to end gender distinction in the workplace. Rather, they explained their practical reasons for taking on coalmining, which echoed the structural, economic concerns of the AWRO: it proved the best single job in the region for a woman to support a family. Sandra Bailey Barber of Kentucky had worked as a waitress, as a school bus driver, in a shoe factory, and in a lunchroom, but those jobs didn't "pay anything at all." Barber had wanted to get a divorce and her new job in the mines "made it possible" by providing financial freedom. Barbara Angle, also of Kentucky, continued to work in the mines even when she was pregnant because she could not risk losing the job. She was single and, in order to receive welfare, she had to "name the father" or claim she had been gang-raped and did not know the paternity. Even if willing to identify the father, she would get only "sixty-some dollars a month." She preferred her financial independence to other options. In charting out their reasons for entering the mines, women argued for the right to well-paying jobs that would allow them autonomy.[58] The CEP drove home the point that access to industrial work would offer women economic security: in a 1978 report, the organization claimed that "the most effective means of eliminating poverty among Appalachian women is to assure they have equal access to jobs in the coal industry."[59]

That the CEP built on the foundations of women's antipoverty and labor activism of the past decade became clear when it linked itself to the Brookside Strike and UMWA unionization drive in Harlan County. Between 1978 and 1980, the Women's Bureau of the Labor Department partnered with CEP on developing a training program for potential women miners. At the initial program, along with basic guidance on tools, labor rights, safety instruction, and physical conditioning, the organizers showed the film *Harlan County, USA*, followed by a panel of women who were its veritable stars. The Brookside women and miners united around a desire to improve their economic situations and to create more democratic and fair workplaces.[60]

Nevertheless, the legal campaigns for women's employment in blue-collar jobs proved different in tone and argument than those of the women antipoverty warriors of the previous decade. Those women had centered the caregiving labor central to so many American women's lives. The culminating forces of a welfare backlash, state divestment, the rise of the women's movement, and the success of Title VII and the various organizations that took up its mandate led to new efforts to solve poverty by expanding women's paid employment. This new approach accepted the liberal idea—one that women activists challenged throughout the 1960s and early 1970s—that jobs programs offered the best solution to the problem of economic instability. In

Figure 10. Maxine Mitchell, UMWA miner, Island Creek #2, Vansant, Virginia, 1976. Courtesy of www.earldotter.com ©.

the new schema, feminists accepted the archetype of worker as breadwinner, but now workers would not be distinguished by sex.

Women Miners and Family Leave Policies

It is little surprise that Appalachian feminists chose to focus their efforts on employment; they had perfected the art of taking advantage of the best opportunities before them. Even as they accepted the citizen-as-worker mantra, women who entered formerly all-male workplaces necessarily changed those spaces. They exposed sexual harassment, demanded access to good-paying jobs, and subverted long-held socialization patterns based on gender. Although their roles as caregivers in society were muted, they had little choice but to force discussions about reproductive labor and worker health and safety within their workplaces and in American society writ large.

The Coal Employment Project's central goal was to gain access to coal-mining jobs, but once women were in the jobs, they faced a range of problems related to the fact that social reproduction continued to fall to them. They lacked child care in their communities; they had concerns over occupational health (especially for pregnant women); and they needed family leave policies. CEP soon began fielding studies based on the problems that women brought to attention at conferences and in surveys and letters to the organization.

Between 1973 and the early 1980s, the coal industry went from having no women miners to having women as 2 percent of the workforce.[61] The majority of women miners held positions as general inside laborers, also known as "brute work" because it entailed hard labor but less skill relative to other jobs. In her study of coalmining women in West Virginia, Suzanne E. Tallichet describes the general inside laborer as doing the most "physically demanding manual jobs" in the mines yet garnering the least respect because it was perceived as low skill. Characterized by flexibility and low prestige, the job consisted of a range of tasks from hanging ventilation curtains and laying track to setting timbers and assembling heavy equipment. Women described how their positions as general inside laborers often mirrored those at home; male workers told them what to do, and they picked up after them or took care of tasks that nobody else wanted to do, like collecting the refuse left behind by other workers. Women often found it difficult to gain promotions because of a lack of training and seniority, as well as a sense among their superiors that they were not capable of operating machinery. By the early 1980s, they began pressing for more access to training that would lead to promotions for women.[62]

Along with gender issues within the workplace, which have been the primary focus of studies of women miners, these workers also continued to take responsibility for the aboveground labor of caring for families, an issue that women brought to the fore as a labor issue. Women miners organized effectively through the Coal Employment Project and within the UMWA (they comprised less than 2 percent of membership) to make caregiving a labor issue. The CEP hired community organizer, June Rostan, as health and safety coordinator, and she began a pregnancy study with women miners. Rostan's work was part of a broader conversation about the rights of pregnant women in the workplace, with the passage of the Pregnancy Discrimination

Act (1978), which prohibited discrimination of pregnant women as long as they could continue their work. Like female industrial workers in other places, women miners argued that the risks that pregnant women faced were not dissimilar to those that all coalminers faced in a dangerous industry and used their positions to broach topics about occupational safety and health in the coal industry. In fact, several women miners would become leaders in their unions and workplaces in demanding safer workplaces for all.[63]

Coalmining women also began to argue for family leave policies almost as soon as they had numbers in the mines. At the second National Conference of Women Miners in 1979, attendees initially adopted a resolution on maternity leave before revising to include parental leave. A group of women leaders then began strategizing about how to convince the UMWA to adopt a parental leave policy, focusing on the upcoming 1984 contract with the Bituminous Coal Operators Association (BCOA). June Rostan recalled that they chose to broaden the policy to parental leave "because they realized that they were such a minority in the union that they'd never get that just for themselves. Then they also said, you know, 'There are men who need off when their wives have babies.' And they also knew that it would be easier to get it passed if it was a demand that they made on behalf of themselves *and* their union brothers."[64] As working-class women, they saw the necessity of collective efforts on behalf of working people that were not always gender distinctive, but, notably, they generalized from the experiences of women.

From the start, working-class women saw the need for cross-sex alliances in building support for women's rights, and they conjoined women's rights to worker rights. They worked within their districts to identify at least one male worker who had a story of taking time off work to support a child or family member. For instance, they identified one man who took leave-of-absence because his son had leukemia, and he had to drive him to a far-away hospital for treatments. The man's employer worked with him, but, without a policy in place, he technically could have been fired. Women miners also convinced UMWA President Cecil Roberts to support a parental leave policy. He stated his support: "Reproduction is a necessary and crucial activity. Employers should be forced to recognize this point."[65]

The organizers for parental leave met with partial success. At the UMWA convention in 1983, miners voted for the UMWA to adopt a parental leave policy as a contract demand in negotiations with the BCOA. They called for a six-month leave policy for mothers or fathers with a child or sick dependent. During leave the worker would continue to receive health care benefits, and her seniority would be intact when she returned to work. While the UMWA ran into barriers in negotiations—the BCOA cited high costs of a parental leave policy—the negotiations led to a study on parental leave. The CEP also joined the chorus of women's groups who put pressure on Congress to adopt a national parental leave policy. CEP believed that "if the issue could be firmly brought up the ladder through the collective bargaining arena in the meantime, the odds would be greatly increased for ultimately getting strong legislation." Numerous other unionists joined them in those efforts.[66]

The tide turned on robust family leave policies as the battle for paternity leave stretched over a decade, into the 1990s. Rather than fighting for a policy that affirmed the positions of caregivers and acknowledged their difficulties in navigating the American workplace, family leave advocates, facing the business community and politicians unsympathetic to the needs of women workers, ultimately sought a much narrower policy. The Family and Medical Leave Act (FMLA) of 1993 paled in comparison to the policy that mining and many other working women had envisioned. Rather than six months of leave, qualifying workers would be allowed twelve weeks of unpaid leave per year in the case of personal illness or to care for a sick family member or newborn child.[67]

Women miners encountered what historian Katherine Turk argues was an ever-narrowing understanding of sex equality law between the 1970s and 1990s, as workers and feminists fought for sex equality within the workplace. A broad understanding of sex equality that took into account the complexity of women's and men's lives was replaced with "unmediated opportunity as the centerpiece of the women's workplace rights agenda." Under the law, workers would enjoy "strong protections against sexist workplace culture" but face a workplace where their reproductive lives were nearly unspoken and invisible.[68] As Turk argues, "Rather than reasoning from the needs of the most vulnerable workers by extending protection to men, as some advocates initially suggested, the archetypal worker in the age of sex equality was the breadwinning male whose main objective was unfettered job access."[69]

Women miners' struggle to remake workplaces showed that they questioned the dominant vision of family and work, which continued to ignore or undermine caregiving labor that usually fell to women. With the strength of the union behind them and an organizing base in the CEP and women miners' conferences, they argued for policies that supported workers as dynamic members of their communities, and they challenged the sexual division of labor that structured their lives. Yet they faced a political establishment and legal system that continued to disavow the necessary work of caregiving and instead created a framework of nondistinction when it came to sex. That allowed for women's entrance into new workplaces, yet failed to alter assumptions about the warp and woof of American society.

As they fought for parental leave well into the 1980s, women miners linked their entrance into new workplaces to the unfinished battle for caregiver rights. They argued, as one organizer wrote, for "an opening to redefine the relation of family and work in a changing workforce, exposing the hollow 'family' rhetoric of the Reagan era and its contempt for working women and the real problems of the American family."[70] Those "real" problems stemmed from the fact that the reproductive and caregiving seams that held communities together were still rendered invisible in the imaginations of policy makers and power brokers. In the early 1990s, the idea of *who* could be a worker had transformed more than the idea of what makes a worker, despite the best efforts of blue-collar women.

Antipoverty and welfare rights activists had demanded that caregiving be part of the vision of American democracy and that it was linked to solving poverty, to environmental battles, to expanding democratic participation in communities, to labor struggles, and to women's rights. Appalachian feminists in the late 1970s backed away—or more aptly were pushed away—from a narrative that centered on caregivers, seeing the path to employment emerge as their best option. Like many women, they soon faced the hard truth that American workplaces were not designed to accommodate them in their roles as caregivers and joined new battles to change workplace environments and, more significantly, Americans' relationship to work.

• • •

The women's movement opened up new vistas where Appalachian activists could continue to extend their arguments for democracy and fairness in coal country. Bringing light to issues that deeply affected women had been a long-standing practice. In the 1960s and '70s, antipoverty activist Edith Easterling broadened the vision of the local war on poverty to include women's interests; Appalachian welfare rights activists demonstrated that welfare was a women's and working-class issue; Eula Hall fought for access to health care; and the Brookside women showed how women's caregiving and the labor strike were interrelated. Appalachian activists' *embrace* of "women's rights" in the 1970s, however, marked a new phase in their activism.

Feminists in Appalachia were white and working-class or middle-class allies of the working class. For the most part, African American women in the mountains were not present in these regional feminist spaces, perhaps due to the risks associated or because they did not feel welcome. With the exception of working women's push into traditionally male work in the region—campaigns that included black and white women—organizing around women's rights in Appalachia did not lead to moments of interracial cooperation the way that antipoverty and welfare rights organizing had: the Appalachian women's movement was whiter than any of the campaigns of the past decade, reflecting the dominance of white liberal women in feminist organizations and the diminishing opportunities for alliance-building.

Yet, white Appalachian feminists did not fit easily into liberal feminism's agenda. Their platform clashed with that promoted by the women who came to lead sex equality efforts statewide and nationwide, many of whom did not see or understand the centrality of class inequality in many women's lives. Turning back to the history shows how mountain feminists did not see themselves in an irresolvable conflict with liberal feminists, however, but as participants who could fashion the goals of the movement.[71] They sought to convince liberal feminists that working within existing structures of capitalism without fighting for dramatic restructuring of the economy and a strong defense of the social safety net was tantamount to ignoring the thousands of women like them who lived in communities in economic crisis.

The short-lived Appalachian Women's Rights Organization and the decade of grassroots activism that it represented called for multifaceted responses to women's poverty and class inequality broadly. This mode of feminist activism (and the many others like it that emerged across the country) complicate the familiar refrain in labor history that identity politics, notably feminism, "eclipsed" class politics in the 1970s. Several scholars have argued that the turn away from class solidarity—the core of New Deal liberalism—combined with other factors to weaken the labor movement.[72] This argument assumes a sharp divide between the old order in which economic justice was central and an era of fragmentation during which feminists and minority groups fought symbols of oppression rather than economic structures that led to stratification. That resultant narrative perilously ignores the full swath of feminist alternatives that circulated in the 1970s, as when CEP, working-class feminists, and their allies sought to build robust feminist platforms that argued for the interrelatedness of class and gender.

By contrast, the strand of liberal feminism that became dominant by the 1980s focused on the composition of the labor market rather than the ways in which the structure of the economy produced inequality. The feminist policies that grew out of that movement served middle-class and professional women more than working-class women and failed to fully incorporate the complexities of class or, as Appalachian feminists named it, "economic and survival problems."[73] The tangle of problems did not go away with access to new jobs, jobs that a majority of working women would not be able to access, especially as mechanization altered the Appalachian economy. The coal industry entered a long, slow death, and coalmining proved to be an untenable career for women and men.[74] As sociologist Leslie McCall has shown, while gender-specific tactics such as antidiscrimination policies led to significant income gains for women at the top, "women's absolute progress in the bottom half occurred in fits and starts."[75] At the same time that the wage gap among women increased, the wages of blue-collar men stagnated, putting working-class families at greater financial risk.

It is impossible to understand that historical development without placing it in the context of the backlash against the welfare state and the federal and grassroots war on poverty, as well as the insistence by policy makers across the political aisle that waged work was the ultimate goal. For many policy makers, employment at any cost was the solution to ending welfare, and for many feminists it was the solution to advancing women. Those twin goals shaped and ultimately restricted the possibilities of feminist policies.

Too often in the political discussions then and in accounts today, the voices of working-class women have been crowded out, their decade of activism dismissed, and their work to place caregivers at the center of social movements and public policy ignored. Histories of the American women's movement have been diminished without them. Although scholars have justly celebrated coalmining and other blue-collar women, they have failed too often to connect their battles against discrimination to the more vexing history of antipoverty activism, welfare rights, and labor struggles. The fuller history of Appalachian feminism—rooted in the gendered class struggles that had characterized the history of the mountains in the twentieth century and built upon ongoing debates about the meaning of economic justice—faded from public view before it was ever fully explored, even as many of their struggles grew in intensity and exceeded regional boundaries. Like many working-class and poor women across the United States, Appalachian feminists offered an important example of *gender justice*, an approach that links gender inequality to various struggles against domination, from gendered violence to corporate power.[76] They imagined a multidimensional transformation of society, one in which care work would be valued and the voices of poor and working-class women would become central to solving social problems.

Epilogue

When we step back and consider the lives of Appalachian women activists, new ways of understanding democratic struggles of the 1960s and '70s come into view. Women leaders who took up the fight for justice ushered in a web of activism that pulsed outward from a core ethic of care. The act of caregiving animated their understanding of politics and activism and infused their movements. Feminist philosophers define *caring* as an "activity that includes everything that we do to maintain, continue, and repair our 'world' so that we can live in it as well as possible. That world includes our bodies, our selves, and our environment, all of which we seek to interweave in a complex, life-sustaining web."[1] The women activists of this history tended to the broken bodies of miners, mourned the dead, raised children, fought for clean water, fed the families of striking workers, carried their neighbors to hospitals, helped relatives navigate welfare offices, implemented school lunch programs, distributed educational resources, sheltered abused women and children, fought for parental leave, and much more. Most caregivers do not become activists, of course. The merging of an ethic of care with democratic struggle, however, yielded a powerful argument that has not been fully appreciated by historians of twentieth-century America.

In linking the various kinds of caring labor that women did in their communities, from sitting at bedsides to exposing environmental destruction to creating local health care networks and fighting for welfare, workers' and women's rights, this book constructs a new narrative of Appalachia through the lens of women's activism. It examines women's politics in relation to, and often as a component of, their caregiving labors. As Ronald D. Eller writes in his influential book on the politics of development in Appalachia, *Uneven*

Ground, "The stories we tell about ourselves can give us a vision for the kind of community we want to become, and building a vision of alternative possibilities is critical if we desire broad-based systemic change." Critical to those stories and visions is a history of women's lives and activism, not simply to include women in an Appalachian or American history but because placing women in history exacts new interpretations.

Taken as a whole, the activism charted in this book's pages reflects *caring* as central to justice, fairness, rights, and democracy. The women who emerged as leaders described themselves as people sustaining life and managing the manifest brutalities of the coal industry. When they joined organizations, walked picket lines, protested in the streets, and testified in public settings, they changed the narrative of democratic progress, what it meant and whom it benefited. The object of Appalachian activists' struggle—to ease the burden of unrestrained capitalism—was not realized but offers important lessons in the era of finance capitalism that matured in the late twentieth century.

In the last thirty years, working-class caregivers have faced an American political economy ever more hostile to their needs and concerns and increasingly demanding of their time and energy. Although overall poverty has decreased since the 1960s, many communities in the Appalachian South, like rural and working-class communities across the United States, have seen the rise of economic inequality, including income gaps and a growing divide between rural and metropolitan.[2] In the Appalachian coalfields, the last decades of the twentieth century ushered in the final and most precipitous decline in the coal industry, as mining jobs dropped by half and more and as the coal industry consolidated and transitioned to surface mining in the form of mountaintop removal. Those changes also spelled disaster for the UMWA, which all but disappeared in the Appalachian coalfields. In the "age of cheap," Walmart and fast-food outlets popped up all over the region, and the coal industry found the least expensive way to produce coal, with few workers, many machines, and little regard for long-term environmental and human costs of cheap energy.[3] Although the coal industry had long exploited workers, mining was nonetheless the best-paying work around. When those jobs disappeared by the hundreds, no other industry filled the gap and more people filed into the service economy where they garnered low wages and survived with little in the way of workplace benefits or economic security. Others worked in the public sector and health care industry, where they faced declining wages as states slashed budgets in a period of divestment.

The loss of mining jobs and the transition to a global market and service-based economy paralleled the unraveling of the social safety net. Helen Matthews Lewis, scholar-activist and trailblazer in Appalachian studies, wrote in the early 1980s, in a reflection on oral history interviews with rural women: "They have soothed and restored those damaged by economic crisis, cared for the victims, helped people migrate away and come back home." She continued, pivoting to the assault on the social safety net in the 1980s: "women's labor is used as a safety valve to maintain the economic system through cycles of inflation and depression. Social programs can be cut because women are back home in the informal, 'non-economic' economy feeding and maintaining family members."[4] In the 1990s, the bipartisan dismantling of Aid to Families with Dependent Children left poor families, and, in particular women, on shaky ground and served a final blow to decades of activism to guarantee welfare rights to all Americans. As sociologists Debra A. Henderson and Ann R. Tickamyer write, welfare reform marked the transition in Appalachia from the war on poverty to "the war on welfare and poor people" and exacerbated problems that stemmed from deindustrialization.[5] Community health clinics, legal aid services, and community organizations—the legacies of the grassroots war on poverty—stood as the only buffers in a political economy increasingly hostile to the interests of poor and working people.

• • •

During the heated and divisive election cycle of 2016, white Appalachia became, as it so often had in the past, the shorthand for an imagined white working class and a raft of related topics. Yet, reports from the region rarely dealt with the longer, complex history of the region. For months before the election, journalists reported on various Trump Countries, as they were dubbed, with Appalachian communities supposedly serving as ground zero for understanding working-class white people's support for a billionaire who claimed to care about the "forgotten people" of America. On the one hand, the focus makes sense. Many of these communities had been Democratic strongholds throughout most of the twentieth century, thus their turn to Republican candidates in recent decades is worthy of analysis. On the other hand, a minority of people voted (in the hundreds of people, not thousands) and many progressives in the region spoke out against Trump's policies, thus undermining any notion of a monolithic Trump Country. As in the past, Appalachia was a way to signal a host of characteristics all at once: white, working-class, postindustrial, impoverished, bigoted, uneducated, and filled with resentment over so-called big government, but also reliant on public assistance programs like Medicaid and disability. Simultaneously, the signposting allowed an evasion of any deep analysis of American racism or growing economic disparity, decades in the making and never contained to one region.[6]

These portraits also relied on tired tropes that almost entirely erased the voices and experiences of working-class women, a multiracial and multi-ethnic group, from history. Moreover, that narrative wiped from historical memory the progressive activism that has been so central to Appalachia's history. And it ignored the legacy of past movements, including ongoing campaigns against mountaintop removal as well as new movements, like health campaigns to expose the pharmaceutical industry's role in perpetuating the opioid epidemic, mobilization of LGBTQ Appalachian youth, and local movements to rejuvenate cooperative and creative local economies that counter corporate, neoliberal regimes.[7]

Yet in 2016, presidential candidates along with mainstream media outlets all propped up the iconic image of the coalminer, a white, able-bodied man, as the representation of Appalachia. Donald J. Trump promised to reignite the coal industry in Appalachia and to "bring back jobs," one of his many mantras. Hillary Clinton said she would help miners transition to a new, sustainable industry. Bernie Sanders, the election cycle's working-class champion, drew upon outmoded images of male industrial workers.[8] This despite the fact that in 2015 employment in the coal industry had declined 92 percent in eastern Kentucky from its peak in 1948, its primary legacy a heavy toll on the environment and public health.[9] In the twenty-first century, the vast majority of workers in Appalachia, and throughout much of America, work in health care support, education, social services, and food services, and many are women who continue to take on the brunt of caregiving labors in their community. They are also rising as the face of the new labor movement: In the spring of 2018, teachers in West Virginia fomented a state-wide, nine-day strike, and teachers in Kentucky and elsewhere soon followed. Along with higher wages, they demanded that their states fund education and renew commitments to public sector workers. Theirs is a fight for the common good.

This body politic requires new political frameworks. Political commitments to breadwinner liberalism, filtered through racial capitalism and underpinned by gender inequality, choked off the ideas of welfare rights and antipoverty activists in the 1960s. They limited the feminist promise of the 1970s. And they continue to ignore the complex realities of most working people's lives. As political rhetoric goes, conceptions of a "worker" that are narrow in scope have little chance of generating the kind of diverse, hopeful coalitional work that emerged in the late 1960s and 1970s, before backlash and internal strife curbed it.

The history recounted here offers up "breathing space and a toolbox," as writer Rebecca Solnit calls the sustaining work of social justice activism and civic participation.[10] People like Florence Reece, Granny Hager, Edith Easterling, Sue Ella Kobak, Mary Rice Farris, Eula Hall, Bessie Smith Gayheart, Sudie Crusenberry, Minnie Lunsford, Lois Scott, Bessie Lou Cornett, members of the Coal Employment Project, and their many allies—civil rights activists, lawyers, doctors, union organizers, feminists, and students—took a chance and stood up for a more just society. To do so was a "privilege and a freedom," Edith Easterling reminisced. With only a few, precious tools at their disposal, Appalachian women activists worked for what they believed was possible—the common good in their communities, the region, and the nation. Their most potent tool was the knowledge that they carried from a lifetime of tending to families, surviving tragedies, bearing witness to the disasters of unregulated capitalism, advocating for their communities, and taking a stand for fairness and justice. And many times over they have shared their life stories, tools for the present, about how they took steps to create the society that they imagined possible, one that centers and values caregiving labor.

Notes

Introduction

1. Alessandro Portelli, *They Say in Harlan County: An Oral History* (New York: Oxford University Press, 2011), 155.

2. Ibid.; Granny Hager, "How I Got My School Girl Figure Back," in Kathy Kahn, *Hillbilly Women: Mountain Women Speak of the Struggle and Joy in Southern Appalachia* (New York: Double Day, 1973), 39–49.

3. Portelli, *They Say in Harlan County*, 308.

4. I use the broader terms *Mountain South* and *Appalachian South* to refer to the region under study here, with eastern Kentucky, and, to a lesser extent, West Virginia, southwest Virginia, and eastern Tennessee, the primary focuses of this study. I rarely use *Appalachia* alone, as it often signifies a particular history and idea of the region, although I do employ it when referring to a particular idea of place or a specific identity. I borrow this pattern from Connie Park Rice, "Introduction: A Tapestry of Voices," in *Women of the Mountain South: Identity, Work, and Activism*, eds., Connie Park Rice and Marie Tedesco (Athens: Ohio University Press, 2015).

5. I stand on the shoulders of scholars who have made visible women and gender in Appalachian history. See especially Barbara Ellen Smith, "Beyond the Mountains: The Paradox of Women's Place in Appalachia," *NWSA Journal* 11.3 (1999): 1–17, 2; Rice and Tedesco, eds., *Women of the Mountain South*; Wilma Dunaway, *Women, Work, and Family in the Antebellum Mountain South* (New York: Cambridge University Press, 2008); Helen M. Lewis with editors Patricia D. Beaver and Judith Jennings, *Helen Matthews Lewis: Living Social Justice in Appalachia* (Lexington: University Press of Kentucky, 2012); Mary K. Anglin, *Women, Power, and Dissent in the Hills of Carolina* (Urbana: University of Illinois Press, 2002); Suzanne E. Tallichet, *Daughters of the Mountain: Women Coal Miners in Central Appalachia* (University Park: Pennsylvania State University Press, 2006); Elizabeth Engelhardt, ed., *Beyond Hill and Hollow:*

Original Readings in Appalachian Women's Studies (Athens: Ohio University Press, 2005); Helen M. Lewis and Monica Appleby, *Mountain Sisters: From Convent to Community in Appalachia* (Lexington: University Press of Kentucky, 2002); Barbara Ellen Smith, ed., *Neither Separate nor Equal: Women, Race, and Class in the South* (Philadelphia: Temple University Press, 1999); special issue on women, *Appalachian Journal* 37 (Spring/Summer 2010); Jacquelyn Dowd Hall, "Disorderly Women: Gender and Labor Militancy in the Appalachian South," *Journal of American History* 73, no. 2 (September 1986): 354–382; and Sally Ward Maggard, "Coal Field Women Making History," in *Back Talk from Appalachia: Confronting Stereotypes*, eds., Dwight B. Billings, Gurney Norman, and Katherine Ledford (Lexington: University of Kentucky Press, 1999), 228–250.

6. Annelise Orleck, "Introduction: The War on Poverty from the Grassroots Up," Annelise Orleck and Lisa Gayle Hazirjian, eds., *The War on Poverty: A New Grassroots History, 1964–1980* (Athens: The University of Georgia Press, 2011), 1–28. For other examples of the grassroots war on poverty, see Annelise Orleck, *Storming Caesar's Palace: How Black Mothers Fought Their Own War on Poverty* (Boston: Beacon Press, 2005); Rhonda Y. Williams, *The Politics of Public Housing: Black Women's Struggles against Urban Inequality* (New York: Oxford University Press, 2004); Kent Germany, *New Orleans after the Promises: Poverty, Citizenship, and the Search for the Great Society* (Athens: University of Georgia Press, 2005); Crystal Sanders, *A Chance for Change: Head Start and Mississippi's Black Freedom Struggle* (Chapel Hill: University of North Carolina Press, 2016); Robert Bauman, *Race and the War on Poverty: From Watts to East L.A.* (Norman: University of Oklahoma Press, 2008); Susan Youngblood Ashmore, *Carry It On: The War on Poverty and the Civil Rights Movement in Alabama, 1964–1972* (Athens: University of Georgia Press, 2008); Tamar W. Carroll, *Mobilizing New York: AIDS, Antipoverty, and Feminist Activism* (Chapel Hill: University of North Carolina Press, 2015); and Greta de Jong, *You Can't Eat Freedom: Southerners and Social Justice after the Civil Rights Movement* (Chapel Hill: University of North Carolina Press, 2016).

7. Evelyn Nakano Glenn, "From Servitude to Service Work: Historical Continuities in the Racial Division of Paid Reproductive Labor," *Signs: Journal of Women in Culture and Society* 18, no. 1 (1992): 1–43.

8. On the history of paid caring work in the United States, see Eileen Boris and Jennifer Klein, *Caring for America: Home Health Workers in the Shadow of the Welfare State* (New York: Oxford University Press, 2012); Evelyn Nakano Glenn, *Forced to Care: Coercion and Caregiving in America* (Cambridge: Harvard University Press, 2012); Eileen Boris and Rachel Salazar Parreñas, eds., *Intimate Labors: Cultures, Technologies, and the Politics of Care* (Stanford: Stanford University Press, 2010).

9. Eva Feder Kittay, *Love's Labor: Essays on Women, Equality, and Dependency* (New York: Routledge, 1999), 1–4.

10. Nancy Fraser, "Contradictions of Capital and Care," *New Left Review* 100 (July/August 2016): 99–117, 101.

11. I draw here upon David Montgomery's conception of "citizen worker" and his analysis of nineteenth-century American workers' understanding of and relationship to citizenship, as well as the historical relationship between democracy and labor. See David Montgomery, *Citizen Workers: The Experience of Workers in the United States with Democracy and the Free Market during the Nineteenth Century* (New York: Cambridge University Press, 1993), 1–12. Scholars who have influenced my thinking on caregiving include Nancy Fraser, *Fortunes of Feminism: From State-Managed Capitalism to Neoliberal Crisis* (New York: Verso, 2013); Berenice Fisher and Joan C. Tronto, "Toward a Feminist Theory of Care," in *Circles of Care: Work and Identity in Women's Lives*, eds., Emily Abel and Margaret Nelson (Albany: State University of New York Press, 1991); Margaret Urban Walker, *Moral Understandings: A Feminist Study in Ethics* (New York: Oxford University Press, 2007); Johanna Oksala, "Affective Labor and Feminist Politics," *Signs: Journal of Women in Culture and Society* 41, no. 2 (2016): 281–303; Cindi Katz, "Vagabond Capitalism and the Necessity of Social Reproduction," *Antipode* 33 (September 2001): 709–728. Scholars who have centered caregiving in their work include Temma Kaplan, *Crazy for Democracy: Women in Grassroots Movement* (New York: Routledge, 1997); Alexis Jetter, Annelise Orleck, and Diana Taylor, eds., *The Politics of Motherhood: Activist Voices from Left to Right* (Hanover, N.H.: University Press of New England, 1997); Laurie B. Green, "Challenging the Civil Rights Narrative: Women, Gender, and Politics of Protection," in *Civil Rights History from the Ground Up: Local Struggles, A National Movement*, ed., Emilye Crosby (Athens: University of Georgia Press, 2011), 52–80; Glenn, *Forced to Care*; Boris and Klein, *Caring for America*.

12. See Dwight B. Billings and Kathleen M. Blee, *The Road to Poverty: The Making of Wealth and Hardship in Appalachia* (Cambridge: Cambridge University Press, 2000).

13. I draw here from Dana Frank, "White Working Class Women and the Race Question," *International Labor and Working-Class History* (Fall 1998): 80–102.

14. Laurie B. Green, "'Where Would the Negro Women Apply for Work?': Gender, Race, and Labor in Wartime Memphis," *Labor: Studies in Working-Class History of the Americas* 3, no. 3 (Fall 2006): 95–118; Katherine Turk, "A Fair Chance to Do My Part of Work: Black Women, War Work, and Rights Claims at the Kingsbury Ordnance Plant," *Indiana Magazine of History* 108, no. 3 (September 2012): 209–244.

15. While much has been written on the racial and gender contours of the New Deal programs, similar issues in the Great Society programs have received less attention. See Alice Kessler-Harris, *In Pursuit of Equity: Women, Men, and the Quest for Economic Citizenship in 20th Century America* (New York: Oxford University Press, 2001); Linda Gordon, *Pitied but Not Entitled: Single Mothers and the History of Welfare, 1890–1935* (New York: Free Press, 1995); Suzanne Mettler, *Dividing Citizens: Gender and Federalism in New Deal Public Policy* (Ithaca: Cornell University Press, 1998); Jill Quadagno, *The Color of Welfare: How Racism Undermined the War on Poverty* (New York: Oxford University Press, 1994). See also Elizabeth Hinton, *From the*

War on Poverty to the War on Crime: The Making of Mass Incarceration in America (Cambridge: Harvard University Press, 2016).

16. See Kieran Walsh Taylor, "Turn to the Working Class: The New Left, Black Liberation, and the U.S. Labor Movement, 1967–1981" (PhD diss., UNC-Chapel Hill, 2007); Gordon Mantler, *Power to the Poor: Black-Brown Coalition and the Fight for Economic Justice, 1960–1974* (Chapel Hill: The University of North Carolina Press, 2013).

17. Activist Si Kahn drew parallels between an "Appalachian movement" and the movements of black, brown, and Indian people across the country. "CSM—New Directions for the '70s," *ML&W*, September 1970.

18. For other examples of interracial, antipoverty campaigns, see Mantler, *Power to the Poor*; Jennifer Frost, *An Interracial Movement of the Poor: Community Organizing and the New Left in the 1960s* (New York: NYU Press, 2001); Christina Greene, *Our Separate Ways: Women and the Black Freedom Movement in Durham, North Carolina* (Chapel Hill: The University of North Carolina Press, 2005); Anne M. Valk, *Radical Sisters: Second-Wave Feminism and Black Liberation in Washington, D.C.* (Chicago: University of Illinois Press, 2010); and Carroll, *Mobilizing New York*.

19. Barbara Ellen Smith, "De-gradations of Whiteness: Appalachia and the Complexities of Race," *Journal of Appalachian Studies* 10, no. 1–2 (2004): 38–57, 42–43.

20. Sarah Ogan Gunning, *Girl of Constant Sorrow*, Folk-Legacy Records FSA-26, 1965; "I Hate the Company Bosses / I Hate the Capitalist System," accessed August 26, 2017, http://www.folkarchive.de/ihate.html. See Sherry Romalis, *Pistol Packin' Mama: Aunt Molly Jackson and the Politics of Folksong* (Urbana: University of Illinois Press, 1999).

21. Interview with Edith Easterling, Shelva Thompson, and John Dollo, SFC Audio Cassette 18853, in the Guy and Candie Carawan Collection #20008, Southern Folklife Collection, Wilson Library, University of North Carolina at Chapel Hill.

22. For an institutional history of the Appalachian Volunteers, see Thomas Kiffmeyer, *Reformers to Radicals: The Appalachian Volunteers and the War on Poverty* (Lexington: The University Press of Kentucky, 2008).

23. Other studies of the Appalachian War on Poverty include Ronald D. Eller, *Uneven Ground: Appalachia since 1945* (Lexington: The University Press of Kentucky, 2008); Robyn Muncy, "Coal-Fired Reforms: Social Citizenship, Dissident Miners, and the Great Society," in *Journal of American History* 96, no. 1 (June 2009); Jerry Bruce Thomas, *An Appalachian Reawakening: West Virginia and the Perils of the New Machine Age, 1945–1972* (Morgantown: West Virginia University Press, 2011).

24. See classics in Appalachian studies, including Ronald D. Eller, *Miners, Millhands, and Mountaineers: Industrialization of the Appalachian South, 1880–1930* (Knoxville: The University of Tennessee Press, 1982); David Whisnant, *Modernizing the Mountaineer: People, Power, and Planning in Appalachia* (Knoxville: The University of Tennessee Press, 1994); Helen M. Lewis, Linda Johnson, and Don Askins, eds., *Colonialism in Modern America: The Appalachian Case* (Boone, N.C.: The Appalachian Consortium Press, 1978); John Gaventa, *Power and Powerlessness:*

Quiescence and Rebellion in an Appalachian Valley (Oxford: Clarendon Press, 1980). See also Kiffmeyer, *Reformers to Radicals* and "Looking Back to the City in the Hills: The Council of the Southern Mountains and a Longer View of the War on Poverty in the Appalachian South, 1913–1970," in *The War on Poverty: A New Grassroots History, 1964–1980*, 359–386. For critiques of the insider/outsider model, see Smith, "Beyond the Mountains"; Barbara Ellen Smith and Stephen L. Fisher, "The Place of Appalachia," in *Southern Spaces*, January 31, 2013, accessed April 1, 2018, http://www.southernspaces.org/2013/place-appalachia#footnote2_8ya8bck. See also Barbara Ellen Smith, "Representing Appalachia," in *Studying Appalachian Studies: Making the Path by Walking*, eds., Chad Berry, Phillip J. Obermiller, and Shaunna L. Scott (Urbana: University of Illinois Press, 2015), 43–48.

25. Jack E. Weller, *Yesterday's People: Life in Contemporary Appalachia* (Lexington: University of Kentucky Press, 1965).

26. On the importance of alliances in antipoverty work, see Robert R. Korstad and James L. Leloudis, *To Right These Wrongs: The North Carolina Fund and the Battle to End Poverty and Inequality in 1960s America* (Chapel Hill: The University of North Carolina Press, 2010), 355.

27. For similar stories in West Virginia and Mississippi, see Huey Perry, *They'll Cut Off Your Project: A Mingo County Chronicle* (Morgantown: West Virginia University Press, 2011) and Sanders, *A Chance for Change*.

28. Eula Hall, interview with the author, September 2012.

29. Little to date has been written about welfare rights organizing in the Appalachian South, or more generally, welfare rights in poor white communities. See Carroll, *Mobilizing New York*, for a recent exception. For the history of black women's antipoverty campaigns, see Guida West, *The National Welfare Rights Movement: The Social Protest of Poor Women* (New York: Praeger, 1981); Lisa Levenstein, *A Movement without Marches: African American Women and the Politics of Poverty in Postwar Philadelphia* (Chapel Hill: The University of North Carolina Press, 2009); Felicia Kornbluh, *The Battle for Welfare Rights: Politics and Poverty in Modern America* (Philadelphia: University of Pennsylvania Press, 2007); Orleck, *Storming Caesar's Palace*; Williams, *The Politics of Public Housing*; Quadagno, *The Color of Welfare*; Premilla Nadasen, *Welfare Warriors: The Welfare Rights Movement in the United States* (New York: Routledge, 2005); Marisa Chappell, *The War on Welfare: Family, Poverty, and Politics in Modern America* (Philadelphia: University of Pennsylvania Press, 2010).

30. For other examples of the intersections between antipoverty activism and feminism, see Carroll, *Mobilizing New York*; Nancy A. Naples, *Grassroots Warriors: Activist Mothering, Community Work, and the War on Poverty* (New York: Routledge, 1998); and Orleck, *Storming Caesar's Palace*.

31. Fraser, *Fortunes of Feminism*, 214–215.

32. See Kimberlé Crenshaw, "Demarginalizing the Intersection of Race and Sex: A Black Feminist Critique of Antidiscrimination Doctrine, Feminist Theory, and Antiracist Politics," *University of Chicago Legal Forum* (1989): 139–167; Leslie McCall,

"The Complexity of Intersectionality," *Signs* 30, no. 3 (Spring 2005): 1771–1800; Evelyn Nakano Glenn, *Unequal Freedom: How Race and Gender Shaped American Freedom and Labor* (Cambridge: Harvard University Press, 2002); Ava Baron, *Work Engendered: Toward a New History of American Labor* (Ithaca: Cornell University Press, 1991); Ruth Milkman, *On Gender, Labor, and Inequality* (Urbana: University of Illinois Press, 2015).

33. They enacted what Alice Kessler-Harris calls the "gendered imagination." See Kessler-Harris, *In Pursuit of Equity*; Dorothy Sue Cobble, *The Other Women's Movement: Workplace Justice and Social Rights in Modern America* (Princeton: Princeton University Press, 2004); Serena Mayeri, *Reasoning from Race: Feminism, Law, and the Civil Rights Revolution* (Cambridge: Harvard University Press, 2011); Katherine Turk, *Equality on Trial: Gender and Rights in the Modern American Workplace* (Philadelphia: University of Pennsylvania Press, 2016).

34. See Korstad and Leloudis, *To Right These Wrongs*; Kathryn Newfont, *Blue Ridge Commons: Environmental Activism and Forest History in Western North Carolina* (Athens: University of Georgia Press, 2011).

35. See Amy Dru Stanley, "Histories of Capitalism and Sex Difference," *Journal of the Early Republic* 36 (Summer 2016): 343–350. See also "Interchange: The History of Capitalism," *Journal of American History* 101, no. 2 (2014): 503–636. On women in the coalfields see Jaclyn J. Gier and Laurie Mercier, eds., *Mining Women: Gender in the Development of a Global Industry, 1670–2005* (New York: Palgrave Macmillan, 2006).

36. Fraser, "Contradictions of Capital and Care." As Fraser argues, reproductive labor and caregiving are not in essence "anticapitalist" but must be understood as part of a capitalist social order.

37. "Eastern Kentucky Women," *ML&W*, April 1975.

38. On emerging frameworks, see Nancy Hewitt's introduction to *No Permanent Waves: Recasting Histories of U.S. Feminism*, ed., Nancy Hewitt (New Brunswick, N.J.: Rutgers University Press, 2010), 1–14. I build on the newest scholarship on the women's movement, including Valk, *Radical Sisters*; Annelise Orleck, *Rethinking American Women's Activism* (New York: Routledge, 2014); Dorothy Sue Cobble, Linda Gordon, and Astrid Henry, *Feminism Unfinished: A Short Surprising History of American Women's Movements* (New York: Liverwright, 2014); Stephanie Gilmore, ed., *Feminist Coalitions: Historical Perspectives on Second-Wave Feminism in the United States* (Urbana: University of Illinois Press, 2008). On the women's movement in the U.S. South, see Katarina Keane, "Second-Wave Feminism in the American South, 1965–1980" (PhD diss., University of Maryland, 2009), and Janet Allured, *Remapping Second-Wave Feminism: The Long Women's Rights Movement in Louisiana, 1950–1997* (Athens: University of Georgia Press, 2016). On "grassroots feminism," see the interview with Barbara Greene, a community organizer in Tennessee and Kentucky, by Jessie Wilkerson, May 8, 2011, U-0537, in the Southern Oral History Program Collection #4007, Southern Historical Collection, Wilson Library, University of North Carolina at Chapel Hill. See also "Long Women's Movement in the American South," oral history interview collection, Southern Oral History Program, UNC-Chapel Hill.

39. With few exceptions, most histories of working-class feminism examine women's entrance into the American workplace and the various battles they fought. Exceptions include Orleck, *Storming Caesar's Palace*; Carroll, *Mobilizing New York*: and Orleck, *Rethinking American Women's Activism*. On the intersections of labor, class, and feminism, see Cobble, *The Other Women's Movement*; Annelise Orleck, *Common Sense and a Little Fire: Women and Working-Class Politics in the United States, 1900–1965* (Chapel Hill: University of North Carolina Press, 1995); Tallichet, *Daughters of the Mountains*; Dennis Deslippe, *Rights Not Roses: Unions and the Rise of Working-Class Feminism, 1945–1980* (Urbana: University of Illinois Press, 2000); Daniel Horowitz, *Betty Friedan and the Making of the Feminine Mystique: The American Left, the Cold War, and Modern Feminism* (Amherst: University of Massachusetts Press, 1998); Nancy Gabin, *Feminism in the Labor Movement: Women and the United Auto Workers, 1935–1975* (Ithaca: Cornell University Press, 1990); Ruth Milkman, *Gender at Work: The Dynamics of Job Segregation by Sex during World War II* (Urbana: University of Illinois Press, 1987); Jane Latour, *Sisters in the Brotherhood: Working Women Organizing for Equality in New York City* (New York: Palgrave MacMillian, 2008); Nancy MacLean, *Freedom Is Not Enough: The Opening of the American Workplace* (Cambridge: Harvard University Press, 2006); Serena Mayeri, *Reasoning from Race*; Turk, *Equality on Trial*; Lisa Levenstein, "Don't Agonize, Organize!": The Displaced Homemakers Campaign and the Contested Goals of 1970s Feminism," *Journal of American History* 100, no. 4 (March 2014): 144–168. For discussions of socialist feminism, see Rosalynn Baxandall and Linda Gordon, eds., *Dear Sisters: Dispatches from the Women's Liberation Movement* (New York: Basic Books, 2001); Myra Marx Ferree and Patricia Yancey Martin, eds., *Feminist Organizations: Harvest of the New Women's Movement* (Philadelphia: Temple University Press, 1995); and Sara Evans, *Tidal Wave: How Women Changed America at Century's End* (New York: Free Press, 2003).

Chapter 1. The Political and Gender Economy of the Mountain South, 1900–1964

1. Florence Reece, *Against the Current: Poems and Stories*, privately printed by F. Reece (Knoxville, Tenn.: 1981), McClung Library, Knoxville, Tenn.; Skye K. Moody (formerly Kathy Kahn), *Hillbilly Women: Struggle and Survival in Southern Appalachia* (New York: Anchor Books, 2014), Location 353, Kindle.

2. Kahn, *Hillbilly Women*, 29.

3. Portelli, *They Say in Harlan County*, 233; Eller, *Miners, Millhands, and Mountaineers*, 82–84.

4. Dexter Collett, "The Musicians of the Mine Wars," *Appalachian Heritage* 34, no. 2 (Spring 2006): 72–81.

5. John W. Hevener, *Which Side Are You On? The Harlan County Coal Miners, 1931–1939* (Urbana: University of Illinois Press), 32.

6. Kahn, *Hillbilly Women*, 36–37; Florence Reece, as told to Kathy Kahn, "They Say Those Child Brides Don't Last," in *Calling Home: Working Class Women's Writings*,

An Anthology, ed., Janet Zady (New Brunswick, N.J.: Rutgers University Press, 1993), 57–62, and, for full lyrics to "Which Side Are You On?" see pages 62–64.

7. Dick Weissman, *Which Side Are You On? An Inside History of the Folk Music Revival in America* (New York: Bloomsbury, 2006), 45–47; The Freedom Voices with Len Chandler, "Which Side Are You On?" (Civil Rights Version), *WNEW's Story of Selma* (Folkways Records, 1965), Smithsonian Center for Folklife and Cultural Heritage; Loyal Jones, "Florence Reece, *Against the Current*," *Appalachian Journal* 12, no. 1 (Fall 1984): 68–72.

8. Reece, "They Say Those Child Brides Don't Last," in *Calling Home*, 64.

9. See Eller, *Miners, Millhands, and Mountaineers*; Robert Weise, *Grasping at Independence: Debt, Male Authority, and Mineral Rights in Appalachian Kentucky, 1850–1915* (Knoxville: University of Tennessee Press, 2001); Ronald L. Lewis, *Transforming the Appalachian Countryside: Railroads, Deforestation, and Social Change in West Virginia, 1880–1920* (Chapel Hill: University of North Carolina Press, 1998).

10. For a comprehensive history, see John Alexander Williams, *Appalachia: A History* (Chapel Hill: University of North Carolina Press, 2002), 253–254.

11. Eller, *Miners, Millhands, and Mountaineers*, 155.

12. Ibid. See list of coalfields and coalmines in Arthur M. Miller, *Geology of Kentucky*, published by the Kentucky Geological Survey in 1919, accessed November 29, 2016, http://www.uky.edu/OtherOrgs/KPS/goky/pages/gokych22.htm; "Kentucky, Population of Counties by Decennial Census: 1900 to 1990," compiled and edited by Richard Forstall (Washington, D.C.: Population Division, U.S. Bureau of the Census, 1995), accessed November 29, 2016, https://www.census.gov/population/cencounts/ky190090.txt.

13. Eller, *Miners, Millhands, and Mountaineers*, xxi, 36–37, 210–211; Weise, *Grasping at Independence*, 234–235.

14. Eller, *Miners, Millhands, and Mountaineers*, 210–219.

15. Williams, *Appalachia: A History*, 253–254.

16. Quoted in Weise, *Grasping at Independence*, 164–165. See also Dunaway, *Women, Work and Family in the Antebellum Mountain South.*

17. Malta Miller, interviewed by Glenna Graves, October 14, 1988, Family and Gender in the Coal Community Oral History Project, Louie B. Nunn Center for Oral History, University of Kentucky Libraries.

18. Mae Frazier, interviewed by Graves, December 8, 1988, Family and Gender in the Coal Community Oral History Project.

19. Miller, interviewed by Graves.

20. Onda Lee Holbrook, interviewed by Graves, September 11, 1988, Family and Gender in the Coal Community Oral History Project.

21. Bertha B. Kretzer interviewed by Graves, November 6, 1988, Family and Gender in the Coal Community Oral History Project.

22. Marjorie Castle, interviewed by Graves, September 11, 1988, Family and Gender in the Coal Community Oral History Project.

23. Grace Litteral, interviewed by Graves, June 14, 1988, Family and Gender in the Coal Community Oral History Project.

24. Portelli, *They Say in Harlan County*, 128–129; Eller, *Miners, Millhands, and Mountaineers*, 190; Shaunna L. Scott, *Two Sides to Everything: The Cultural Construction of Class in Harlan County, Kentucky* (New York: State University of New York Press, 1995), 13–14.

25. Portelli, *They Say in Harlan County*, 166–175; W. Fitzhugh Brundage, "Racial Violence, Lynching, and Modernization in the Mountain South," in *Appalachians and Race: The Mountain South from Slavery to Segregation*, ed., John C. Inscoe (Lexington: University Press of Kentucky, 2001), 302–316.

26. See the "Eastern Kentucky African American Migration Project," #5585, Southern Historical Collection, The Wilson Library, University of North Carolina at Chapel Hill.

27. Billings and Blee, *The Road to Poverty*, 22–24, 216.

28. See Smith, "De-gradations of Whiteness," 42–43, and John Inscoe, *Appalachians and Race*. For comprehensive data on the free and enslaved population by county, see the website and database, "Notable Kentucky African Americans," accessed August 20, 2017, http://nkaa.uky.edu/nkaa/about.

29. On the history of African Americans in Appalachian coalfields, see Inscoe, *Appalachians and Race*; Joe William Trotter, *Coal, Class, and Color: Blacks in Southern West Virginia, 1915–32* (Urbana: University of Illinois Press, 1990); William H. Turner and Edward J. Cabbell, eds., *Blacks in Appalachia* (Lexington: The University Press of Kentucky, 1985); and David Corbin, *Life, Work, and Rebellion in the Coalfields: The Southern West Virginian Miners, 1880–1922* (Urbana: University of Illinois Press, 1981), 61–86. On the history of String Town, see Mary Music, "Years of Service, History under One Roof," *Appalachian News-Express*, June 1, 2007.

30. Reece, *Against the Current*, xi.

31. Knoxville *News-Sentinel*, May 19 and May 21, 1902; *Journal and Tribune* (Knoxville), May 22, 1902, archived at "Disasters in Tennessee," an online exhibit, Tennessee State Library and Archives, accessed on November 29, 2016, http://share.tn.gov/tsla/exhibits/disasters/fraterville.htm.

32. James Green, *The Devil Is Here in These Hills: West Virginia's Coal Miners and Their Battle for Freedom* (New York: Atlantic Monthly Press, 2015); "All Coal Mining Disasters: 1839–present," The National Institute for Occupational Safety and Health, Centers for Disease Control, accessed November 29, 2016, https://www.cdc.gov/niosh/mining/statistics/content/coaldisasters.html.

33. Eller, *Uneven Ground*, 163–164; "Buffalo Creek Flood: An Act of Man," directed by Mimi Pickering (Whitesburg: Appalshop, 1975).

34. Opal Goble, interviewed by Graves, July 19, 1988, Family and Gender in the Coal Community Oral History Project.

35. Barbara Ellen Smith, *Digging Our Own Graves: Coal Miners and the Struggle over Black Lung Disease* (Philadelphia: Temple University Press, 1987); James R.

Carroll, "Severe Black Lung Returns to 1970s Levels," *Courier-Journal*, September 15, 2014.

36. Portelli, *They Say in Harlan County*, 156.

37. Hevener, *Which Side Are You On?* 4–5.

38. Richard J. Callahan Jr., *Work and Faith in the Kentucky Coal Fields: Subject to Dust* (Bloomington: University of Indiana Press, 2008), 113–114.

39. Green, *The Devil Is Here In These Hills*.

40. John C. Hennen, "Introduction to the New Edition," Members of the National Committee for the Defense, *Harlan Miners Speak: Report on Terrorism in the Kentucky Coal Fields* (Lexington: University of Kentucky Press, 2008); Portelli, *They Say in Harlan County*, 183–208; Hevener, *Which Side Are You On?* 55–93.

41. Hevener, *Which Side Are You On?* 37.

42. Ibid., 33–93.

43. Ibid. See also Portelli, *They Say in Harlan County*, 198–201.

44. Hennen, *Harlan Miners Speak*, 90, 164.

45. Aunt Molly Jackson, "Hungry Ragged Blues," *The Songs and Stories of Aunt Molly Jackson* (Washington, D.C.: Folkways, 1960), archived at Smithsonian Center for Folklife and Cultural Heritage.

46. Keith Dix, *What's a Coal Miner to Do? The Mechanization of Coal Mining* (Pittsburgh: University of Pittsburgh Press, 1988), 199.

47. Jerry Bruce Thomas, *An Appalachian New Deal: West Virginia In the Great Depression* (Lexington: The University Press of Kentucky, 1998), 92–94; Dix, *What's a Coal Miner to Do?*, 191–193.

48. James Gregory, *The Southern Diaspora: How the Great Migrations of Black and White Southerners Transformed America* (Chapel Hill: University of North Carolina Press, 2005); Chad Berry, *Southern Migrants, Northern Exiles* (Urbana: University of Illinois Press, 2000).

49. Sue Ella Kobak, interview with the author, March 6, 2011.

50. Three million people from Appalachia migrated to cities between 1940 and 1970 in search of economic opportunities. See Eller, *Uneven Ground*, 20–21.

51. Ibid., 11, 16.

52. Muncy, "Coal-Fired Reforms," 72–98, 73.

53. The plan covered "any miner employed by signatures to the coal wage agreements; unemployed miners who were last employed by a signatory; disabled miners; retired miners receiving pensions from the fund; and dependents, including wives, children to age eighteen, and parents of the miner or his wife if they lived with the miner and had been dependent on him for a year." Eller, *Uneven Ground*, 81.

54. See Robyn Muncy, *Relentless Reformer: Josephine Roche and Progressivism in Twentieth Century America* (Princeton: Princeton University Press, 2015), 254–262. See also Muncy, "Coal-Fired Reforms," and Richard P. Mulcahy, *A Social Contract for the Coal Fields: The Rise and Fall of the United Mine Workers of America Welfare and Retirement Fund* (Knoxville: University of Tennessee Press, 2001).

55. Muncy, "Coal-Fired Reforms."

56. Portelli, *They Say in Harlan County*, 4–5; Kahn, *Hillbilly Women*, 41.

57. For a comprehensive history of surface mining in Appalachia, see Chad Montrie, *To Save the Land and People: A History of Opposition to Surface Coal Mining in Appalachia* (Chapel Hill: University of North Carolina Press, 2003).

58. Ibid., 79, 82–83.

59. See "War on Poverty: Portraits from an Appalachian Battleground, 1964," *Time and Life* Pictures/Getty Images, accessed February 3, 2014, http://life.time.com/history/war-on-poverty-appalachia-portraits-1964/#1; Michael Harrington, *The Other America: Poverty in the United States* (New York: Macmillan, 1962); Harry Caudill, *Night Comes to the Cumberlands: A Biography of a Depressed Area* (Boston: Little, Brown, 1963); Homer Bigart, "Kentucky Miners: A Grim Winter," *New York Times*, October 19, 1963; Michael L. Gillette, *Launching the War on Poverty: An Oral History* (New York: Oxford University Press, 2010), 1. On the history of implementation, see Eller, *Uneven Ground*.

60. Eller, *Uneven Ground*, 15–20; Appalachian Regional Commission, *Appalachian Data Book* (Washington, D.C.: ARC, 1967); U.S. Bureau of Labor Statistics, *Technology, Productivity, and Labor in the Bituminous Coal Industry 1950–79*, Bulletin 2072 (Washington, D.C.: GPO, 1981).

61. The most popular of the photographs was taken by Walter Bennett for *Time and Life* and captured President Lyndon Johnson's visit to Tom Fletcher's home in Kentucky as part of his tour of poverty-stricken areas in the U.S. Photo by Walter Bennett, *Time and Life* Pictures/Getty Images.

62. "Guidelines, Remarks at Inez, Kentucky," folder poverty trip #1, part 2, box 39, Office Files of the White House Aides-Moyers, Lyndon B. Johnson Presidential Library, Austin, Texas (hereafter LBJ Library).

63. See Orleck, "Introduction: The War on Poverty," in *The War on Poverty*, 1–28, 2–3; Pam Fessler, "Kentucky County That Gave War on Poverty a Face Still Struggles," Morning Edition, National Public Radio, January 8, 2014; Allen G. Breed, "Poster Father Weary of Sour Fate," *LA Times*, June 26, 1994; Eller, *Uneven Ground*, 81–82.

64. Lyndon B. Johnson, "Remarks upon Signing the Appalachia Bill," March 9, 1965, digitized by Gerhard Peters and John T. Woolley, *The American Presidency Project*, accessed February 3, 2014, http://www.presidency.ucsb.edu/ws/?pid=26801.

65. Gillette, *Launching the War on Poverty*, 118.

66. Senators John Sherman Cooper and Jennings Randolph, "The Appalachian Development Act: A Statement for the 40th Anniversary of ML&W," *ML&W* XL, 1, Summer 1965.

67. Orleck, "Introduction: The War on Poverty," in *The War on* Poverty, 10.

68. Act of August 20, 1964 (Economic Opportunity Act of 1964), Public Law 88-452, 78 STAT 508, Enrolled Acts and Resolutions of Congress, 1789–2011, Record Group 11, National Archives, accessed February 4, 2017, http://research.archives.gov/description/299896.

69. See Ashmore, *Carry It On*, 29–30; Alyosha Goldstein, *Poverty in Common: The Politics of Community Action during the American Century* (Durham: Duke University Press, 2012), 115–116; William M. Epstein, *Democracy without Decency: Good Citizenship and the War on Poverty* (University Park: The Pennsylvania State University Press, 2010), 58–63.

70. Statement made by Assistant Secretary representing the U.S. Department of Agriculture John Baker, quoted in Ashmore, *Carry It Forward*, 30.

71. See David E. Whisnant, *All That Is Native and Fine: The Politics of Culture in an American Region* (Chapel Hill: University of North Carolina Press, 1983); On women's role in particular, see Penny Messinger, "Professionalizing 'Mountain Work' in Appalachia: Women in the Conference of Southern Mountain Workers," in *Women in the Mountain South*, 217–243.

72. See Whisnant, *Modernizing the Mountaineer*; Eller, *Uneven Ground*, 41–42; Kiffmeyer, *Reformers to Radicals*, 17–18; Kiffmeyer, "Looking Back to the City in the Hills"; Messinger, "Professionalizing 'Mountain Work' in Appalachia"; "Guide to the Council of the Southern Mountain Records, 1912–1970," The Council of the Southern Mountain Records, Southern Appalachian Archives, Berea College Special Collections and Archives.

73. "The Council of the Southern Mountains: Their Training Program, VISTA Volunteers," folder VISTA Rural Projects, box 17; Office of Inspection; Office of Domestic and Antipoverty Operations; Records Concerning the VISTA Program, 1965–1971 (VISTA Program); Records of the Corporation for National and Community Service; RG 362; National Archives at College Park, College Park, Maryland (NACP).

74. Eller, *Uneven Ground*, 97–99.

75. "The Council of the Southern Mountains: Their Training Program, VISTA Volunteers."

76. Some historians have criticized these early programs as misguided liberal policies that failed to address structural problems and instead focused on the culture of poor individuals and families, but those critiques underestimated the ways in which early War on Poverty programs laid the groundwork for a longer and broader social movement in the region. See Kiffmeyer, *Reformers to Radicals*, and Whisnant, *Modernizing the Mountaineer*. Ronald D. Eller has argued that despite their flaws, 1960s antipoverty programs in Appalachia were important factors in the developing social justice movements in Appalachia. See Eller, *Uneven Ground*.

77. Gillette, *Launching the War on Poverty*, 282–284; Eller, *Uneven Ground*, 97–99.

78. See Kiffmeyer, *Reformers to Radicals*, 109–111.

79. "The Council of the Southern Mountains: Their Training Program, VISTA Volunteers."

80. In other key sites of antipoverty organizing in Appalachia, such as West Virginia, the population was a bit higher, but still low at 5 percent. William H. Turner, "The Demography of Black Appalachia: Past and Present," in *Blacks in Appalachia*, 237–261.

81. Ibid.

82. Edward J. Cabbell, "Black Invisibility and Racism in Appalachia: An Informal Survey," in *Blacks in Appalachia*, 3–10.

83. See Jack Guillebeaux, "Not Just Whites in Appalachia," *in Blacks in Appalachia*, 207–201, and Linda Elkington, interviewed by Gibbs Kinderman, August 8, 1987, War on Poverty Oral History Project, Louie B. Nunn Center for Oral History, University of Kentucky Libraries. There were also exceptions, including in Harlan County, where an interracial youth group organized with the assistance of antipoverty workers; in Floyd County, where interracial community meetings took place; and community action efforts in black communities in West Virginia and southwest Virginia. For examples, see *Cloverfork Newsletter*, January 22, 1968, March 21, 1968, and May 27, 1968, folder 16, box 129; "Preface," White Papers, 1966, folder 4, box 8, Appalachian Volunteers Records, Southern Appalachian Archives, Berea College (hereafter cited as AV Records); Kiffmeyer, *Reformers to Radicals*, 169; Perry, *They'll Cut Off Your Project.*

84. For discussion of various conflicts that emerged between the CSM and the AVs, see Kiffmeyer, chapter five, *Reformers to Radicals*; see also Eller, *Uneven Ground*, 116–118.

85. Appalachian Community Meeting, Washington, D.C., "The Problem of Participation in Community Action Programs: Impressions and Suggestions," August 21–22, 1966, folder 7, box 8, AV Records. The *Charleston Gazette* reported about 300 representatives planned to attend the meeting, James A. Haught, "300 Poor Map Trip to Capital," *Charleston Gazette*, August 2, 1966.

86. Joseph T. Mulloy interviewed by Thomas Kiffmeyer, November 10, 1990, War on Poverty Oral History Project.

87. "Report on Appalachian Volunteers Activities, 1965," folder 1, box 8, AV Records.

Chapter 2. "I Was Always Interested in People's Welfare"

1. Edith Easterling, interviewed by Carrie Kline, March 12, 2011, Southern Appalachian Archives, Berea College.

2. See, for example, John Dominis's photographs, from a photo essay, "The Valley of Poverty," *LIFE*, January 31, 1964; "War on Poverty: Portraits from an Appalachian Battleground, 1964," *Time and Life* Pictures/Getty Images, accessed February 3, 2014, http://life.time.com/history/war-on-poverty-appalachia-portraits-1964/#1.

3. Edith Easterling and Jake Easterling, interviewed by Nyoka Hawkins, August 2, 1987, Social History and Cultural Change in the Elkhorn Coal Fields Oral History Project, Louie B. Nunn Oral History Center, University of Kentucky.

4. Anthropologist Oscar Lewis outlined the culture of poverty theory in *Five Families: Mexican Case Studies in the Culture of Poverty* (New York: Basic Books, 1959); Daniel Patrick Moynihan applied it to black families in the United States. See Chappell, *The War on Welfare*, 35–41, 45–50.

5. Jack E. Weller, *Yesterday's People: Life in Contemporary Appalachia* (Lexington: University of Kentucky Press, 1965). See also Billings and Blee, *The Road to Poverty*, 10–11.

6. For similar stories of local organizing in West Virginia, see Perry, *They'll Cut Off Your Project.* For case studies that focus on women in antipoverty organizing, see Orleck, *Storming Caesar's Palace*; Germany, *New Orleans after the Promises*; Carroll, *Mobilizing New York*; Naples, *Grassroots Warriors*; Christina Greene, *Our Separate Ways: Women and the Black Freedom Movement in Durham, North Carolina, 1940–1970* (Chapel Hill: University of North Carolina Press, 2005); Williams, *The Politics of Public Housing.*

7. Edith Easterling's narrative is drawn from three oral history interviews: Edith Easterling, interviewed by Carrie Kline, March 12, 2011; Edith Easterling, interviewed by Gibbs Kinderman, October 10, 1989, War on Poverty Oral History Collection; Edith Easterling and Jake Easterling, interviewed by Nyoka Hawkins, August 2, 1987.

8. "150 Years of Pike County," Pike County Historical Society, accessed on November 30, 2016, https://archive.org/details/150yearspikecoun01pike.

9. Easterlings, interviewed by Hawkins.

10. Easterling, interviewed by Kinderman.

11. While in service, Isaac died of typhoid fever, leaving behind eight children (four of whom were dependents) from his second wife, Mary, who had died around 1860. Just before the war, he married a woman named Polly, and she bore a son the same year Isaac died. Polly received a bounty of $100 following Isaac's death, and several years later claimed a pension of $10 a month for herself and her son. Mary Whitt Coleman, Index of Special Examiners Report, Claim of Nancy Hunt, et al. Children of Isaac Coleman, January 13, 1907, widow's pension application no. WC144300; service of Isaac Coleman (Kentucky Infantry Regiment 39, Company D, Civil War); Case Files of Approved Pension Applications of Widows and Other Veterans of the Army and Navy Who Served Mainly in the Civil War and the War with Spain, compiled 1861–1934, Department of Veterans Affairs, Record Group 15, National Archives, Washington, D.C. For Joseph Coleman's statement, see Deposition H.

12. Theda Skocpol, *Protecting Soldiers and Mothers: The Political Origins of Social Policy in the United States* (Cambridge: Harvard University Press, 1995).

13. See 1930 U.S. census, Pike County, Kentucky, Poor Bottom, ED 98-13, dwelling 39, family 39, Vina J. Coleman; digital image, Ancestry.com, accessed September 4, 2016, http://ancestory.com; 1920 U.S. census, Pike County, Lookout Precinct 30, ED 115, dwelling 186, family 186, Vina J. Coleman; digital image, Ancestry.com, accessed September 4, 2016, http://ancestry.com; 1910 U.S. census, Pike County, Kentucky, Hellier, ED 164, dwelling 243, family 244, Joseph Coleman; digital image, Ancestry.com, accessed September 14, 2016, http://ancestry.com. Vina Coleman claimed a pension until her death in 1945. See Joseph Coleman, Organization Index to Pension Files of Veterans Who Served between 1861 and 1900, pension certificate nos. 214077 (invalid), 729996 (widow), 740076 (dependent); service of Joseph Coleman (Kentucky Infantry Regiment 39, Company H, Civil War); Organization Index to Pension Files of Veterans Who Served between 1861 and 1900, compiled 1949–1949, documenting the period 1861–1942, Department of Veterans Affairs, Record Group 15; National Archives, Washington, D.C.

14. Easterling, interviewed by Kline.
15. Easterlings, interviewed by Hawkins.
16. Easterling, interviewed by Kline.
17. Easterlings, interviewed by Hawkins.
18. Ibid.
19. Ibid.
20. Ibid.
21. Easterling, interviewed by Kinderman.
22. Easterlings, interviewed by Hawkins.
23. Ibid.
24. Easterlings, interviewed by Hawkins.
25. Easterling, interviewed by Kline.
26. Sue Ella Kobak, interviewed by the author, March 6, 2011; Easterlings, interviewed by Hawkins.
27. Kobak, interviewed by the author; Easterling, interviewed by Kinderman.
28. Kobak, interviewed by the author.
29. Easterling, interviewed by Kinderman.
30. Based on a chart compiled by Jeanette Knowles, in author's possession.
31. Kobak, interviewed by the author, March 6, 2011.
32. Easterling, interviewed by Kinderman.
33. Kobak, interviewed by the author, March 6, 2011.
34. Kiffmeyer, *Reformers to Radicals*, 89.
35. Kobak, interviewed by author, March 6, 2011; Kobak, interviewed by Kinderman.
36. See John M. Glen, *Highlander: No Ordinary School, 1932–1962* (Lexington: The University Press of Kentucky, 1988).
37. Press Release, Highlander Center, March 2, 1964, "Grassroots Social Activism: Records of the Highlander Folk School and Highlander Research and Education Center, 1932–1978," microfilm (Woodbridge, Conn.: Primary Source Microfilm, 2007).
38. "Southern Student Organizing Committee," Civil Rights Movement Veterans, online archive, hosted by Tougaloo College, accessed February 7, 2017, http://www.crmvet.org/tim/timhis64.htm#1964ssoc.
39. See Emmie Shrader, "Poor Whites and the Movement," and Kimberly Moody, "Organizing Poor Whites," as well as "SSOC conference notes," folder 10, box 58, Southern Student Organizing Committee, 1965–1966, AV Records.
40. Kobak, interviewed by the author, March 6, 2011.
41. Kobak, interviewed by the author, March 6 and May 20, 2011.
42. Kobak, interviewed by Kinderman, October 28, 1985, War on Poverty Oral History Project.
43. Thomas Rhodenbaugh, interviewed by Thomas Kiffmeyer and Harry Rice, March 11, 2011, Appalachia Oral History Collection, Special Collections, Berea College.

44. Kobak, interviewed by author, March; Easterling, interviewed by Kinderman; Joe Mulloy, "Community Action Efforts in Pike and Letcher Counties," (1966), folder 4, box 8, AV Records.

45. Mulloy, interviewed by Kiffmeyer.

46. Easterling, interviewed by Kinderman. See also Kiffmeyer, *Reformers to Radicals*, 174–175.

47. Ibid.; See also Kiffmeyer, *Reformers to Radicals*, 174–175.

48. VISTA Roster, Pike and Floyd Counties," folder 6, box 42, AV Records; "Project Guideline Report, 1965–1966, folder 2, box 8, AV Records; Joe Mulloy, "Report on Intern Activities of Edith Easterling," January 4, 1967, folder 1, box 25, AV Records; description of interns (and quotation) from Kiffmeyer, *Reformers to Radicals*, 152.

49. Mulloy, "Community Action Efforts in Pike and Letcher Counties."

50. Easterling, interviewed by Kline. For other examples of cross-generational alliances, see Charles Payne, *I've Got the Light of Freedom: The Organizing Tradition and the Mississippi Freedom Struggle*, 2nd edition (Berkeley: University of California Press, 2007) and Sara Evans, *Personal Politics: The Roots of Women's Liberation in the Civil Rights Movement and the New Left* (New York: Vintage Books, 1979).

51. Guy and Candie Carawan, "Sowing on the Mountain: Nurturing Cultural Roots and Creativity for Community Change," in *Fighting Back in Appalachia: Traditions of Resistance and Change*, ed., Stephen L. Fisher (Philadelphia: Temple University Press, 1993), 245–261, 247.

52. Easterling, interviewed by Kinderman; Easterling, interviewed by Kline.

53. Easterling, interviewed by Kinderman.

54. On Easterling's work history, see David Walls, Response to Tom Bethell, folder 5, box 42, AV Records; Marrowbone Folk School Pamphlet, folder 8, box 95, Council of the Southern Mountains Records, 1970–1989, Southern Appalachian Archives, Berea College (hereafter cited as CSM Records); "The Marrowbone News," folder 9, box 130, AV Records.

55. For other examples of creating community meeting spaces, see "White Papers," Preface, 1966, AVs, folder 4, box 8, AV Records; "Report on Appalachian Volunteers Activities, 1965," folder 1, box 8, AV Records; "History of the AV Eastern Kentucky Program," AV Quarterly Report, October 1967, folder 9, box 8, AV Records.

56. Marrowbone Folk School Pamphlet, folder 8, box 95, CSM Records; "The Marrowbone News," folder 9, box 130, AV Records.

57. "Pike County," report by Edith Easterling, May 1968, folder 3, box 9, AV Records.

58. Marrowbone Folk School Pamphlet; Marrowbone News, August 1967 and September 1968, folder 15, box 15, AV Records.

59. Eller, *Uneven Ground*, 148, and Montrie, *To Save the Land and People*, 88–90; The Appalachian Volunteers' staff maintained that in taking up the issue of strip mining, they were following the lead of community members. See "The Appalachian Volunteers: A Report to the Public," August 17, 1967, folder 1, box 10, AV Records.

60. Montrie, *To Save the Land and People*, 65–66, 72, 91–96.

61. Easterling, interviewed by Kinderman.

62. "Press Release, July 13, 1967" and "Press Release, Monday, July 24," folder 12, box 40, AV Records; Easterling, interviewed by Kinderman; Easterling, interviewed by Anne Lewis, "Outtakes—Appalachian Group to Save the Land and People," Appalshop Archive.

63. "Owensboro Symposium on Stripmining," 1967, folder 2, box 55, AV Records; "Press Release, July 24, 1967," folder 12, box 40, AV Records.

64. Ratliff's Testimony at Criminal Trial, folder 60, subseries 2.2, McSurely Papers; FBI Report, July 24, 1969, folder 222, subseries 2.3.2, in the Alan McSurely Papers, #4928, Southern Historical Collection of the University of North Carolina at Chapel Hill and the African American Resources Collection of North Carolina Central University (hereafter McSurely Papers).

65. "Quarterly Report, October 1967, Special Report to Governor Breathitt," folder 9, box 8, AV Records.

66. Amended Pages: Alan McSurely Security Matter, folder 212, subseries 2.3.2, McSurely Papers; Eller, *Uneven Ground*, 149–151.

67. Amended Pages: Alan McSurely Security Matter, McSurely Papers.

68. Easterling, interviewed by Kinderman; Easterling, interviewed by Kline.

69. Ratliff told one reporter: "Frankly, I laughed about these things when I first heard them. Then I got into this material, and I became convinced." In James C. Millstone, "Late Night Arrest Began Kentucky Sedition Case," *St. Louis Post*, September 18, 1967.

70. Amended Pages: Alan McSurely Security Matter, McSurely Papers.

71. "Report of the September 1967 Pike County Grand Jury," folder 1, box 10, AV Records.

72. Easterling, interviewed by Kinderman; President of the Pike County Chamber of Commerce told reporters that "some local persons, including a woman antipoverty employee who heretofore led an exemplary life," had been converted to Communism. See James C Millston, "Kentucky Grand Jury Charged Antipoverty Workers with Sedition," *St. Louis Post*, September 16, 1967.

73. Edith Easterling, "Why I Voted for Joe Mulloy to Be Fired," December 6, 1967, folder 1, box 11, AV Records. The firing of Mulloy led to a series of resignations. See letters by Thomas Bethel, Steve Daugherty, and Mike Clark, and the press release, "Appalachian Volunteers Fire Joe Mulloy," folder 1, box 11, AV Records. See also Eller, *Uneven Ground*, 149–151; Kiffmeyer, *Reformers to Radicals*, 194–195.

74. Letters between 1965–1969, folder 1, box 59, AV Records.

75. Thelma Parker Witt, interviewed by Jo Crockett Zingg, November 11, 2010, Southern Appalachian Archives, Berea College.

76. Before the sedition arrests, Joe Mulloy was in conversation with a local about buying an unused one-room schoolhouse. The deal fell through when he was arrested. See Mulloy, interviewed by Kiffmeyer.

77. Quarterly report by Edith Easterling, May 14, 1968, folder 3, box 9, AV Records.

78. Governor Breathitt to Sargent Shriver, September 19, 1967, and Shriver to Breathitt, August 26, 1967, folder Kentucky, Mid-Atlantic Region, box 14; VISTA Program; RG 362; NACP.

79. Bill Cook, "Memo to Sargent Shriver," September 8, 1967, folder Kentucky, Mid-Atlantic Region, box 14; VISTA Program; RG 362; NACP.

80. Al Whitehouse, "Statement on Appalachian Volunteers," September 20, 1967, and note to Leveo Sanchez from Jestyn Portugill, and the memorandum, "Appalachian Volunteers Meeting with Governor Breathitt," October 5, 1967, in which OEO officials note that Breathitt's "confidence in Whitehouse" is "discouraging" and will "take some time to change," folder Kentucky, Mid-Atlantic Region, box 14; VISTA Program; RG 362; NACP.

81. "White Papers, Preface," 1966, folder 4, box 8, AV Records.

82. Easterling, interviewed by Kinderman.

83. Marrowbone News, August 16, 1967, folder 15, box 15, AV Records.

84. Marrowbone News, August 16, 1967, and November 1967, folder 15, box 15, AV Records.

85. The Robert F. Kennedy Performance Project, accessed April 11, 2017, http://rfkineky.org/project/tour/fleming-neon.htm (hereafter RFK Performance Project); Thelma Parker Witt, Jeannette Knowles, and Mildred Shackleford, interviewed by author, January 21, 2013, in the author's possession.

86. See The Food Stamp Act of 1964, Public Law 88–525, August 31, 1964, accessed February 5, 2017, http://www.fns.usda.gov/sites/default/files/PL_88-525.pdf.

87. "Transcript of Evidence, Hearing Held at Fleming-Neon, Kentucky," Field Hearings—Eastern Kentucky, U.S.S. Subcommittee on Employment, Manpower, and Poverty, archived in The RFK Performance Project.

88. "MLK Public Statement on the Poor People's Campaign," The King Center, accessed August 3, 2017, http://www.thekingcenter.org/archive/document/mlk-public-statement-poor-peoples-campaign.

89. King quoted in Mantler, *Power to the Poor*, 90.

90. Ibid., 97.

91. "Appalachian People's Meeting, 1966–1968," folder 15, box 40, AV Records; "Mountain People Attend Poor People's Conference," *The Hawkeye*, May 20, 1968, folder 1, box 130, AV Records.

92. Mantler, *Power to the Poor*, 152.

93. "More than 700 People Came to the Appalachian People's Meeting," May 25, 1968, folder 15, box 40, AV Records.

94. "Statements of Demands for Rights of the Poor" presented to Agencies of the U.S. Government by the SCLC and its Committee of 100, April 29–30, May 1, 1968, folder 5, box 55, AV Records.

95. Southern Christian Leadership Conference, 1968–1969, folder 6, box 59, AV Records.

96. Eric Metzner, "Partial Report on the Trip to Washington," June 3, 1968, folder 15, box 40, AV Records.

97. Kobak, phone interview with the author, March 29, 2017.

98. Mantler, *Power to the Poor*, 211–212.

99. Since its inception, the NWRO had taken the stance that "poverty and poor people, not just black people" could benefit from the organization. It also worked to

overturn the associations between welfare and African American women, pointing out that the majority of welfare recipients were white. West, *The National Welfare Rights Movement*, 22, 60, 83–83.

100. Easterling to fellow organizers, July 22, 1968, and Easterling to Tim Sampson, July 1968, folder 15, box 51, AV Records.

101. Meeting notes on the Tim Sampson Sunday Session, August 6, 1968, folder 5, box 51, AV Records.

102. Easterling, Sue, Volunteer, 1968, AVs, folder 6, box 4, AV Records.

103. Knowles, Witt, and Shackleford, interviewed by the author.

104. Ibid.

105. Witt, interviewed by Zingg; Kentucky Mountain Welfare Rights Organization, folder 40, box 49, CSM Records.

Chapter 3. "In the Eyes of the Poor, the Black, the Youth"

1. Easterlings, interviewed by Hawkins; Easterling, interviewed by Kline. See also Kentucky Un-American Activities Committee, 1968, files, folder 8, box 50, AV Records.

2. Easterling, interviewed by Kinderman.

3. Louie B. Nunn, "Opening of the Kentucky Republican Campaign," London, September 14, 1968, Robert F. Sexton and Lewis Bellardo, eds., *The Public Papers of Louie B. Nunn, 1967–1971* (Lexington: University of Kentucky Press, 1965), 183–185.

4. Louie B. Nunn, interviewed by Thomas Kiffmeyer, July 6, 1963, War on Poverty Oral History Project.

5. Karen Tani, *States of Dependency: Welfare, Rights, and American Governance, 1935–1972* (New York: Cambridge University Press, 2016).

6. Nunn, interviewed by Kiffmeyer.

7. Catherine Fosl, *Subversive Southerner: Anne Braden and the Struggle for Racial Justice in the Cold War South* (New York: Palgrave Macmillan, 2002); Catherine Fosl and Tracy E. K'Meyer, eds., *Freedom on the Border: An Oral History of the Civil Rights Movement in Kentucky* (Lexington: University Press of Kentucky, 2009); Robert R. Korstad, *Civil Rights Unionism and the Struggle for Democracy in the Mid-Twentieth Century South* (Chapel Hill: University of North Carolina Press, 2003); Robin D. G. Kelley, *Hammer and Hoe: Alabama Communists during the Great Depression*, 2nd edition (Chapel Hill: University of North Carolina Press, 2015); Glenda Gilmore, *Defying Dixie: The Radical Roots of Civil Rights, 1919–1950* (New York: W. W. Norton and Company, 2009).

8. Fosl, *Subversive Southerner*, 145.

9. Ibid., 145; Glen, *Highlander*, 184.

10. Fosl, *Subversive Southerner*, 135–173.

11. Ibid., 232–234, 282–283, 287.

12. See "Mountain Feminist: Helen Matthews Lewis, Appalachian Studies, and the Long Women's Movement," compiled and eds. Jessica Wilkerson and David P. Cline, *Southern Cultures* (Fall 2011); Gregg L. Michel, *Struggle for a Better South: The Southern Student Organizing Committee, 1964–1969* (New York: Palgrave Macmil-

lan, 2004); Appalachian Workshops and White Community Project Workshops, in "Grassroots Social Activism," microfilm.

13. Southern Mountain Project, Prospectus 1965–1966, "Grassroots Social Activism," microfilm.

14. Fosl, *Subversive Southerner*, 306–308.

15. See Hasan Kwame Jeffries, *Bloody Lowndes: Civil Rights and Black Power in Alabama's Black Belt* (New York: New York University Press, 2009).

16. On the history of black power in Louisville, see K'Meyer, *Civil Rights in the Gateway to the South: Louisville, Kentucky, 1945–1980* (Lexington: The University Press of Kentucky, 2009), chapter 6.

17. Ibid., 217–250.

18. "KUAC File," Kentucky Un-American Activities Committee, 1968, files, folder 8, box 50, AV Records; Easterling, interviewed by Kline; Transcripts of Hearings and Exhibits, boxes 1 and 2, Joint Committee on Un-American Activities, General Assembly, Legislative Research Commission, Kentucky Department of Library and Archives (hereafter KDLA).

19. Transcripts of Hearings, Pikeville, October 15–16, 1968, box 1, Joint Committee on Un-American Activities, General Assembly, Legislative Research Commission, KDLA.

20. "KUAC Will Continue Hearing after Election," *Courier-Journal*, October 17, 1968.

21. Transcripts of Hearings, Pikeville, October 15–16, 1968, Joint Committee on Un-American Activities.

22. Press Release, Dave Walls, October 14, 1968, folder 8, box 50, AV Records.

23. Transcripts of Hearings, Pikeville, October 15–16, 1968, Joint Committee on Un-American Activities.

24. Ibid.

25. "Internal Fight Splits Pikeville as KUAC Probe Nears," *Courier-Journal*, October 14, 1968.

26. "KUAC Will Continue Hearing after Election," *Courier-Journal*, October 17, 1968.

27. "Statement by David Walls, Acting Director, AV," Press Release, October 14, 1968, folder 8, box 50, AV Records.

28. Transcript of Hearings, Pikeville, December 3, 1968, box 2, Joint Committee on Un-American Activities.

29. "Witness Scolds Probers for Attacks on AVs," *Courier-Journal*, December 4, 1968.

30. Transcript of Hearings, Pikeville, December 3, 1968, box 2, Joint Committee on Un-American Activities.

31. Ibid. Thanks to Sue Ella Kobak for pointing out the significance of Easterling's use of "brother."

32. Ibid.

33. Ibid.

34. Ibid.

35. Easterling, interviewed by Kinderman.

36. "KUAC Delivers Mid-Trial Verdict," *ML&W*, December 1968; "KUAC Urges Nunn: Oust Appalachian Volunteers," *Courier Journal*, November 30, 1968; Kiffmeyer, *Reformers to Radicals*, 204–205.

37. Memo from Pike County Citizens' Association, folder 9, box 55, AV Records; Letters in support of Edith Easterling, October 1968, folder 5, box 46, AV Records; on the AVs' closure, see Kiffmeyer, *Reformers to Radicals*, 204–205.

38. Letters in support of Edith Easterling, October 1968, folder 5, box 46, AV Records.

39. See Whisnant, *Modernizing the Mountain*; Kiffmeyer, *Reformers to Radicals* and "Looking Back to the City in the Hills: The Council of the Southern Mountains and a Longer View of the War on Poverty in the Appalachian South," in *The War on Poverty: A New Grassroots History*, 359–386.

40. Quoted in Eller, *Uneven Ground*, 152.

41. Edith Easterling, "Three Months Report," February 1969, folder 9, box 9, AV Records.

42. Edith Easterling to Conrad Browne, May 1969, folder 9, box 95, Highlander Research and Education Center Papers, The State Historical Society of Wisconsin, Archival Division (hereafter Highlander Records).

43. "Fifty-Fifth Annual Conference, 1967," folder 4, box 145, Council of the Southern Mountains, 1913–1970, Southern Appalachian Archives, Berea College.

44. See Kiffmeyer, "Looking Back to the City in the Hills," 362.

45. "Greetings from the Youth Commission of the Council of the Southern Mountains," folder 6, box 46, AV Records; Sue Ella Kobak interviewed by Margaret Brown, January 2, 1991, War on Poverty Oral History Collection.

46. Kobak, interviewed by the author; Easterling, interviewed by Kinderman; Karen Mulloy, interviewed by Margaret Brown, November 10, 1990, War on Poverty Oral History Collection.

47. Memo on meeting attended by CSM Community Action Committee and FOCIS, October 1968, folder 14, box 109, Highlander Records.

48. "The Rundown," folder 4, box 20, AV Records. The rhetoric and goals of the Youth Commission parallel one of the major goals of the Black Studies Movement: to build black consciousness among black students. Student activists from Appalachia reflected on how to build pride and class-consciousness among Appalachian youth. On the Black Student Movement, see Martha Biondi, *The Black Revolution on Campus* (Berkeley: University of California Press, 2012).

49. "Youth Commission, Neighborhood Youth Corp Proposal, n.d.," folder 2, box 226, AV Records; Kobak interviewed by the author, March and May 2011. See "The Rundown," April 9, 1969, "CSM Newsletters, 1968–1969," folder 4, box 20, AV Records.

50. See Amy Sonnie and James Tracie, *Hillbilly Nationalists, Urban Race Rebels, and Black Power: Community Organizing in Radical Times* (Brooklyn: Melville House, 2011).

51. Sue Ella Easterling to Milton Ogle, January 26, 1968, folder 6, box 46, AV Records.

52. *ML&W*, May 1969.

53. "Youth Commission, Neighborhood Youth Corp Proposal, n.d.," folder 2, box 226, AV Records.

54. Mary Rice Farris, "Ten Feet Tall," *ML&W*, May 1969.

55. Mary Farris interviewed by Leroy Wimbush, Madison County, Kentucky, January 1973, Record Group No. 14.03, box 2, Oral Histories, His 190/App Oral History, Berea College Archives.

56. "Mary Rice Farris, Application," folder 46, box 109, AV Records; Mary Farris to Diane London, folder 6, box 50, AV Records.

57. "Transcript of Evidence, Hearing Held at Vortex, Kentucky," Field Hearings—Eastern Kentucky, U.S.S. Subcommittee on Employment, Manpower, and Poverty, archived in The RFK Performance Project.

58. Ibid.

59. See Chana Kai Lee, *For Freedom's Sake: The Life of Fannie Lou Hamer* (Urbana: University of Illinois Press, 2000); Nadasen, *Welfare Warriors*; Orleck, *Storming Caesar's Palace.*

60. See Smith, "Degradations of Whiteness," and Barbara Ellen Smith, "Representing Appalachia: The Impossible Necessity of Appalachian Studies," in *Studying Appalachian Studies: Making the Path by Walking*, eds., Chad Berry, Philip J. Obermiller, and Shaunna L. Scott (Urbana: University of Illinois Press, 2015), 42–61.

61. Farris, "Ten Feet Tall."

62. "Fontana: The Formal Record," *ML&W*, May 1969; Kobak, interviewed by the author, May 2010 and August 2011; Loyal Jones, interviewed by the author, June 2012.

63. Kiffmeyer, *Reformers to Radicals*, 123–124, 205.

64. Loyal Jones, Resignation letter to the Board of Commissioners, May 28, 1970, folder 29, box 63, CSM Records.

65. Eula Hall, interviewed by Harry Rice, November 10, 2004, Council of the Southern Mountains Oral History Project, Southern Appalachian Archives, Berea College.

66. Loyal Jones to Donald Rumsfeld, April 1 and April 16, 1970, folder 23, box 63, CSM Records; Loyal Jones, Resignation letter to the Board of Commissioners. See Korstad and Leloudis, *To Right These Wrongs*, 338–340. For other examples of how the reorganization of the OEO affected antipoverty organizations, see Greta de Jong, "Plantation Politics: The Tufts-Delta Health Center and Intraracial Class Conflict in Mississippi, 1965–1972," in *The War on Poverty*, 270–273; Daniel M. Cobb, "The War on Poverty in Mississippi and Oklahoma: Beyond Black and White," in *The War on Poverty*, 401–402.

67. See Lewis, et al., *Colonialism in Modern America.*

68. Appalachian Studies Conference, 1970, Clinch Valley College, folder 12, box 102, Highlander Records.

69. See Lewis, et al., *Colonialism in Modern America.*

70. Phone interview with Sue Ella Kobak, March 29, 2017; Obituary for John Kobak, folder 14, box 96, Highlander Records; Stephen Parks, "State Man Finds Wealth amidst Poverty," *Hartford Courant*, January 5, 1970.

71. Easterling to Conrad Browne, 1970 and 1971, folder 9, box 95, Highlander Records.

72. Edith Easterling to John Rosenberg, John Rosenberg's personal papers, Prestonsburg, Kentucky; Easterling, interviewed by Kinderman.

Chapter 4. March for Survival

1. Eula Hall, interviewed by Neil Boothby and Robert Korstad, September 5, 1992, Southern Rural Poverty Collection, DeWitt Wallace Center for Media and Democracy, Duke University, accessed October 22, 2017, http://dewitt.sanford.duke.edu/rutherfurd-living-history/southern-rural-poverty-collection; Eula Hall, interviewed by the author, March 10, 2011.

2. Hall, interviewed by the author, March 10, 2011.

3. Ibid.

4. Hall, interviewed by Boothby and Korstad.

5. Hall, interviewed by the author; interviewed by Boothby and Korstad.

6. Hall, interviewed by Boothby and Korstad.

7. Ibid.; "What Is Welfare?" (Teaberry, Ky.: Hawkeye Press, Inc., May 1968), folder 9, box 63, AV Records.

8. Elizabeth M. Schneider, "The Violence of Privacy," in *The Public Nature of Private Violence: The Discovery of Domestic Abuse*, eds., Martha Albertson Fineman and Roxanne Mykitiuk (New York: Routledge, 1994).

9. Hall, interviewed by Boothby and Korstad.

10. U.S. Department of Commerce, Bureau of the Census, *1970 Census of the Population: General Social and Economic Characteristics*, Kentucky, vol. 1, pt. 19; Richard A. Couto, *Poverty, Politics, and Health Care: An Appalachian Experience* (New York: Praeger Publishers, 1975), 63.

11. Community Profile: Floyd County, Kentucky, Office of Economic Opportunity Information Center (Washington, D.C.: Office of Economic Opportunity, 1966), box 193; Office of Economic Opportunity; Information Center, 1964–1967; Records of the Community Services Administration; RG 381; NACP.

12. Hall, interviewed by Boothby and Korstad.

13. On "breadwinner liberalism," see Robert O. Self, *All in the Family: The Realignment of American Democracy since 1960* (New York: Macmillan, 2012). On the history of welfare rights, see Levenstein, *A Movement without Marches*; Felicia Kornbluh, *The Battle for Welfare Rights: Politics and Poverty in Modern America* (Philadelphia: University of Pennsylvania Press, 2007); Orleck, *Storming Caesar's Palace*; Quadagno, *The Color of Welfare*; Nadasen, *Welfare Warriors*.

14. Caudill, *Night Comes to the Cumberlands*. In his next book, *Watches of the Night*, Caudill hammered the welfare regime from the New Deal to the expansion

of welfare under Johnson's War on Poverty measures. Harry Caudill, *Watches of the Night* (Ashland, Ky.: Jesse Stuart Foundation, 1976), 178.

15. Caudill, *Night Comes to the Cumberlands*, 280–287, 286.

16. Quoted in Orleck, Introduction, *The War on Poverty*, 10.

17. Ibid., 18–19.

18. Chappell, *The War on Welfare*, 1, 5.

19. Witt, Knowles, and Shackleford, interviewed by author.

20. See Nadasen, *Rethinking the Welfare Rights Movement*, 16–19.

21. On the history of the welfare rights movement and the racialization of welfare recipients, see Quadagno, *The Color of Welfare*, and Patricia Hill Collins, *Black Feminist Thought: Knowledge, Consciousness, and the Politics of Empowerment* (New York: Routledge, 2000).

22. Report on Floyd and Knott Counties by Flem Messer, folder 2, box 8, AV Records.

23. Colleen LeBlanc, telephone interview with the author, October 2016.

24. LeBlanc, telephone interview with the author.

25. Hall, interviewed by the author, September 15, 2012.

26. William G. Poole, A Citizen's Report on Volunteers in Service to America and Appalachian Volunteers in Floyd County, Kentucky, November 11, 1966, folder 3, box 8, AV Records.

27. LeBlanc, telephone interview with the author.

28. Hall, interviewed by Boothby and Korstad.

29. *The Hawkeye*, August 4, 1966, folder 1, box 130, AV Records.

30. The Problem of Participation in Community Action Programs: Impressions and Suggestions, August 21–22, 1966, folder 7, box 8, AV Records; Hall, interviewed by the author, 2011.

31. Tom Hamilton, Hank Zingg, and Nick Frasure, Floyd County Reports, AV Activity Reports, folder 2, box 9, AV Records.

32. Steve Brooks, interviewed by the author, November 18, 2013.

33. Hall, interviewed by the author, 2011 and 2013; Floyd CAP Opposes AV Activity, *The Hawkeye*, April 22, 1968. During the KUAC hearings, Harry Eastburn testified against AV activities. See "KUAC File," *Appalachian Lookout*, December 1968.

34. Hall, interviewed by Rice.

35. Brooks, interviewed by the author; "Welfare Rights," *The Hawkeye*, May 1, 1969.

36. "Eastern Kentucky Welfare Rights Organization Constitution and By-Laws," folder 14, box 46, AV Records.

37. Ibid.

38. See Muncy, "Coal-Fired Reforms."

39. "Eastern Kentucky Welfare Rights Organization Constitution and By-Laws," folder 14, box 46, AV Records.

40. Letter to Julian Mosley from Steve Brooks, January 8, 1970, folder 40, box 49, CSM Records.

41. Men and Jobs, The Problem of Participation in Community Action Programs: Impressions and Suggestions, August 21–22, 1966, folder 7, box 8, AV Records.

42. Vivian Keathley, telephone interview with author, March 2012.

43. Hall, interviewed by the author, September 2012.

44. Ibid., March 2012.

45. Ibid., 2013.

46. Ibid., 2011, 2013.

47. Thorkelson, interviewed by Zingg, October 11, 2008.

48. Ricki Solinger, "The First Welfare Case: Money, Sex, Marriage, and White Supremacy in Selma, 1966, A Reproductive Justice Analysis," *Journal of Women's History* 22, no. 3 (Fall 2010): 13–38.

49. See Martha F. Davis, *Brutal Need: Lawyers and the Welfare Rights Movement* (New Haven: Yale University Press, 1993); Thorkelson, interviewed by Zingg.

50. Thorkelson, interviewed by Zingg; Status Report on Lawyers, n.d. box 1, folder VISTA lawyers, VISTA Program; RG 362; NACP.

51. Thomas Rhodenbaugh to William L. Robinson, and Howard Thorkelson to Richard L. Huffman, January 24, 1969, folder 5, box 51, AV Records.

52. Role of Law Students in AV Program: Appraisal and Recommendations, folder 4, box 51, AV Records.

53. Ibid.

54. Letters to Milton Ogle, July 22, 1968, and Distribution List, folder 9, box 63, AV Records.

55. I borrow this phrase from Felicia Kornbluh, "Food as a Civil Right: Hunger, Work, and Welfare in the South after the Civil Rights Act," *Labor: Studies in Working-Class History* 1–2 (2015): 135–158.

56. Hall, interviewed by the author, 2013.

57. Ibid.

58. Linda L. Hamilton to Carl Perkins, August 7, 1969, folder 14, box 46, AV Records.

59. For history of the National School Lunch Program, see Susan Levine, *School Lunch Politics: The Surprising History of America's Favorite Welfare Program* (Princeton: Princeton University Press, 2008). See also Committee on School Lunch Participation, *Their Daily Bread: A Study of the National School Lunch Program* (Atlanta: McNelly-Rudd, 1968) and Citizens' Board of Inquiry into Hunger and Malnutrition in the United States, *Hunger, U.S.A.: A Report* (Boston: Beacon Press, 1968).

60. "LBJ Wraps Up His Poverty Tour of the Appalachian States," film, LBJ Library, accessed September 4, 2016, www.lbjlib.utexas.edu/johnson/lbjforkids/pov_media.shtm.

61. Levine, *School Lunch Politics*, 105.

62. Ibid., 113.

63. Ibid., 128.

64. Ibid., 113–116. Gordon W. Gunderson, "National School Lunch Program, Child Nutrition Act," accessed November 26, 2013, http://www.fns.usda.gov/nslp/history_6#child.

65. Levine, *School Lunch Politics*, 143; "EKWRO Denied Access to School Lunch Regulations," *The Hawkeye*, July 15, 1969; "History of the School Lunch Issue," *The Hawkeye*, August 1969. See also *Appalachian Lookout*, January–February 1969 and April 1969.

66. Levine, *School Lunch Politics*, 143.

67. "Report Assails East Kentucky School-Lunch 'Failure,'" *The Hawkeye*, July 15, 1969.

68. Hall, interviewed by Boothby and Korstad; Hall, interviewed by the author, March 2011.

69. "Report Assails East Kentucky School-Lunch 'Failure'"; Letter to Charles Remsberg requesting copies of magazine article, folder 16, box 46, AV Records.

70. "Report Assails East Kentucky School-Lunch 'Failure.'"

71. Hall, interviewed by Boothby and Korstad; Hall, interviewed by author, March 2011.

72. Ibid.

73. Letter from Clark, published in *The Hawkeye*, September 1969.

74. Hall, interviewed by Boothby and Korstad; Board of Education Declaration, July 21, 1969, and Declaration published in the *Sandy Valley Shopper*, folder 16, box 46, AV Records. See also "AVs as Subversives," *The Hawkeye*, and "KUAC File," *Appalachian Lookout*.

75. Ibid.

76. EKWRO Textbook Committee to Charles Clark, October 10, 1969, reprinted in *The Hawkeye*, October 1969.

77. Thorkelson, interviewed by Zingg.

78. Brooks, interviewed by the author.

79. "Mountain Women Join Negro Mothers to Push for Welfare," *Courier-Journal*, January 28, 1968.

80. Ibid.

81. Bill Peterson, "150 Poor People Air Complaints at Capitol," *Courier-Journal*, June 21, 1969.

82. "Governors Get Shares in Colt," *Courier-Journal*, May 1, 1969.

83. "Hope—The Thoroughbred Mule," *ML&W*, May 1969.

84. "Nunn, Smiling Grimly, Accepts 'Hope,' the Mule," *Courier-Journal*, May 2, 1969; Louie B. Nunn, "Republican Governors' Conference, Acceptance of Poor People's Mule, May 1, 1969," *The Public Papers of Governor Louie B. Nunn, 1967–1971*, 276–277; "Mayor Applied Pressure for Swift End to Sit-in," *Courier-Journal*, May 1, 1969; "Governors Drop ABM, Criticize Welfare Policy," and "Small Protest Group Jeers GOP Governors," *Courier-Journal*," May 3, 1969.

85. Louie B. Nunn, "Welfare Reform," March 11, 1970, *The Public Papers of Governor Louie B. Nunn, 1967–1971*, 76–77; See Jennifer Mittelstadt, Marisa Chappell, and Premilla Nadasen, *Welfare in the United States: A History with Documents, 1935–1966* (New York: Routledge, 2009), 32–37.

86. "Appalachian Roundup, Kentucky WRO Meets New Welfare Commissioner," *ML&W*, June-July 1972, 34; "Appalachian Roundup, KY WRO Wins on Food Stamps,"

ML&W, August 1972; "Appalachian Roundup, Kentucky, Commissioner Huecker Addressed State Welfare Rights Group," *ML&W*, November 1972.

87. Hall, interviewed by the author, 2013; *ML&W*, May-June 1971 and September-October 1971; "Report from March Planning Committee," September 1971, and "The Appalachian Welfare March," folder 7, box 96, CSM Records.

88. See Chappell, *The War on Welfare*, 65–66.

89. Nadasen, *Rethinking the Welfare Rights Movement*, 79–81, 84–87.

90. Survival March, Information Packet, folder 7, box 96, CSM Records.

91. "A Summary of the Survival March," *ML&W*, November 1971; "Washington March," *Mountain Eagle*, November 11, 1971.

92. "A Summary of the Survival March," *ML&W*, November 1971.

93. Survival March, Information Packet; Leonard Pardue, "HEW Chief Hears Appalachian Marchers," *Courier-Journal*, November 9, 1971.

94. Pardue, "HEW Chief Hears Appalachian Marchers."

95. A Summary of the Survival March, *ML&W*, November 1971.

96. Smith, *Digging Our Own Graves*, 119–127, 168–171, 173.

97. "Eyeing Faceless Bureaucrats," Washington, D.C., *The Evening Star*, November 9, 1971.

98. A Summary of the Survival March, *ML&W*.

99. Nadasen, *Welfare Warriors*, 158–159.

100. March for Survival, Washington Impressions, November 21, 1971, Recording, CD, SM-CT-005-001, CSM Records.

101. Hall, interviewed by Boothby and Korstad.

Chapter 5. "The Best Care in History"

1. Hall, interviewed by Boothby and Korstad.

2. LeBlanc, interviewed by the author; Hall interviewed by the author, March 2011, September 2012.

3. Hall, interviewed by Boothby and Korstad.

4. Jennifer Nelson, "'Hold Your Head Up and Stick Out Your Chin': Community Health and Women's Health in Mound Bayou, Mississippi," *NWSA Journal* 1 (Spring 2005): 99–118. See also John Dittmer, *The Good Doctors: The Medical Committee for Human Rights and the Struggle for Social Justice in Health Care* (Jackson: University Press of Mississippi, 2017).

5. Description of Organizations, folder 9, box 91, CSM Records; Health Fairs—1970 Annual Report, folder 5, box 92, CSM Records; Report of the Health Commission Staff, 1971–1971, folder 6, box 92, CSM Records.

6. See "About Us," Big Sandy Health Care, Inc., accessed February 18, 2014, http://www.bshc.org/index.php?page=how-cmsms-works.

7. Nelson, "Hold Your Head Up and Stick Out Your Chin," 105.

8. Dr. H. Jack Geiger, "Community Health Centers: Health Care as an Instruments of Social Change," in *Reforming Medicine: Lessons of the Last Quarter Century*, eds., Victor W. Sidel and Ruth Sidel (New York: Pantheon Books, 1984), 12–13. Dittmer, *The Good Doctors*; Greta de Jong, "Plantation Politics: The Tufts-Delta Health Center

and Intraracial Class Conflict in Mississippi, 1965–1972," in Orleck and Hazirjian, *The War on Poverty*, 256–299.

9. "David Allen is," folder "Appalachian Volunteers, 1969," box 2S417, Field Foundation Records, Briscoe Center, Austin, Texas.

10. Howard Thorkelson, Mountain Legal Rights Association Report, folder AV Community Organization and Disability Projects, box 2S426, Field Foundation. See Edward Berkowitz, *Disability Policy: America's Programs for the Handicapped, A Twentieth Century Fund Report* (New York: Cambridge University Press, 1987), 78.

11. Thorkelson, Mountain Legal Rights Association Report.

12. Dittmer, *The Good Doctors*, 82–83.

13. Thorkelson, Mountain Legal Rights Association Report.

14. Howard Thorkelson to Leslie Dunbar, July 17, 1970, folder AV Community Organization and Disability Projects.

15. Merlin Chowkwanyun, "The New Left and Public Health: The Health Policy Advisory Center, Community Organizing, and the Big Business of Health, 1967–1975," *American Journal of Public Health* 101, no. 2 (February 2011): 238–249, accessed October 2013, http://www.ncbi.nlm.nih.gov/pmc/articles/PMC3020214/; "Rob Burlage Papers, 1956–1973," Biography/History, Wisconsin Historical Society.

16. "Intro," The Health/PAC Digital Archive, accessed February 7, 2017, http://www.healthpacbulletin.org.

17. Chowkwanyun, "The New Left and Public Health," and Personal Papers, in Maxine Kenny's possession.

18. Personal Papers, in Maxine Kenny's possession.

19. Eller, *Uneven Ground*, 158–159.

20. On the movement, see Alan Derickson, "Extreme Solidarity," chap. 7, in *Black Lung: Anatomy of a Public Health Disaster* (Ithaca: Cornell University Press, 1998), 79–80.

21. Des Callan, "Ole King Cole," *Health/PAC Bulletin (September 1971)*, The Health/PAC Digital Archive, accessed September 9, 2017, http://www.healthpacbulletin.org.

22. Derickson, "Extreme Solidarity," chap. 7 in *Black Lung*.

23. Comprehensive Health Services Program, as of February 1, 1968, and Comprehensive Neighborhood Health Services Program, Guidelines, February 1967, folder Health Programs; box 7; Records of the Field Coordination Division; Records of the OEO; RG 381; NACP.

24. Couto, *Poverty, Politics, and Health Care*, 58–59.

25. Ibid., 124.

26. Quoted in ibid., 125; Hall, interviewed by the author, September 2012; Geiger, "Community Health Centers," 20; Homer Bigart, "Antipoverty Programs Imperiled in Appalachia," *New York Times*, June 15, 1971.

27. Couto, *Poverty, Politics, and Health Care*, 71.

28. Ibid., 75.

29. Ibid., 134.

30. Martin Jean Schecter, representing Dr. Arnold Schecter, to Mel Goldstein, Office of General Counsel, OEO, box 5, folder "Floyd County Comprehensive Health

Services Program"; General Counsel, Inspection and Investigation Files; RG 381; NACP. See also Couto, *Poverty, Politics, and Healthcare*, 123–125.

31. Maxine Kenny, "Mountain Health Care: Politics, Power, and Profits," *ML&W*, April 1971; Press Release, "Area Health Services Criticized at Public Hearing," folder 7, box 93, CSM Records II; Bigart, "Antipoverty Programs Imperiled in Appalachia."

32. "Bill of Health Rights," folder 9, box 107, CSM Records; Couto, *Poverty, Politics, and Health Care*, 183–185.

33. P. A. Paul Shaheen and Harry Perlstadt, "Class Action Suits and Social Change: The Organization and Impact of the Hill-Burton Cases," *Indiana Law Journal* 57 (1982), in Digital Repository at Maurer Law, Maurer School of Law, Indiana University, accessed September 9, 2017, http://www.repository.law.indiana.edu/ilj/vol57/iss3/2/; "EKWRO Wins Health Care Suit," *ML&W*, March 1974.

34. Muncy, *Relentless Reformer*, 257–261.

35. F. T. Billings, "A Teaching Relationship: Students in Rural Health Care," *Transactions of the American Clinical and Climatological Association* 21 (1980): 167–176, PubMed Central, accessed September 9, 2017, http://www.ncbi.nlm.nih.gov/pmc/articles/PMC2279449/.

36. "Why a Health Fair? Discussion with Floyd County, Kentucky People," *ML&W*, July–August 1971.

37. Billings, "A Teaching Relationship."

38. Proposals for a Mud Creek Health Program, folder 11, box 107, CSM Records.

39. Description of Organizations, folder 8, box 91, CSM Records.

40. Galit M. Sacajiu and Aaron Fox, "Still Marching in a White Coat," *Health Affairs* 27 (March 2008): 583–584, HealthAffairs.org, accessed September 9, 2017, http://content.healthaffairs.org/content/27/2/583.full.

41. Elinor Graham, interviewed by Kline; Elinor Graham, interviewed by the author, March 12, 2011.

42. Graham, interviewed by the author; Personal Papers, in Maxine Kenny's possession.

43. Medical Summary for Summer Health Project, folder 11, box 107, CSM Records.

44. Ibid.

45. Ibid.

46. Ibid., and Graham, interviewed by Kline.

47. Application for a Health Team from National Health Service Corps, folder 11, box 107, CSM Records.

48. Hall, interviewed by Rice; Graham, interviewed by Kline; David Walls, Keynote address to the 34th Annual Conference of the Appalachian Studies Association, Eastern Kentucky University, Richmond, Kentucky, March 11, 2011, *Journal of Appalachian Studies* 17 (Spring/Fall 2011): 9–13, 23–25.

49. "Sick for Clinics," *Southern Exposure* VI (Summer 1978).

50. Graham, interviewed by Kline; Hall, interviewed by Boothby and Korstad.

51. "Mountain Health Care," *ML&W*, February 1973.

52. Ibid.

53. Ibid.

54. Ibid.

55. "Any Problem, We'll Work on It," *ML&W*, January 1973.

56. Graham, interviewed by Kline; Hall, interviewed by Boothby and Korstad.

57. "Knott County CSEJ Hosts Kentucky Black Lung Association," *ML&W*, November 1974.

58. Hall, interviewed by Boothby and Korstad.

59. Ibid.

60. Maxine Kenny, "Stripping: Pillage for Profit," *Health Rights News*, October 1971.

61. Mary Beth Bingman, "Stopping the Bulldozers: What Difference Did It Make?" *Fighting Back in Appalachia*, 17–30, 17–19.

62. "People's Democracy," *ML&W*, November 1971.

63. "Notes from Two Meetings," *ML&W*, May 1970.

64. Sally Ward Maggard, interviewed by the author, July 29, 2016.

65. Bingman, "Stopping the Bulldozers."

66. Montrie, *To Save the Land and People*, 4.

67. Maggard, interviewed by the author.

68. Bingman, "Stopping the Bulldozers"; Montrie, *To Save the Land and People*, 104–105.

69. Maggard, interviewed by the author.

70. Peter Mullins, "Kentuckians Risk Lives in War on Strip-Mining," *Washington Post*, January 31, 1972; George Vescey, "20 Women Occupy Strip Mining Site," *New York Times*, January 23, 1972; "Appalachian Roundup, Floyd County Strippers Attacked," *ML&W*, May 1972; "Strip Mining Fight Goes National," *ML&W*, June-July 1972.

71. Bingman, "Stopping the Bulldozers," 29.

72. Montrie, *To Save the Land and People*, 109.

73. Few studies examine women's health in Appalachia. The comprehensive volume, *Health and Well-Being in Appalachia* (Lexington: University of Kentucky Press, 2012) edited by Robert L. Ludke and Phillip J. Obermiller, contains brief sections on "women's health," but it does not offer a study or analysis of family planning, birth control, or access to abortion.

74. Graham, interviewed by author.

75. "Five Profiles of Women," *ML&W*, November 1972.

76. Ibid.

77. Graham, interviewed by the author.

78. Linda Elkington, "Women," *ML&W*, December 1972.

79. See Finn Enke, *Finding the Movement: Sexuality, Contested Space, and Feminist Activism* (Durham: Duke University Press, 2007), 199.

80. *ML&W*, Special Women's Issue, June 1974.

81. Ibid.

82. Linda Johnson, "Alternatives," and Jan Chapin, "Facts for Women," *ML&W*, June 1974.

83. Geiger, "Community Health Centers." See also Lily M. Hoffman, *The Politics of Knowledge: Activist Movements in Medicine and Planning* (Albany: State University of

New York Press, 1987) and Richard A. Couto, with Stephanie C. Eken, *To Give Their Gifts: Health, Community, and Democracy* (Nashville: Vanderbilt University Press, 2002).

84. Hall, interviewed by the author, September 2012.

Chapter 6. "I'm Fighting for My Own Children That I'm Raising Up"

1. Sudie Crusenberry, Scrapbooks, Appalachian Archive, Southeast Kentucky Community and Technical College, Cumberland, Kentucky; photo by Earl Dotter for *UMW Journal*, December 1973. See also Carol A. B. Giesen, *Coal Miners' Wives: Portraits of Endurance* (Lexington: University of Kentucky Press, 1995), 68. On the strike narrative, see Portelli, *They Say in Harlan County*, and Sally Ward Maggard, "Gender Contested: Women's Participation in the Brookside Coal Strike," in *Women and Social Protest*, eds., Guida West and Rhoda Blumberg (New York: Oxford University Press, 1990), 75–90; "Women's Participation in the Brookside Coal Strike: Militance, Class, and Gender in Appalachia," *Frontiers* 9, no. 3 (1987): 16–21; Sally Ward Maggard, "Eastern Kentucky Women on Strike: A Study of Gender, Class, and Political Action in the 1970s" (PhD diss., University of Kentucky, 1989); Lynda Ann Ewen, *Which Side Are You On? The Brookside Mine Strike in Harlan County, Kentucky, 1973–1974* (New York: Vanguard Books, 1979).

2. See Maxine Molyneux, "Mobilisation without Emancipation? Women's Interests, the State and Revolution in Nicaragua," in *Women's Movements in International Perspective: Latin America and Beyond* (New York: Palgrave, 2001), 38–59; Temma Kaplan, *Crazy for Democracy: Women in Grassroots Movement* (New York: Routledge, 1997) and her discussion of "female consciousness," 6–7.

3. Nancy Fraser, "Behind Marx's Hidden Abode," *New Left Review* 86 (March–April 2014), accessed March 5, 2017, https://newleftreview.org/II/86/nancy-fraser-behind-marx-s-hidden-abode.

4. Ibid.

5. Portelli, *They Say in Harlan County*, 128.

6. Scott, *Two Sides to Everything*, 53, 62.

7. Portelli, *They Say in Harlan County*, 119–120.

8. On the relationship between individual and collective memories, see Anna Green, "Individual Remembering and 'Collective Memory': Theoretical Presuppositions and Contemporary Debates," *Oral History Society* 32, no. 2 (2004): 35–44. For the contested memories of the 1930s miners' strikes, see Portelli, *They Say in Harlan County*.

9. Unless otherwise noted, Lois Scott's life narrative is drawn from the oral history, Lois Scott, interviewed by Melissa Scott, March 27, 1995, Appalachian Archive, Southeast Kentucky Community and Technical College, Cumberland, Kentucky.

10. Hevener, *Which Side Are You On?*

11. Ibid., 15.

12. *Liberation News Service*, October 23, 1976.

13. Ibid.

14. "Brookside Women," produced by Nona Hall, and "Brookside Women," *Journal of Current Social Issues* 11, no. 6 (Spring 1974).

15. Bessie Lou Cornett later changed her name to Bessie Lou Parker. Because she went by Cornett at the time of the strike, I refer to her by that name.

16. Southern Appalachian Leadership Training interns, Cornett, Bessie, Cumberland, Ky., folder 21, box 28, Highlander Records.

17. *Harlan County, USA*, Criterion Collection, DVD, directed by Barbara Kopple (New York: Cabin Creek Films, 1976, 2006).

18. Portelli, *They Say in Harlan County*, 310–311; Scott, *Two Sides to Everything*, 54–55; Ewen, *Which Side Are You On?* 137–139.

19. For a history of the reform efforts, see *The United Mine Workers of America: A Model of Industrial Solidarity?* ed., John H. M. Laslett (University Park: Pennsylvania State University Press, 1996).

20. Matt Witt, "Organize! The UMWA Comes Back to Eastern Kentucky," *UMW Journal* (September 1973): 16–19; Matt Witt, "UMWA Plans Eastern Organizing Drive," *UMW Journal* (May 1, 1973).

21. Maggard, "Eastern Kentucky Women on Strike," 314; "Hard Times in Harlan County," *Journal of Current Social Issues* 11, no. 6 (Spring 1974).

22. Scott, *Two Sides to Everything*, 55.

23. Tom Bethell and Bob Hall, "The Brookside Strike," in *Southern Exposure*, special issue on Harlan County, 1931–1976 (1976).

24. Lois Scott, interviewed by Katie Gilliam, April 3, 1987, Appalachian Archive, Southeast Kentucky Community and Technical College; Ewen, *Which Side Are You On?* 39; Minnie Lunsford, interviewed by Sally Ward Maggard; *Harlan County, USA*; Marat Moore, "Hard Labor: Voices of Women from the Appalachian Coalfields," *Yale Journal of Law & Feminism* 2, no. 2 (1989): 199–238.

25. Moore, "Hard Labor," 203.

26. Interview with Minnie Lunsford, Betty Eldridge, and Gussie Mills, "Brookside Women," produced by Nona Hall, Appalshop Archive; Maggard, "Eastern Kentucky Women on Strike," 315; Ewen, *Which Side Are You On?* 39.

27. "Disturbance Reported at Eastover," *Harlan Daily Enterprise*, September 28, 1973.

28. Eastover Mining Company: Brookside Women Strike, folder 13, box 156, CSM Records.

29. Ewen, *Which Side Are You On?* 101–107.

30. *Harlan County, USA*, and "The Making of Harlan County USA," extras, *Harlan County, USA*.

31. Maggard, "Eastern Kentucky Women on Strike," 316.

32. "Brookside Women," produced by Hall.

33. "Records Indicate Hogg Had Mine Interest," *Courier-Journal*, January 9, 1974.

34. "Brookside Women," produced by Hall.

35. "Women, Children Jailed in Harlan County," *UMW Journal* (October 16–31, 1973).

36. "Women Save the Strike," *The Southern Patriot*, November 1973.
37. Jim Somerville, "Harlan Speaks Again," *ML&W*, March 1974.
38. Maggard, "Eastern Kentucky Women on Strike," 240.
39. Ewen, *Which Side Are You On?* 105–107.
40. "In Harlan County Women Take Up the Fight," *Great Speckled Bird*, January 14, 1974; "The Organizing Department," *UMW Journal* (December 1973): 22.
41. Nancy Fraser, "Behind Marx's Hidden Abode."
42. Moore, "Hard Labor," 204–205.
43. Ibid., 205.
44. *Great Speckled Bird*, November 12, 1973.
45. *Harlan County, USA.*
46. "Citizen's Inquiry in Harlan County," *Great Speckled Bird*, April 1, 1974.
47. Portelli, *They Say in Harlan County*, 126; Scott, *Two Sides to Everything*, 14–16.
48. See Hennen, *Harlan Miners Speak.*
49. *Journal of Current Social Issues* 11, no. 6 (Spring 1974).
50. "Hard Times in Harlan County," *Journal of Current Social Issues*, 11.
51. "Brookside Women," *Journal of Current Social Issues.*
52. Somerville, "Harlan Speaks Again."
53. "Brookside Women," *Journal of Current Social Issues.*
54. Scott, *Two Sides to Everything*, 50–51.
55. Nora Howard, interviewed by the author, August 31, 2011; *UMW Journal* (April 1–15, 1974); "Brookside Women," *Journal of Current Social Issues.*
56. Howard, interviewed by the author.
57. Ibid.
58. *UMW Journal* (April 1–15, 1974); Portelli, *They Say in Harlan County*, 46.
59. Howard, interview by the author.
60. *Harlan County, USA.*
61. James M. Jasper, *The Art of Moral Protest: Culture, Biography, and Creativity in Social Movements* (Chicago: The University of Chicago Press, 1997), 186.
62. "Veteran of the '30s Visits Harlan Strikers," *Southern Patriot* (November 1973).
63. Hall, interview with author, September 15, 2012; Sally Ward Maggard, "Coal Field Women Making History," in *Back Talk from Appalachia: Confronting Stereotypes*, 228–250; Matt Witt, "Union Rallies behind Brookside Strikers," *UMW Journal* (August 1–15, 1974): 3–5; "Unions, Churches Join 'Dump Duke Campaign,'" June 1–15, 1974, 19. For coverage of these events, see also *The Southern Patriot* and *Mountain Life and Work*, 1974.
64. Judy Klemesrud, "Coal Miners Started the Strike—Then Their Women Took Over," *New York Times*, May 15, 1974.
65. "Brookside Women," produced by Hall.
66. Klemesrud, "Coal Miners Started the Strike."
67. Quoted in Maggard, "Eastern Kentucky Women on Strike," 237.
68. See Ewen, *Which Side Are You On?* 106–107.

69. See Richard M. Barsam, *Nonfiction Film: A Critical History*, revised and expanded (Bloomington: Indiana University Press, 1992).

70. Maggard, "Eastern Kentucky Women on Strike," 159.

71. *Salt of the Earth*, written by Michael Wilson, directed by Herbert J. Biberman (New York: Independent Productions, 1954); Ellen R. Baker, *On Strike and on Film: Mexican American Families and Blacklisted Filmmakers in Cold War America* (Chapel Hill: University of North Carolina Press, 2007).

72. Barbara Winslow, *Voices of Women Historians: The Personal, the Political, the Professional* (Bloomington: Indiana University Press, 1999), 228.

73. Moore, "Hard Labor," 202.

74. Matt Witt, "The Bribe at Brookside," *UMW Journal*, May 16–31, 1974: 8–9.

75. Matt Witt, "Victory in Harlan!" *UMW Journal* (September 1–15, 1974): 4–6; Matt Witt, "Gun Thugs Shoot Up Strikers' Homes," *UMW Journal (*August 16–31, 1974); Matt Witt, "Company, Police Violence Erupts at Brookside," *UMW Journal* (July 16–31, 1974).

76. Eileen Whalen, "Women Save the Strike, Harlan Miners Fight for Union," *Southern Patriot* (November 1973).

77. Portelli, *They Say in Harlan County*, 324–330.

78. Ibid.

79. Maggard, "Eastern Kentucky Women on Strike," 243–247.

80. "Labor/Women: LNS Interview with Harlan County Women: Organizing in Aftermath of Brookside Miner's Strike," *Liberation News Service*, October 23, 1976.

81. Biographies of Southern Appalachian Leadership Training Interns, Cornett, Bessie.

82. Ewen, *Which Side Are You On?* 115–116; "Labor/Women."

83. Ibid.

84. Ibid., 114–115.

85. On taboos, see Jennifer Ritterhouse, *Growing Up Jim Crow: How Black and White Southern Children Learned Race* (Chapel Hill: University of North Carolina Press, 2006), and Lillian Eugenia Smith, *Killers of the Dream* (New York: W. W. Norton and Company, 1994).

86. See Robert H. Zieger, *For Jobs and Freedom: Race and Labor in America Since 1865* (Lexington: University of Kentucky Press, 2007), 115–116.

87. Portelli, *They Say in Harlan County*, 166–175.

88. Ewen, *Which Side Are You On?* 116–117; "Labor/Women."

89. Ibid., 114–117; "Kentuckians Oppose Klan," *Southern Patriot* (June–July 1975).

90. "Harlan Youths Are Fearful That They're Targets of Klan," *Courier-Journal*, August 13, 1976; "Klan Leader Says Whites Face Bias," *Courier-Journal*, July 21, 1975.

91. Portelli, *They Say in Harlan County*, 323.

92. "Labor/Women."

93. Ewen, *Which Side Are You On?* 117–118; "Bessie Lou Provided Voice for Dissent," *Harlan Daily Enterprise*, March 11, 2010.

Chapter 7. "Nothing Worse than Being Poor and a Woman"

1. "Eastern Kentucky Women," *ML&W*, April 1975.

2. Ibid.

3. Leon Fink, "When Community Comes Home to Roost: The Southern Milltown as Lost Cause," *Journal of Social History* 40 (Autumn 2006): 122–123; *Constitution of the October League (Marxist-Leninist)* (October 1975), in "Encyclopedia of Anti-Revisionism On-Line," accessed March 6, 2014, https://www.marxists.org/history/erol/ncm-3/ol-constitution.htm.

4. "Eastern Kentucky Women," *ML&W*, April 1975; Sudie Crusenberry, Scrapbooks.

5. See Cobble, et al., *Feminism Unfinished*; Orleck, *Rethinking American Women's Activism*; Gilmore, ed., *Feminist Coalitions: Historical Perspectives on Second-Wave Feminism in the United States* (Urbana: University of Illinois Press, 2008); Hewitt, ed., *No Permanent Waves*.

6. Jocelyn Olcott, *International Women's Year: The Greatest Consciousness-Raising Event in History* (New York: Oxford University Press, 2017), 6. By 1977, and the National Women's Conference in Houston, Texas, the politics of feminism—and how they fit in American politics more broadly—had shifted. See Marjorie Spruill, *Divided We Stand: The Battle over Women's Rights and Family Values That Polarized American Politics* (New York: Bloomsbury, 2017).

7. See Cobble, et al., *Feminism Unfinished*; Hewitt, *No Permanent Waves*; Gilmore, *Groundswell*, 4–5.

8. See also Carroll, *Mobilizing New York*, 106.

9. On the history of feminist policy in the workplace, see Turk, *Equality on Trial*; Mayeri, *Reasoning from Race*, and MacLean, *Freedom Is Not Enough*.

10. Cobble, et al., *Feminism Unfinished*, 52. For a history of the PCSW, see Kessler-Harris, *In Pursuit of Equity*.

11. *American Women: Report on the President's Commission on the Status of Women* (Washington, D.C.: 1963), digital version at Hathi Trust Digital Library, accessed January 28, 2017, https://catalog.hathitrust.org/Record/003047127.

12. "About the Kentucky Commission on Women," Women.KY.gov, accessed January 28, 2017, http://women.ky.gov/About/Pages/default.aspx.

13. "Memo to Governor Nunn, July 9, 1968," folder "Commission Meeting, July 1968," box "Commission on Women, 1964–1971," Kentucky Department of Library and Archives (KDLA).

14. "No Cinderellas," section "Paging Women," *Jefferson Reporter* (Buechel, Kentucky), April 16, 1970, accessed March 1, 2017, http://nyx.uky.edu/dips/xt7sf766513r/data/0567.pdf.

15. "Conference Proceedings," Second Annual Conference on Women in the War on Poverty, May 15–17, 1968, Hathi Trust Digital Library, accessed January 28, 2017, https://babel.hathitrust.org/cgi/pt?id=pur1.32754081231890;view=1up;seq=4.

16. Ibid.

17. Marie Humphries, Memo to Governor Nunn, July 9, 1968, and Memo July 12, 1968, folder "OEO, Washington, D.C. Meeting," box "Commission on Women, 1964–1971," KDLA.

18. Ibid.

19. Ibid.

20. Ibid.

21. "A Woman for Women," *Voice-Tribune*, Louisville, Ky., January 22, 2015.

22. For the Commission Meeting of August 17, 1968, folder "Commission Meeting, July 9, 1968," box "Commission on Women, 1964–1971."

23. Ibid.

24. "Appalachian Women's Rights Organization Forms," *ML&W*, March 1975.

25. Ibid. On "channels" of feminist activism in the 1970s, see Melissa Estes Blair, *Revolutionizing Expectations: Women's Organizations, Feminism, and American Politics, 1965–1980* (Athens: University of Georgia Press, 2014), 7.

26. "Appalachian Women's Rights Organization Forms," *ML&W*, March 1975.

27. Ibid.

28. Hall, interviewed by the author, 2011, 2013.

29. Kathryn Nasstrom, *Everybody's Grandmother and Nobody's Fool: Frances Freeborn Pauley and the Struggle for Social Justice* (Ithaca: Cornell University Press, 2000); Orleck, *Storming Caesar's Palace*; Carroll, *Mobilizing New York*; Chappell, *The War on Welfare*, 171.

30. Program, Kentucky Commission on Women, Public Hearing IV, March 18, 1975, folder 18, box 128, CSM Records.

31. Sally Ward Maggard, "Women's Hearings Held at Hazard, KY," and Appalachian Women's Rights Organization, "Women's Statements on Problems in East Kentucky," *ML&W*, April 1975.

32. Minutes of the Fourth Hearing of the Kentucky Commission on Women, March 18, 1975," folder "Minutes—Public Hearings, 1974–1975," box "Commission on Women, minutes, public hearings," KDLA.

33. Newsletter, Appalachian Women's Rights Organization, n.d., folder 16, box 28, CSM Records.

34. Ibid.

35. Chappell, *The War on Welfare*, 126.

36. Ibid., 181.

37. Cobble, et al., *Feminism Unfinished*, 11.

38. See Kentucky Commission on Women, *News Bulletin*, folder "Kentucky Commission on Women, Newsletters," box 6, Commissions on the Status of Women collection, 1967–2004, Schlesinger Library.

39. See Chappell for similar developments at the policy level, in *The War on Welfare*, 181.

40. For a history of affirmative action efforts, see MacLean, *Freedom Is Not Enough*; "The Hidden History of Affirmative Action: Working Women's Struggles in the 1970s and the Gender of Class," *Feminist Studies* 25 (Spring 1999); Turk, *Equality on Trial*; Mayeri, *Reasoning from Race*.

41. Fosl and K'Meyer, eds., *Freedom on the Border*, 84–85, 109–110.

42. Marie Abrams, interviewed by Sue Wylie, July 17, 1991, Kentucky Commission on Women Oral History Project, Louie B. Nunn Center for Oral History.

43. "Timeline," Kentucky Commission on Human Rights, kchr.gov, accessed January 1, 2014, http://www.kchr.ky.gov/kchr1970.htm.

44. Newsletter, Appalachian Women's Rights Organization.

45. "Women Fight for Jobs in Coal Fields," *ML&W*, September 1975. See also "Women Seek Jobs in Kentucky Coal Mines," *ML&W*, May 1975.

46. In 1977, 98.7 percent of all people working in the coal industry were men. See Betty Jean Hall, "Women Miners Can Dig It, Too!" in *Communities in Economic Crisis: Appalachia and the South*, eds., John Gaventa, Barbara Ellen Smith, and Alex Willingham (Philadelphia: Temple University Press, 1990), 54.

47. Kentucky Commission on Human Rights, "Commission's Class Action Approval in Pyro Mining Case Marks Breakthrough for Coal Mining Women," *Human Rights Report*, October 1981. Portelli, *They Say in Harlan County*, 160; Marat Moore, *Women in the Mines: Stories of Life and Work* (New York: Twayne Publishers, 1996), xxvi–xxxii.

48. "Nearly $45,000 in Back Wages Paid to Women in Coal Mining Cases," *Human Rights Report*, November 1976.

49. "Women Seek Jobs in Kentucky Coal Mines," *ML&W*, May 1975.

50. "Nearly $45,000 in Back Wages."

51. "Commission's Class Action Approval in Pyro Mining."

52. Jenny Montgomery, "Women Miners: Complaints of Sex Discrimination Force Coal Industry to End 'Male Only' Tradition," Staff Report, 86-4, Kentucky Commission on Human Rights, September 24, 1986, Kentucky Documents, Government Documents Dept., University of Louisville Libraries; Moore, "Hard Labor," 199–238.

53. Leslie Lilly, "Bringing Sister Home: The Fight for Job Equity in Appalachia," February 14, 1980, folder 2, box 2, Helen Matthews Lewis Papers, 1894–2000, Collection 103A, W. L. Eury Appalachian Collection, Appalachian State University.

54. Hall, "Women Miners Can Dig It, Too!" 53–54; Chris Weis, "Appalachian Women Fight Back," in *Fighting Back in Appalachia*, 153–154; Montgomery, "Women Miners."

55. Hall, "Women Miners Can Dig It, Too!" 56–57.

56. Moore, "Hard Labor," 232.

57. Moore, *Women in the Mines*. See cover image, "Miners for the ERA," and article, "Women Push Coal Employment," *ML&W*, August 1978; Judith Wollmer, "Victory for Women Underground," *Ms. Magazine*, March 1985, 17.

58. Moore, "Hard Labor," 209, 215, 222.

59. "Government and TVA Asked to Support Jobs for Women Miners," *ML&W*, July 1978.

60. Women's Bureau (DOL), "The Coal Employment Project—How Women Can Make Breakthroughs into Nontraditional Industries" (1985), eric.ed.gov, accessed March 1, 2017, http://files.eric.ed.gov/fulltext/ED271601.pdf.

61. Harold Wood, "Coal Industry Resurgence Attracts Variety of New Workers," *Monthly Labor Review* (January 1981): 3–8.

62. Tallichet, *Daughters of the Mountain*, 72–90.

63. Rostan, interviewed by the author. See Turk, *Equality on Trial*, 184–185. On how "fetal protection" displaced workers' rights, see Sara Dubow, *Ourselves Unborn: The History of the Fetus in Modern America* (New York: Oxford University Press, 2011), 130–131.

64. June Rostan, interviewed by the author, July 6, 2009.

65. Cosby Totten, Goldie Totten, and June Rostan, "Women Miners' Fight for Parental Leave," *Labor Research Review* 1, no. 11 (1988): 89–95, 93.

66. Ibid., 95.

67. See Turk, *Equality on Trial*, 189.

68. Ibid., 176

69. Ibid., 185.

70. Totten, Totten, and Rostan, "Women Miners' Fight for Parental Leave," 95.

71. On the "hegemony of white, middle-class understandings of feminism," see Introduction, in Hewitt, ed., *No Permanent Waves*, 6.

72. See Nelson Lichtenstein, *State of the Union: A Century of American Labor* (Princeton: Princeton University Press, 2003); Jefferson Cowie, *Stayin' Alive: The 1970s and the Last Days of the Working Class* (New York: The New Press, 2012); Jefferson Cowie and Nick Salvatore, "The Long Exception: Rethinking the Place of the New Deal in American History," *International Labor and Working Class History* 74 (Fall 2008): 3–32; and the response by Nancy MacLean, "Getting New Deal History Wrong," *International Labor and Working Class History* 74 (Fall 2008): 49–55. On identity politics and feminism specifically, see Marisa Chappell, "Demanding a New Family Wage: Feminist Consensus in the 1970s Full Employment Campaign," in *Feminist Coalitions: Historical Perspectives on Second-Wave Feminism in the United States*, ed., Stephanie Gilmore (Urbana: University of Illinois Press, 2008), and Dorothy Sue Cobble, "A 'Tiger by the Toenail': The 1970s Origins of the New Working-Class Majority," *Labor: Studies in Working-Class History of the Americas* 2, no. 3 (2005): 103–114. On the "full working-class promise" of the 1970s, see Lane Windham, *Knocking on Labor's Door: Union Organizing in the 1970s and the Roots of a New Economic Divide* (Chapel Hill: University of North Carolina Press, 2017).

73. Sally Maggard to Gail Falk, n.d., folder 26, box 70, CSM Records.

74. Moore, *Women in the Mines*, 313. Moore includes a table of numbers of women hired in mines. Between 1973 and 1989, 3,965 women were hired out of 162,186 workers. New mining technologies along with industrial decline led to layoffs in the early 1990s, and women have never regained the numbers they had in the industry. See also Tallichet, *Daughters of the Mountain*, 7.

75. Lisa McCall, "Increasing Class Disparities among Women," in *The Sex of Class: Women Transforming American Labor*, ed., Dorothy Sue Cobble (Ithaca: ILR Press, 2007), 15–34.

76. Fraser, *Fortunes of Feminism*, 159–74.

Epilogue

1. Berenice Fisher and Joan C. Tronto, "Toward a Feminist Theory of Care," in *Circles of Care: Work and Identity in Women's Lives*, eds., Emily Abel and Margaret Nelson (Albany: State University of New York Press, 1991), 40.

2. See Eller, *Uneven Ground*, 232–233.

3. On the "age of cheap," see Bryant Simon, *The Hamlet Fire: A Tragic Story of Cheap Food, Cheap Government, and Cheap Lives* (New York: The New Press, 2017), 231–243.

4. Helen Matthews Lewis, *Living Social Justice*, 139–140.

5. Deborah Thorne, Ann Tickamyer, and Mark Thorne, "Poverty and Income in Appalachia," *Journal of Appalachian Studies* 10, no. 3 (2004): 341–358, 341. See also Debra A. Henderson and Ann R. Tickamyer, "Lost in Appalachia: The Unexpected Impact of Welfare Reform on Older Women in Rural Communities," *The Journal of Sociology and Social Welfare* 35, no. 3 (2008): 153–171.

6. Roger Cohen, "We Need Somebody Spectacular," *New York Times*, September 9, 2016; John Saward, *Vanity Fair*, "Welcome to Trump County, USA," February 24, 2016, accessed March 8, 2017, http://www.vanityfair.com/news/2016/02/donald-trump-supporters-west-virginia; "In the Heart of Trump Country," Larissa MacFarquhar, *New Yorker*, October 10, 2016, accessed March 8, 2017, http://www.newyorker.com/magazine/2016/10/10/in-the-heart-of-trump-country. For a full list and analysis of this coverage, see Elizabeth Catte, "There Is No Neutral There: Appalachia as Mythic Trump Country," accessed April 14, 2018, https://elizabethcatte.com/2016/10/16/appalachia-as-trump-country/. See also Elizabeth Catte, *What You're Getting Wrong about Appalachia* (Cleveland, OH: Belt Publishing, 2018).

7. For examples of more recent progressive campaigns in the Appalachian South, see Stephen L. Fisher and Barbara Ellen Smith, eds., *Transforming Places: Lessons from Appalachia* (Urbana: University of Illinois Press, 2012).

8. For a gender analysis of Clinton and Sanders's messaging about work and welfare, see Namara Smith, "The Woman's Party: On Hillary Clinton and Welfare," *n+1* (Fall 2016), accessed September 30, 2017, https://nplusonemag.com/issue-26/the-intellectual-situation/the-womans-party/; and "Namara Smith Responds to Connor Kilpatrick," *n+1* (Winter 2017): 209.

9. See Matt Klesta, "Eastern Kentucky: A Region in Flux," *Forefront*, accessed January 25, 2017, https://www.clevelandfed.org/newsroom-and-events/publications/forefront/ff-v7n01/ff-20160302-v7n0105-eastern-kentucky-a-region-in-flux.aspx. See also "Coal Production and Employment Trends," Kentuckians for the Commonwealth, accessed January 25, 2017, http://kftc.org/campaigns/appalachian-transition/coal-production-and-employment-trends.

10. Rebecca Solnit, *Hope in the Dark: Untold Histories, Wild Possibilities*, E-book, updated edition (Chicago: Haymarket Books, 2016), location 574.

Bibliography

Manuscript Collections

Appalachian State University, Boone, N.C.
Eury Appalachian Collection
Helen Matthews Lewis Papers, 1894–2000
Berea College, Berea, Ky.
Appalachian Volunteers Oral History Collection
Appalachian Volunteers Papers
Council of the Southern Mountains, 1913–1970
Council of the Southern Mountains, 1970–1989
Council of the Southern Mountains Oral History Project Collection
Southern Appalachian Archives
Briscoe Center, Austin, Tex.
Field Foundation Records
East Tennessee State University, Johnson City, Tenn.
Archives of Appalachia
Coal Employment Project Records
June Rostan Records
Marat Moore Oral History Collection
Kentucky Department of Libraries and Archives, Frankfort, Ky.
Commission on Women
Legislative Research Commission
Lyndon Baines Johnson Presidential Library, Austin, Tex.
Presidential Papers
White House Central Files
National Archives at College Park
Community Services Administration Records
OEO Records

Radcliffe Institute, Harvard University, Cambridge, Mass.
Arthur and Elizabeth Schlesinger Library on the History of Women in America
Commissions on the Status of Women
Rockefeller Center Archives
Ford Foundation Records
Southeast Kentucky Community and Technical College, Cumberland, Ky.
Appalachian Archive
Oral History Collection
Sudie Crusenberry Scrapbooks
State Historical Society of Wisconsin, Madison, Wis.
Archival Division
George Wiley Papers
Highlander Research and Education Center Papers
University of Kentucky, Lexington, Ky.
Louie B. Nunn Center for Oral History
Family and Gender in the Coal Community Oral History Project
Kentucky Commission on Women Oral History Project
Kentucky Legislature Oral History Project
Social History and Cultural Change in the Elkhorn Coal Fields Oral History Project
War on Poverty Oral History Project
University of North Carolina–Chapel Hill, Chapel Hill, N.C.
Southern Folklife Collection, Wilson Library
Guy and Candie Carawan Collection
Southern Historical Collection, Wilson Library
Alan McSurely Papers
Southern Oral History Program
Long Women's Movement in the American South Oral History Project

Newspapers, Magazines, and Journals

Appalachian Lookout
Courier-Journal (Louisville, Kentucky)
Good Housekeeping
Great Speckled Bird
The Hawkeye
Health/PAC Bulletin
Health Rights News
Human Rights Report (Kentucky Commission on Human Rights)
Impact
Journal of Current Social Issues
Liberation News Service
The Mountain Eagle
Mountain Life & Work
Ms. Magazine

News-Sentinel (Knoxville)
New York Times
Southern Exposure
Southern Patriot
TIME magazine
United Mine Workers Journal
Washington Post

Film and Sound Archives

Appalshop Archive, Whitesburg, Ky.
"Bessie Lou, Coal Camp." 16mm film.
"Brookside Women." VHS.
"Buffalo Creek Flood: An Act of Man." Directed by Mimi Pickering, 1975. VHS.
"Outtakes—Appalachian Group to Save the Land and People." Directed by Anne Lewis. VHS.
CBS Reports, "Hunger in America." Produced by Martin Carr. Aired May 21, 1968. CBS News, 1968.
Harlan County, USA, Criterion Collection. Directed by Barbara Kopple. New York: Cabin Creek Films, 1976, 2006. DVD.
"LBJ Wraps Up His Poverty Tour of the Appalachian States." Lyndon Baines Johnson Library, www.lbjlib.utexas.edu/johnson/lbjforkids/pov_media.shtm.
Salt of the Earth. Written by Michael Wilson. Directed by Herbert J. Biberman. Narberth, Penn.: Alpha Video Distributors, 2004. DVD.
Smithsonian Center for Folklife and Cultural Heritage
"Songs and Stories of Aunt Molly Jackson"
"WNEW's Story of Selma"
You Got to Move. Directed by Lucy Massie Phenix and Veronica Selver. Cumberland Mountain Educational Cooperative. Harrington Park, N.J.: Milliarum Zero, 2009.

Digital Collections

Atlanta Cooperative News Project, 1968–1985. Great Speckled Bird Collection. Southern Labor Archives, Georgia State University, Atlanta, Ga.

Microfilm

Records of the Highlander Folk School and Highlander Research and Education Center, 1933–1978. Woodbridge, Conn.: Primary Source Microfilm, 2007.

Oral Histories by Author

Carla Barrett, August, 19, 2011, Harlan, Kentucky.
Mary Beth Bingman, August 5, 2010, Whitesburg, Kentucky.
Steve Brooks, November 18, 2013, Nickelsville, Virginia.
Candie Carawan, August 18, 2010, New Market, Tennessee.

Elinor Graham, Helen Rentch, Ruth Yarrow, and Penelope Crandall, March 12, 2011, Richmond, Kentucky.

Barbara Greene, May 8, 2011, Williamsburg, Kentucky.

Eula Hall, March 10, 2011, Prestonsburg, Kentucky, and September 15, 2012, Grethel, Kentucky.

Louellen Hall, March 8, 2011, Grethel, Kentucky.

Nora Howard, August 31, 2011, by telephone.

Loyal Jones, June 1, 2012, Berea, Kentucky.

Vivian Keathley, March 2012, by telephone.

Maxine Kenny, November 18, 2013, Nickelsville, Virginia.

Jeanette Knowles, Mildred Shackleford, and Thelma Parker Witt, January 21, 2013, Stanford, Kentucky.

Sue Ella Kobak, March 6, 2011, and May 20, 2011, Dryden, Virginia.

Sue Ella Kobak, March 29, 2017, by telephone.

Anne Lewis, April 8, 2011, Atlanta, Georgia.

Helen Matthews Lewis, May 28, 2010, Morganton, Georgia.

Sally Ward Maggard, July 29, 2016, Pocahontas County, West Virginia.

Neil McBride, May 27, 2010, Oak Ridge, Tennessee.

Helen Rentch, June 29, 2011, Midway, Kentucky.

June Rostan, July 6, 2009, Greenback, Tennessee.

Flossie Sloan, March 8, 2011, Grethel, Kentucky.

Other Oral Histories

Marie Abrams, interviewed by Sue Wylie, July 17, 1991. Kentucky Commission on Women Oral History Project.

Marjorie Castle, interview by Glenna Graves, Sept. 11, 1988. Family and Gender in the Coal Community Oral History Project.

Edith Easterling, interview by Carrie Kline, March 12, 2011. Southern Appalachian Archives.

Edith Easterling, interview by Gibbs Kinderman, October 10, 1989. War on Poverty Oral History Project.

Edith Easterling, Shelva Thompson, and John Dollo, SFC Audio Cassette 18853. In the Guy and Candie Carawan Collection.

Jake and Edith Easterling, interview by Nyoka Hawkins, August 2, 1987. Social History and Cultural Change in the Elkhorn Coal Fields Oral History Project.

Linda Elkington, interview by Gibbs Kinderman, August 8, 1987. War on Poverty Oral History Project.

Mary Rice Farris, interview by Leroy Wimbush, January 1973. Oral Histories, His 190/App Oral History, Berea College Archives.

Mae Frazier, interview by Glenna Graves, December 8, 1988. Family and Gender in the Coal Community Oral History Project.

Opal Goble, interview by Glenna Graves, July 19, 1988. Family and Gender in the Coal Community Oral History Project.

Elinor Graham, interview by Carrie Kline, March 11, 2011. Southern Appalachian Archives.

Eula Hall, interview by Neil Boothby and Robert Korstad, September 5, 1992. Southern Rural Poverty Collection, DeWitt Wallace Center for Media and Democracy, Duke University.

Eula Hall, interview by Harry Rice, November 10, 2004. Southern Appalachian Archives.

Onda Lee Holbrook, interview by Glenna Graves, September 11, 1988. Family and Gender in the Coal Community Oral History Project.

Marie Humphries, interview by Sue Wiley, n.d. Kentucky Commission on Women Oral History Project.

Jeanette Knowles, interview by Jo Crockett Zingg, June 16, 2009. Southern Appalachian Archives.

Sue Ella Kobak, interview by Gibbs Kinderman, October 28, 1985. War on Poverty Oral History Project.

Sue Ella Kobak, interview by Margaret Brown, January 2, 1991. War on Poverty Oral History Project.

Bertha B. Kretzer, interview by Glenna Graves, November 6, 1988. Family and Gender in the Coal Community Oral History Project.

Grace Litteral, interview by Glenna Graves, June 14, 1988. Family and Gender in the Coal Community Oral History Project.

Minnie Lunsford, interview by Sally Ward Maggard, Harlan County, Kentucky. Sally Ward Maggard's personal collection.

Malta Miller, interviewed by Glenna Graves, October 14, 1988. Family and Gender in the Coal Community Oral History Project.

Scott Miller, interview by Jan Romond, March 6, 2006. Kentucky Legislature Oral History Project.

Joseph T. Mulloy, interview by Thomas Kiffmeyer, November 10, 1990. War on Poverty Oral History Project.

Karen Mulloy, interview by Margaret Brown, November 10, 1990. War on Poverty Oral History Project.

Louie B. Nunn, interview by Thomas Kiffmeyer, July 6, 1963. War on Poverty Oral History Project.

Thomas Rhodenbaugh, interview by Thomas Kiffmeyer and Harry Rice, March 11, 2011. War on Poverty Oral History Project.

Lois Scott, interview by Katie Gilliam, April 3, 1987. Appalachian Archive. Southeast Kentucky Community and Technical College.

Lois Scott, interview by Melissa Scott, March 27, 1995. Appalachian Archive. Southeast Kentucky Community and Technical College.

Howard Thorkelson, interview by Jo Crockett Zingg, October 11, 2008. Southern Appalachian Archives.

Thelma Parker Witt, interview by Jo Crockett Zingg, November 11, 2010. Southern Appalachian Archives.

Privately Held Collections

Maxine Kenny Papers
John Rosenberg Papers

Online Archives

Civil Rights Movement Veterans, online archive, hosted by Tougaloo College, http://www.crmvet.org.

"Eastern Kentucky African American Migration Project," Southern Historical Collection, UNC–Chapel Hill, http://ekaamp.web.unc.edu.

Records of the Council of the Southern Mountains, 1970–1989, exhibition.http://community.berea.edu/hutchinslibrary/specialcollections/exhibit/xhibitsaaintroasp.

The Robert F. Kennedy Performance Project, http://www.rfkineky.org.

Reports, Presentations, and Government Publications

"All Coal Mining Disasters: 1839-present." The National Institute for Occupational Safety and Health, Centers for Disease Control.

"AVs: Women and Activism in Appalachia." Panel at Thirty-Fourth Annual Appalachian Studies Conference, "River of Earth: Action, Scholarship, Reflection, and Renewal," March 11, 2011.

Black, Dan. A., Mark Mather, and Seth G. Sanders. *Standards of Living in Appalachia, 1960–2000*. Washington, D.C.: Appalachian Regional Commission, 2007.

Citizens' Board of Inquiry into Hunger and Malnutrition in the United States. *Hunger, U.S.A: A Report*. Boston: Beacon Press, 1968.

Committee on School Lunch Participation. *Their Daily Bread: A Study of the National School Lunch Program*. Atlanta: McNelly-Rudd, 1968.

Gunderson, Gordon W. "National School Lunch Program, Child Nutrition Act." http://www.fns.usda.gov/nslp/history_6#child.

Harlan Miners Speak: Report on Terrorism in the Kentucky Coal Fields. Prepared by members of the National Committee for the Defense of Political Prisoners, 1932. Lexington: The University Press of Kentucky, 2008.

Isserman, Andrew. *Socio-Economic Review of Appalachia, Appalachia Then and Now: An Update of "The Realities of Deprivation" Reported to the President in 1964, Revised November 1996*. Washington, D.C.: Appalachian Regional Commission, 1996.

Montgomery, Jenny. "Women Miners: Complaints of Sex Discrimination Force Coal Industry to End 'Male Only' Tradition." Staff Report, 86-4, Kentucky Commission Human Rights, September 24, 1986. Kentucky Documents, Government Documents Department, University of Louisville Libraries.

U.S. Bureau of Labor Statistics. *Technology, Productivity, and Labor in the Bituminous Coal Industry 1950–79*, Bulletin 2072. Washington, D.C.: GPO, 1981.

U.S. Department of Commerce, Bureau of the Census. *1970 Census of the Population: General Social and Economic Characteristics*. Kentucky, vol. 1, pt. 19.

Index

Jessica Wilkerson is an assistant professor of history and Southern studies at the University of Mississippi.

The Working Class in American History

Worker City, Company Town: Iron and Cotton-Worker Protest in Troy and Cohoes, New York, 1855–84 *Daniel J. Walkowitz*
Life, Work, and Rebellion in the Coal Fields: The Southern West Virginia Miners, 1880–1922 *David Alan Corbin*
Women and American Socialism, 1870–1920 *Mari Jo Buhle*
Lives of Their Own: Blacks, Italians, and Poles in Pittsburgh, 1900–1960 *John Bodnar, Roger Simon, and Michael P. Weber*
Working-Class America: Essays on Labor, Community, and American Society *Edited by Michael H. Frisch and Daniel J. Walkowitz*
Eugene V. Debs: Citizen and Socialist *Nick Salvatore*
American Labor and Immigration History, 1877–1920s: Recent European Research *Edited by Dirk Hoerder*
Workingmen's Democracy: The Knights of Labor and American Politics *Leon Fink*
The Electrical Workers: A History of Labor at General Electric and Westinghouse, 1923–60 *Ronald W. Schatz*
The Mechanics of Baltimore: Workers and Politics in the Age of Revolution, 1763–1812 *Charles G. Steffen*
The Practice of Solidarity: American Hat Finishers in the Nineteenth Century *David Bensman*
The Labor History Reader *Edited by Daniel J. Leab*
Solidarity and Fragmentation: Working People and Class Consciousness in Detroit, 1875–1900 *Richard Oestreicher*
Counter Cultures: Saleswomen, Managers, and Customers in American Department Stores, 1890–1940 *Susan Porter Benson*
The New England Working Class and the New Labor History *Edited by Herbert G. Gutman and Donald H. Bell*
Labor Leaders in America *Edited by Melvyn Dubofsky and Warren Van Tine*
Barons of Labor: The San Francisco Building Trades and Union Power in the Progressive Era *Michael Kazin*
Gender at Work: The Dynamics of Job Segregation by Sex during World War II *Ruth Milkman*
Once a Cigar Maker: Men, Women, and Work Culture in American Cigar Factories, 1900–1919 *Patricia A. Cooper*
A Generation of Boomers: The Pattern of Railroad Labor Conflict in Nineteenth-Century America *Shelton Stromquist*
Work and Community in the Jungle: Chicago's Packinghouse Workers, 1894–1922 *James R. Barrett*
Workers, Managers, and Welfare Capitalism: The Shoeworkers and Tanners of Endicott Johnson, 1890–1950 *Gerald Zahavi*

Men, Women, and Work: Class, Gender, and Protest in the New England Shoe Industry, 1780–1910 *Mary Blewett*

Workers on the Waterfront: Seamen, Longshoremen, and Unionism in the 1930s *Bruce Nelson*

German Workers in Chicago: A Documentary History of Working-Class Culture from 1850 to World War I *Edited by Hartmut Keil and John B. Jentz*

On the Line: Essays in the History of Auto Work *Edited by Nelson Lichtenstein and Stephen Meyer III*

Labor's Flaming Youth: Telephone Operators and Worker Militancy, 1878–1923 *Stephen H. Norwood*

Another Civil War: Labor, Capital, and the State in the Anthracite Regions of Pennsylvania, 1840–68 *Grace Palladino*

Coal, Class, and Color: Blacks in Southern West Virginia, 1915–32 *Joe William Trotter Jr.*

For Democracy, Workers, and God: Labor Song-Poems and Labor Protest, 1865–95 *Clark D. Halker*

Dishing It Out: Waitresses and Their Unions in the Twentieth Century *Dorothy Sue Cobble*

The Spirit of 1848: German Immigrants, Labor Conflict, and the Coming of the Civil War *Bruce Levine*

Working Women of Collar City: Gender, Class, and Community in Troy, New York, 1864–86 *Carole Turbin*

Southern Labor and Black Civil Rights: Organizing Memphis Workers *Michael K. Honey*

Radicals of the Worst Sort: Laboring Women in Lawrence, Massachusetts, 1860–1912 *Ardis Cameron*

Producers, Proletarians, and Politicians: Workers and Party Politics in Evansville and New Albany, Indiana, 1850–87 *Lawrence M. Lipin*

The New Left and Labor in the 1960s *Peter B. Levy*

The Making of Western Labor Radicalism: Denver's Organized Workers, 1878–1905 *David Brundage*

In Search of the Working Class: Essays in American Labor History and Political Culture *Leon Fink*

Lawyers against Labor: From Individual Rights to Corporate Liberalism *Daniel R. Ernst*

"We Are All Leaders": The Alternative Unionism of the Early 1930s *Edited by Staughton Lynd*

The Female Economy: The Millinery and Dressmaking Trades, 1860–1930 *Wendy Gamber*

"Negro and White, Unite and Fight!": A Social History of Industrial Unionism in Meatpacking, 1930–90 *Roger Horowitz*

Power at Odds: The 1922 National Railroad Shopmen's Strike *Colin J. Davis*

The Common Ground of Womanhood: Class, Gender, and Working Girls' Clubs, 1884–1928 *Priscilla Murolo*
Marching Together: Women of the Brotherhood of Sleeping Car Porters *Melinda Chateauvert*
Down on the Killing Floor: Black and White Workers in Chicago's Packinghouses, 1904–54 *Rick Halpern*
Labor and Urban Politics: Class Conflict and the Origins of Modern Liberalism in Chicago, 1864–97 *Richard Schneirov*
All That Glitters: Class, Conflict, and Community in Cripple Creek *Elizabeth Jameson*
Waterfront Workers: New Perspectives on Race and Class *Edited by Calvin Winslow*
Labor Histories: Class, Politics, and the Working-Class Experience *Edited by Eric Arnesen, Julie Greene, and Bruce Laurie*
The Pullman Strike and the Crisis of the 1890s: Essays on Labor and Politics *Edited by Richard Schneirov, Shelton Stromquist, and Nick Salvatore*
AlabamaNorth: African-American Migrants, Community, and Working-Class Activism in Cleveland, 1914–45 *Kimberley L. Phillips*
Imagining Internationalism in American and British Labor, 1939–49 *Victor Silverman*
William Z. Foster and the Tragedy of American Radicalism *James R. Barrett*
Colliers across the Sea: A Comparative Study of Class Formation in Scotland and the American Midwest, 1830–1924 *John H. M. Laslett*
"Rights, Not Roses": Unions and the Rise of Working-Class Feminism, 1945–80 *Dennis A. Deslippe*
Testing the New Deal: The General Textile Strike of 1934 in the American South *Janet Irons*
Hard Work: The Making of Labor History *Melvyn Dubofsky*
Southern Workers and the Search for Community: Spartanburg County, South Carolina *G. C. Waldrep III*
We Shall Be All: A History of the Industrial Workers of the World (abridged edition) *Melvyn Dubofsky, ed. Joseph A. McCartin*
Race, Class, and Power in the Alabama Coalfields, 1908–21 *Brian Kelly*
Duquesne and the Rise of Steel Unionism *James D. Rose*
Anaconda: Labor, Community, and Culture in Montana's Smelter City *Laurie Mercier*
Bridgeport's Socialist New Deal, 1915–36 *Cecelia Bucki*
Indispensable Outcasts: Hobo Workers and Community in the American Midwest, 1880–1930 *Frank Tobias Higbie*
After the Strike: A Century of Labor Struggle at Pullman *Susan Eleanor Hirsch*
Corruption and Reform in the Teamsters Union *David Witwer*
Waterfront Revolts: New York and London Dockworkers, 1946–61 *Colin J. Davis*

Black Workers' Struggle for Equality in Birmingham *Horace Huntley and David Montgomery*
The Tribe of Black Ulysses: African American Men in the Industrial South *William P. Jones*
City of Clerks: Office and Sales Workers in Philadelphia, 1870–1920 *Jerome P. Bjelopera*
Reinventing "The People": The Progressive Movement, the Class Problem, and the Origins of Modern Liberalism *Shelton Stromquist*
Radical Unionism in the Midwest, 1900–1950 *Rosemary Feurer*
Gendering Labor History *Alice Kessler-Harris*
James P. Cannon and the Origins of the American Revolutionary Left, 1890–1928 *Bryan D. Palmer*
Glass Towns: Industry, Labor, and Political Economy in Appalachia, 1890–1930s *Ken Fones-Wolf*
Workers and the Wild: Conservation, Consumerism, and Labor in Oregon, 1910–30 *Lawrence M. Lipin*
Wobblies on the Waterfront: Interracial Unionism in Progressive-Era Philadelphia *Peter Cole*
Red Chicago: American Communism at Its Grassroots, 1928–35 *Randi Storch*
Labor's Cold War: Local Politics in a Global Context *Edited by Shelton Stromquist*
Bessie Abramowitz Hillman and the Making of the Amalgamated Clothing Workers of America *Karen Pastorello*
The Great Strikes of 1877 *Edited by David O. Stowell*
Union-Free America: Workers and Antiunion Culture *Lawrence Richards*
Race against Liberalism: Black Workers and the UAW in Detroit *David M. Lewis-Colman*
Teachers and Reform: Chicago Public Education, 1929–70 *John F. Lyons*
Upheaval in the Quiet Zone: 1199/SEIU and the Politics of Healthcare Unionism *Leon Fink and Brian Greenberg*
Shadow of the Racketeer: Scandal in Organized Labor *David Witwer*
Sweet Tyranny: Migrant Labor, Industrial Agriculture, and Imperial Politics *Kathleen Mapes*
Staley: The Fight for a New American Labor Movement *Steven K. Ashby and C. J. Hawking*
On the Ground: Labor Struggles in the American Airline Industry *Liesl Miller Orenic*
NAFTA and Labor in North America *Norman Caulfield*
Making Capitalism Safe: Work Safety and Health Regulation in America, 1880–1940 *Donald W. Rogers*
Good, Reliable, White Men: Railroad Brotherhoods, 1877–1917 *Paul Michel Taillon*

Spirit of Rebellion: Labor and Religion in the New Cotton South *Jarod Roll*
The Labor Question in America: Economic Democracy in the Gilded Age *Rosanne Currarino*
Banded Together: Economic Democratization in the Brass Valley *Jeremy Brecher*
The Gospel of the Working Class: Labor's Southern Prophets in New Deal America *Erik Gellman and Jarod Roll*
Guest Workers and Resistance to U.S. Corporate Despotism *Immanuel Ness*
Gleanings of Freedom: Free and Slave Labor along the Mason-Dixon Line, 1790–1860 *Max Grivno*
Chicago in the Age of Capital: Class, Politics, and Democracy during the Civil War and Reconstruction *John B. Jentz and Richard Schneirov*
Child Care in Black and White: Working Parents and the History of Orphanages *Jessie B. Ramey*
The Haymarket Conspiracy: Transatlantic Anarchist Networks *Timothy Messer-Kruse*
Detroit's Cold War: The Origins of Postwar Conservatism *Colleen Doody*
A Renegade Union: Interracial Organizing and Labor Radicalism *Lisa Phillips*
Palomino: Clinton Jencks and Mexican-American Unionism in the American Southwest *James J. Lorence*
Latin American Migrations to the U.S. Heartland: Changing Cultural Landscapes in Middle America *Edited by Linda Allegro and Andrew Grant Wood*
Man of Fire: Selected Writings *Ernesto Galarza, ed. Armando Ibarra and Rodolfo D. Torres*
A Contest of Ideas: Capital, Politics, and Labor *Nelson Lichtenstein*
Making the World Safe for Workers: Labor, the Left, and Wilsonian Internationalism *Elizabeth McKillen*
The Rise of the Chicago Police Department: Class and Conflict, 1850–1894 *Sam Mitrani*
Workers in Hard Times: A Long View of Economic Crises *Edited by Leon Fink, Joseph A. McCartin, and Joan Sangster*
Redeeming Time: Protestantism and Chicago's Eight-Hour Movement, 1866–1912 *William A. Mirola*
Struggle for the Soul of the Postwar South: White Evangelical Protestants and Operation Dixie *Elizabeth Fones-Wolf and Ken Fones-Wolf*
Free Labor: The Civil War and the Making of an American Working Class *Mark A. Lause*
Death and Dying in the Working Class, 1865–1920 *Michael K. Rosenow*
Immigrants against the State: Yiddish and Italian Anarchism in America *Kenyon Zimmer*
Fighting for Total Person Unionism: Harold Gibbons, Ernest Calloway, and Working-Class Citizenship *Robert Bussel*
Smokestacks in the Hills: Rural-Industrial Workers in West Virginia *Louis Martin*

Disaster Citizenship: Survivors, Solidarity, and Power in the Progressive Era
Jacob A. C. Remes
The Pew and the Picket Line: Christianity and the American Working Class
Edited by Christopher D. Cantwell, Heath W. Carter, and Janine Giordano Drake
Conservative Counterrevolution: Challenging Liberalism in 1950s Milwaukee
Tula A. Connell
Manhood on the Line: Working-Class Masculinities in the American Heartland
Steve Meyer
On Gender, Labor, and Inequality *Ruth Milkman*
The Making of Working-Class Religion *Matthew Pehl*
Civic Labors: Scholar Activism and Working-Class Studies
Edited by Dennis Deslippe, Eric Fure-Slocum, and John W. McKerley
Victor Arnautoff and the Politics of Art *Robert W. Cherny*
Against Labor: How U.S. Employers Organized to Defeat Union Activism
Edited by Rosemary Feurer and Chad Pearson
Teacher Strike! Public Education and the Making of a New American Political Order *Jon Shelton*
Hillbilly Hellraisers: Federal Power and Populist Defiance in the Ozarks
J. Blake Perkins
Sewing the Fabric of Statehood: Garment Unions, American Labor, and the Establishment of the State of Israel *Adam Howard*
Labor and Justice across the America *Edited by Leon Fink and Juan Manuel Palacio*
Frontiers of Labor: Comparative Histories of the United States and Australia
Edited by Greg Patmore and Shelton Stromquist
Women Have Always Worked: A Concise History, Second Edition
Alice Kessler-Harris
Remembering Lattimer: Labor, Migration, and Race in Pennsylvania Anthracite Country *Paul A. Shackel*
Disruption in Detroit: Autoworkers and the Elusive Postwar Boom
Daniel J. Clark
To Live Here, You Have to Fight: How Women Led Appalachian Movements for Social Justice *Jessica Wilkerson*

The University of Illinois Press
is a founding member of the
Association of American University Presses.

Composed in 10.5/13 Minion Pro
by Kirsten Dennison
at the University of Illinois Press
Cover designed by Dustin J. Hubbart
Cover illustration by Katie Ries

University of Illinois Press
1325 South Oak Street
Champaign, IL 61820-6903
www.press.uillinois.edu